Portrait of the Kings

Portrait of the Kings

The Davidic Prototype in Deuteronomistic Poetics

Alison L. Joseph

Fortress Press
Minneapolis

PORTRAIT OF THE KINGS

The Davidic Prototype in Deuteronomistic Poetics

Cover design: Tory Herman

Cover image: King David (Detail of Interior Mosaics in the St. Mark's Basilica), 12th century. Found in the collection of the Saint Mark's Basilica, Venice.

Library of Congress Cataloging-in-Publication Data

Print ISBN: 978-1-4514-6566-2

eBook ISBN: 978-1-4514-6958-5

The paper used in this publication meets the minimum requirements of American National Standard for Information Sciences — Permanence of Paper for Printed Library Materials, ANSI Z329.48-1984.

Manufactured in the U.S.

This book was produced using PressBooks.com, and PDF rendering was done by PrinceXML.

For my parents, Susan and Charles Joseph

Contents

Acknowledgments

This study began as a doctoral dissertation submitted to the department of Near Eastern Studies at the University of California, Berkeley. The evolution of this work benefited from the help and advice of many individuals. My dissertation committee, Robert Alter, Erich Gruen, and Steven Weitzman, offered helpful and thought-provoking feedback on the dissertation and continue to mentor me. My advisor, Ron Hendel, generously read every iteration of these chapters, long after the ink on my degree was dry. Mark Leuchter and Gary Knoppers reviewed several chapters and offered thoughtful and invaluable comments. Neil Elliott, the biblical studies acquisitions editor at Fortress Press, gave careful attention to my manuscript.

My parents, Susan and Charles Joseph, to whom this volume is dedicated, have given me a lifetime of support and always encouraged and fostered a love of learning and a love of Torah. Without them I would never have gotten here. My family, Matt, Caleb, Eliana, and Orli (who arrived at just the right time), always provided inspiration and distractions (both needed and unsolicited). Their love and willingness to eat pizza and Chinese takeout made the completion of this book possible.

To all I say a deeply heartfelt thank you.

Abbreviations

AB   Anchor Bible

ABN   Robert Alter. *The Art of Biblical Narrative.* New York: Basic Books, 1981.

BAR   *Biblical Archaeology Review*

CBQ   *Catholic Biblical Quarterly*

CMHE   Frank Moore Cross. *Canaanite Myth and Hebrew Epic: Essays in the History of the Religion of Israel.* Cambridge, MA: Harvard University Press, 1973.

DBF   Death and burial formula

Dtr   The Deuteronomist

Dtr^1 The preexilic Deuteronomist

Dtr^2 The exilic Deuteronomist

DtrG   Deuteronomistic *Geschichtsschreiber* (the historiographer), the exilic, Deuteronomistic Historian

DtrH   The Deuteronomistic History

DtrN   The exilic or early postexilic, nomistic redactor(s) of the Deuteronomistic History

DtrP   The exilic, prophetic redactor of the Deuteronomistic History

FRLANT   Forschungen zur Religion und Literatur des Alten und Neuen Testaments

GKC   E. Kautzsch, ed. *Gesenius' Hebrew Grammar.* Translated by A. E. Cowley. 2nd ed. Oxford: Clarendon, 1910.

HTR   *Harvard Theological Review*

HUCA   *Hebrew Union College Annual*

JAOS   *Journal of the American Oriental Society*

JBL   *Journal of Biblical Literature*

JHS   *Journal of Hebrew Scriptures*

JQR   *Jewish Quarterly Review*

JSOT   *Journal for the Study of the Old Testament*

JSOTSup Journal for the Study of the Old Testament Supplement Series

LXX   Septuagint

MT   Masoretic Text

OBO   Orbis biblicus et orientalis

RF   Regnal formula

TZ   *Theologische Zeitschrift*

VT   *Vetus Testamentum*

VTSup   Supplements to *Vetus Testamentum*

ZAW   *Zeitschrift für die alttestamentliche Wissenschaft*

1

The Davidic Prototype in Deuteronomistic Poetics

Listen, my children, and you shall hear
Of the midnight ride of Paul Revere,
On the eighteenth of April, in Seventy-Five:
Hardly a man is now alive
Who remembers that famous day and year.

So begins Henry Wadsworth Longfellow's mythic poem "Paul Revere's Ride."[1] Writing in 1860, on the eve of the Civil War, Longfellow attempts to evoke a shared sense of cultural and moral values among Americans. Longfellow's now famous poem has come to replace the historical account of that important night in the common American memory, demonstrating how the author's ideology and intentions in a literary text can reshape the common conception of history. It also testifies to the blurry line between the genres of literature and historiography.

---

1. Henry Wadsworth Longfellow, "Paul Revere's Ride," in *Selected Poems*, Penguin Classics (New York: Penguin, 1988), 148–52.

Historians have long criticized Longfellow's loose portrayal of historical detail, which exaggerates Revere's singular role in the event, the length of his ride, and his accomplishments.[2] Yet, if Paul Revere were not the one to carry the message, "One, if by land, and two, if by sea," why have most Americans heard only of Revere, while others are forgotten? The answer lies in Longfellow's portrayal of the unassisted role of Revere. The well-planned chain of warnings was very much a team effort, yet Longfellow focused solely on the role of his hero, Paul Revere.[3] His poem created a national Revolutionary legend of Revere, who previously had been little known.

This poem, which presents an account of the beginning of the Revolutionary War, takes on the role of a historical document even though it was intended as a literary one. It presents events in the past and conveys the intentions and imagination of an author. This demonstrates that the process of historiography is complex, even when the goal of a text is not strictly to report a historical event. Historiography is often ideological. The power of the continued life of a historical document after its composition can be seen in this

2. The historical record is as follows: On April 18, 1775, as the British prepared to march on Boston, Paul Revere and William Dawes rode from Boston (Charlestown) toward Lexington to warn John Hancock and Samuel Adams that the Royal troops were coming, knocking on doors and sending previously planned lines of communication into alert. Longfellow narrates that Revere continued the ride on to Concord, even though the truth is quite the opposite. After fulfilling their initial mission in Lexington, Dawes and Revere set out for Concord, and Samuel Prescott joined them on the way, until all three were stopped by British troops. Prescott and Dawes managed to escape, but the British officers detained, questioned, and escorted Revere at gunpoint back to Lexington. Of the three riders, only Prescott arrived at Concord in time to warn its militia of the British approach. (Paul Revere, "A Letter from Col. Paul Revere to the Corresponding Secretary [Jeremy Belknap]," 1798, Manuscript Collection, Massachusetts Historical Society, http://www.masshist.org/cabinet/april2002/reveretranscription.htm). Revere rode a total of thirteen miles that night from Boston to Lexington, and an additional two miles from Lexington before he was stopped by the British patrol. David Hackett Fischer, *Paul Revere's Ride* (New York: Oxford University Press, 1994), 130. Revere's ride pales in comparison to that of the unknown Israel Bissell, who rode from Watertown, MA, to New York City, 225 miles in four days (ibid., 270–71).

3. Fischer, *Paul Revere's Ride*, 332.

example of American historical memory. Revere is acclaimed as an American hero.

As consumers of history, we must consider how a poetic hero can replace a historical one in the historical record. How can an event and one of its actors be completely rewritten and be absorbed as history? Until recently, historians of the American Revolution as well as textbook writers relied almost entirely on Longfellow's poem as historical evidence. This is likely a result of the popularity of the poem, as Longfellow was one of the most prominent American poets of the nineteenth century. Despite Longfellow's disregard for historical fact, the poem has become part of the historical record. It is only in recent years that historians (with limited success) have attempted to dissuade Americans from relying on Longfellow's version of the story.

The success of the poem likely lies in both the quality of the poetry and the meaningful connection Longfellow made with his contemporary audience, an engagement that continues throughout American history. Longfellow's Paul Revere (as opposed to the historical Paul Revere) became a national symbol of the fight for freedom. The powerful images of the event and the hero have become our national memory. They have overshadowed and eclipsed the original event and have formed a new collective American memory. According to American historian David Hackett Fischer, Longfellow "appealed to the evidence of history as a source of patriotic inspiration, but was utterly without scruple in his manipulation of historical fact."[4]

"Paul Revere's Ride" offers a powerful example of the process of historiography and its reception history. A beautifully written poem that sets itself up as the transmission of a historical memory creates a character who appeals to the poet/historian's contemporary audience.

4. Ibid., 331.

The people hold fast to an inflated minor player because Longfellow's depiction speaks to them. The hero becomes a meaningful symbol, representative of the memory of historical experience, even if he does not necessarily reflect the historical experience itself. This is the process of historiography—the historian interprets the past in a way that is meaningful to him and his audience.

Longfellow's poem and its questionable role in the received tradition of American collective memory pose a worthwhile example for the study of biblical historiography. Longfellow's ideological commitments influence the way his narrative is constructed; he is interested in patriotism and creating a mythic hero. He interprets the historical facts in order to support his ideological goals, depicting a morale-boosting, unifying figure at a moment when the country was about to divide. While he may (or may not) have intended for his poem to be taken as a replacement for a more accurate historical account, it has claimed such a place in American collective memory. This occurrence requires us to consider the modes of historiography. Does a narrative need to be intended as history to be history? Where do we draw the boundaries between fiction and history? How do we deal with the differences between history and collective memory? Can history be presented without an ideological perspective?[5] The trackable reception history of Longfellow's poem provides a strong example of how collective memories are constructed to re-create a past that is relevant for the present. This is neither strictly historical nor wholly fiction.[6]

---

5. John Van Seters begins to address these questions in *In Search of History: Historiography in the Ancient World and the Origins of Biblical History* (Winona Lake, IN: Eisenbrauns, 1997). Also, Johan Huizinga, "A Definition of the Concept of History," in *Philosophy and History: Essays Presented to Ernst Cassirer*, ed. Raymond Klibansky and Herbert James Paton (New York: Harper & Row, 1963), 1–10; Hugo Gressmann, *Die Älteste Geschichtsschreibung Und Prophetie Israels* (Göttingen: Vandenhoeck & Ruprecht, 1910). Robert Alter, "Imagining History in the Bible," in *History and—: Histories Within the Human Sciences*, ed. Ralph Cohen and Michael S. Roth (Charlottesville: University Press of Virginia, 1995), 53–72.

This book will address the process of historiography in the book of Kings. As Longfellow does in "Paul Revere's Ride," the historian of Kings analyzes and interprets historical events and creates a history reflective of his (deuteronomistic) ideology, raising a "historical" figure to heroic status, in line with his ideological purpose. The Deuteronomistic Historian devises a prototype of a covenantally adherent king in the portrait of David, who provides the cultic model for subsequent kings to follow. This historian intends to present a historical past, as he sees it, through the purview of his ideological perspective and with a didactic function, specifically through the model of a hero, as in the case of Longfellow's Revere.

In this volume, I will adopt a modified version of Frank Moore Cross's theory of a double redaction of the book of Kings, according to which the Deuteronomistic History is understood as having been compiled, through the redaction of a number of sources, by an author during the reign of Josiah, and updated in a second redaction during the exile. (This theory will be discussed more thoroughly below.) My interest is in examining the creation of the historical past and exploring the historiographical style and method of the preexilic Deuteronomist in Kings.[7] Throughout, I will use the siglum Dtr for this Deuteronomist, or deuteronomistic redactor, whom Cross identifies as Dtr[1], and like Cross, I will identify the exilic redactor as Dtr[2]. I will use DtrH for the Deuteronomistic History in its received form of the books of Deuteronomy through Kings.

The Deuteronomist (here, Dtr) was a collector, author, and redactor. He inherited several self-contained and comprehensive

6. Ronald S. Hendel, "Culture, Memory, and History: Reflections on Method in Biblical Studies," in *Historical Biblical Archaeology and the Future: The New Pragmatism*, ed. Thomas E. Levy (London: Equinox, 2010), 255.
7. See Frank Moore Cross, "The Themes of the Book of Kings and the Structure of the Deuteronomic History," in *Canaanite Myth and Hebrew Epic Essays in the History of the Religion of Israel* (Cambridge, MA: Harvard University Press, 1973), 274–89.

documents that he adopted and reshaped to suit his purposes. Consideration of the process of historiography is plagued by many problems, including the use of sources—their reliability, objectivity, and provenance. We need to take questions of methodology seriously when examining the "historical" works in the Hebrew Bible like the Deuteronomistic History (or Chronicles, for that matter). These works have either been mined for historical data (the old "Bible as history" approach) or reduced to tendentious constructions of a "usable past," but rarely studied as the product of an author sifting among sources, deciding what to include in his history and how to structure what is included not only on the basis of the theological or ideological, but also on the basis of literary considerations.

This inquiry into the process of historiography both integrates the work of biblical scholars who consider issues of style and deals with biblical history in order to discover and prove its historicity or ahistoricity and to designate its sources. This also takes into account the methods developed through the revolution in the literary study of the Bible that began in the 1970s. In this book, I consider the process of historiography and the choices that the Deuteronomist as editor and author had to make in order to craft his history. In a recent essay, Ron Hendel criticizes the trajectory the historical-critical method has taken. It "has too often devolved to tired debates about the dating or historicity of the biblical sources, or has balkanized itself into a variety of methods that take little cognizance of each other, each presuming conceptual autonomy."[8] My goal is to take into account both the historical contextualization of redactional layers and the intentional and conscious literary choices made by the author/redactor.

---

8. Hendel, "Culture, Memory, and History," 250.

History of Scholarship

Since the work of Martin Noth (1943), the Deuteronomistic History (DtrH)—the books of Deuteronomy through Kings—has largely been considered a unified literary work.[9] Noth begins by offering the question of consistency and coherence: "Do we in fact have here a comprehensive framework indicating a larger literary unit which has adopted much traditional material?"[10] In response, he sets out to prove that the work is a self-contained whole. He shows that this author uses language and ideology similar to that found in deuteronomic law.[11] On a linguistic basis, it is possible to see either the work of a single deuteronomistic editor or different editors with a similar style. It is the linguistic uniformity—the use of a characteristic vocabulary, diction, repetition of phrases and sentence structure—that suggests that the work is self-contained.[12]

Initially, Noth's theory of unity was widely accepted, yet it generated multiple opinions on the compositional and redactional history of these books. Scholars have further divided the history, which Noth attributed to a single author, into multiple redactors and various historical contexts. More recently, in the past decade, the study of the "Deuteronomistic History" has been focused on questioning whether such a "unified" work exists. If it does, is the

9. Martin Noth, *Überlieferungsgeschichtliche Studien. Die Sammelnden Und Bearbeitenden Geschischtswerke Im Alten Testement* (Tübingen: Max Niemeyer, 1957); Noth, *The Deuteronomistic History* (Sheffield: JSOT Press, 1981). Noth is preceded by Ewald (1869) in identifying a unity of composition, but with two Deuteronomistic Historians and a preexilic date for the primary history (Heinrich Ewald, *Geschichte Des Volkes Israel*, 6 vols. [Göttingen: Dieterichs Buchhandlung, 1843]; Ewald, *The History of Israel*, trans. R. Martineau [London: Longmans, Green, 1869], 1:156–68). Noth's work sets a new standard for scholarship. For a survey of the history of the Deuteronomistic History, see Albert de Pury and Thomas Römer, "Deuteronomistic Historiography (DH): History of Research and Debated Issues," in *Israel Constructs Its History: Deuteronomistic Historiography in Recent Research* (Sheffield: Sheffield Academic, 2000), 24–141.

10. Noth, *Deuteronomistic History*, 15.

11. Ibid., 17.

12. Ibid., 18.

shadowy figure of the Deuteronomist an incompetent scribe, a slavish collector, a royal lackey, an astute literary bard, or a figment of the modern scholar's imagination?[13] Many scholars have focused on the origins and number of redactors to such an extent that some even deny the existence of DtrH, arguing that the redactional layers get so separated, amplified, and multiplied that it is difficult to maintain that the work of so many hands, at varying times, can possibly be unified. In a volume on *The Future of the Deuteronomistic History*,[14] John Van Seters writes an essay titled "The Deuteronomistic History: Can it Avoid Death by Redaction?". He argues that instead of using redaction criticism to chop up the text into small fragments, it should be used to identify long additions and the core work—and so to restore, rather than destroy, Noth's theory.[15]

Heuristic value has also been placed on reading a (semi-)unified narrative by applying literary considerations to the historical narratives. Literary critics have approached these narratives as historical fiction and have challenged the various tactics scholars have used in assessing the historicity of the historical or "history-like" narratives of DtrH.[16] Increasingly, with the discovery of extrabiblical

---

13. Recent collected works demonstrate the interest in these questions, such as Thomas Römer, ed., *The Future of the Deuteronomistic History* (Leuven: Leuven University Press, 2000); Thomas Römer, *The So-Called Deuteronomistic History: A Sociological, Historical, and Literary Introduction* (New York: T&T Clark, 2007); Linda Schearing and Steven L. McKenzie, eds., *Those Elusive Deuteronomists: The Phenomenon of Pan-Deuteronomism*, JSOTSup 268; Sheffield: Sheffield Academic, 1999); Gary N. Knoppers and J. Gordon McConville, eds., *Reconsidering Israel and Judah: Recent Studies on the Deuteronomistic History* (Winona Lake, IN: Eisenbrauns, 2000); Albert de Pury, Jean-Daniel Macchi, and Thomas Römer, eds., *Israel Constructs Its History: Deuteronomistic Historiography in Recent Research,* JSOT (Sheffield: Sheffield Academic, 2000); Lester L. Grabbe, ed., *Good Kings and Bad Kings: The Kingdom of Judah in the Seventh Century BCE* (New York: T&T Clark, 2005); Mark Leuchter and Klaus-Peter Adam, eds., *Soundings in Kings: Perspectives and Methods in Contemporary Scholarship* (Minneapolis: Fortress Press, 2010).
14. Thomas Römer, ed., *The Future of the Deuteronomistic History* (Leuven-Louvain: Leuven University Press, 2000).
15. John Van Seters, "The Deuteronomistic History: Can It Avoid Death by Redaction?," in *The Future of the Deuteronomistic History*, ed. Thomas Römer (Leuven: Leuven University Press, 2000), 213–22.

evidence that either undermines or verifies the historicity of the biblical narrative, scholars have taken sides on the veracity and acuity of biblical historiography and the reliability and competency of the biblical redactor as historian.

My inquiry moves beyond the discussion of historicity and of identifying redactors and redactions. I explore how we understand the Deuteronomistic text and the method(s) of the Deuteronomistic historian(s) who created it. Is it possible to explore historical meanings without getting bogged down in historical "fact"? And can we use a more objective record of the past to elucidate the subjective narration of it? I will deal with the intention of the author, the use of sources as can be discerned, the relationship of the historiography to historical events, and the theological and literary shaping of the text. My analysis devises a methodological schema that reflects the historiographical poetics in Kings. My goal is not to demonstrate historicity, "truth," and date, but rather to consider representation, meaning, and interpretation.[17]

The subtitle of this book, *The Davidic Prototype in Deuteronomistic Poetics*, describes the areas this volume will address. In chapter 2, I explore the historiographical process of the Deuteronomist, building on the theories of Martin Noth and others since the middle of the twentieth century; lay out a prescriptive style or poetics of the historian; and derive stylistic criteria for identifying the preexilic Deuteronomist. In chapter 3 and following, I consider the construction of the Davidic prototype as the literary model for the kings of Israel and Judah, a signature framing strategy of the Deuteronomist.

16. Alter, "Imagining History"; Alter, *ABN*, chap. 2; Meir Sternberg, *The Poetics of Biblical Narrative* (Bloomington: Indiana University Press, 1985), chap. 1.
17. Hendel, "Culture, Memory, and History," 251.

Historiography

Biblical historiography takes quite seriously the task of presenting an understandable past, but until recently, the history of scholarship has not included serious considerations of how the historian works. In the past two decades, three scholars who have dealt with these issues in an attempt to understand the process of biblical historiography are Baruch Halpern, Marc Brettler, and Gary Knoppers.

Halpern, in his book *The First Historians: The Hebrew Bible and History*, bases his arguments on Noth's premise of narrative unity, but does not directly address the question of the unity of the history.[18] Instead, he reacts to the work of scholars who debate the historicity or ahistoricity of the work, the generic identification of literature or historiography, and provenance of composition and redaction. In response, Halpern attempts to qualify and quantify the historiographical process of ancient Israel. He addresses the question of the general nature of biblical history and the role of the historian. He believes that the history writer's intention is to "lead the reader to believe that the work is a valid representation of the past." The narrative does not necessarily have to be historically accurate, but the author must intend to present it as true and the reader believe that it is valid.[19] The author's historical intention is one of the major characteristics of biblical historiography that Halpern highlights; this view comes under attack by other scholars.

Halpern's work responds to an absence of scholarship, following Noth, on the importance of discussing the historical intention of the historian as author and redactor. Many historical-critical scholars, in reconstructing the prehistory of the text as we have it, deal with the identification of multiple sources or editorships, asserting that

---

18. Baruch Halpern, *The First Historians: The Hebrew Bible and History* (San Francisco: Harper & Row, 1988).
19. Ibid., xxii.

perhaps the ancient editors were not able to see the contradictions in the text that moderns can see.[20] This is a simplistic perspective. Instead, Halpern urges us to understand that the biblical editors were competent and that the biblical historians were aware of the contradictions inherent in the texts.[21]

Halpern also addresses the general question of historiography: the relationship between the writing of history and historical events. He contends that

> history is not what happened. . . . History is our way of organizing particle configurations into perceptible fictional blocks, such as individuals, groups, and the environment. . . . Historians deal with people, and with societies, as though these were the atoms of causation. The historian's job is to expound human causes to the reader. . . . [History] is a form of human perception about the subatomic past. It is not accurate; like all memory, it is a useful form of organizing knowledge.[22]

Halpern identifies the process of history writing as metaphoric. In this way, historiography inherently lacks scientific objectivity, yet need not be fictional. Halpern's work, especially his conception of Dtr as maintaining "antiquarian" interests (to be discussed below), is important to my arguments here; Dtr inherits a collection of source documents that he faithfully employs in the writing of his history. Halpern's understanding of the selectional work of Dtr contributes greatly to my approach to Dtr's historiographical method.

In contrast, Marc Brettler looks more to the form-critical elements of the biblical historian. In *The Creation of History in Ancient Israel*, he seeks to highlight the central factors responsible for the production of the biblical texts of ancient Israel.[23] Brettler finds Halpern's approach

20. Ibid., xxv.
21. Ibid., xxv–xxvi.
22. Ibid., xxxiii.
23. Marc Zvi Brettler, *The Creation of History in Ancient Israel* (New York: Routledge, 1995).

to history, relying on the intention of the author to deem it historical, problematic. Brettler counters, "How do we know if an elaboration goes beyond the evidence the author had, especially when that evidence is no longer available to us?" How can we know the intentions of the author? How can we know if the narrator believed what he wrote?[24] Brettler contends that "it is difficult, if not impossible, to judge whether a biblical author was working from sources." It is for this reason that he focuses on the Chronicler's history as his paradigm because we know that the Chronicler used some version of Kings as his primary source. Also, Brettler argues that "Halpern's model is especially problematic because it places intentionality in such a central role." Brettler clearly defines history as "a narrative that presents a past," and not merely a narrative whose author intends it to be historical.[25] These two perspectives are not mutually exclusive. An author who intends to write history would indeed by its nature be creating a "narrative that presents a past."

Brettler's arguments against Halpern fly in the face of the history of scholarship on the Deuteronomistic History beginning with Noth. Noth believed strongly in the competence of the Israelite historian, while Brettler questions his motives, first suggesting that historical intention does not make a text historiographical, and second that we cannot know the intentions of the Deuteronomist. More recently, some scholars, especially those deemed literary critics of the Bible, have given up on historical-critical biblical study and only use synchronic approaches, deeming the text unhistorical.[26] These approaches were likely influenced by the intellectual development in the world of critical theory of the mid-twentieth century, beginning with the doctrine of intentional fallacy in the 1940s, which denied

24. Ibid., 11.
25. Ibid., 12.
26. *ABN*; Sternberg, *Poetics of Biblical Narrative*; Robert Polzin, *Samuel and the Deuteronomist: 1 Samuel* (Bloomington: Indiana University Press, 1993).

that the interpreter has access to the author's intentions.[27] This prohibited scholars from considering the intentions of the biblical authors. Literary criticism is important in the interpretation of the aesthetic quality of the biblical text, but it should not inhibit historical interpretation. It is foolhardy and nihilistic to dismiss reasoned speculation because we can never achieve certainty. This would discredit much important and convincing interpretation of ancient texts. We will always reach a point of indeterminacy, but that should not prevent us from exploration, throwing up our hands that we cannot know anything about the past. Instead, we must make reasoned assessments, methodological speculation, and recognize the differences between the objective and subjective. While Brettler's hesitation about the question of intention, especially of an ancient author, is warranted as it is extremely difficult to qualify and quantify, my schema of historiographical poetics offers observation-based criteria for determining intention. It is by no means definitive, but presents a systematic range of considerations.

While their approaches appear mutually exclusive, Brettler's presentation of ideological construction and Halpern's antiquarian interests must both be considered.[28] The work of Halpern and Brettler comes down to the same question: how did the biblical historian see/use his sources?[29] They approach this question in two

---

27. William K. Wimsatt and Monroe C. Beardsley, "The Intentional Fallacy," in *The Verbal Icon: Studies in the Meaning of Poetry*, ed. William K. Wimsatt (Lexington: University of Kentucky Press, 1954), 3–18. Reprinted from *Sewanee Review* 54 (1946).

28. H. G. M. Williamson, "Review of The Creation of History in Ancient Israel, by Marc Z. Brettler," *Journal of Jewish Studies* 47, no. 2 (1996): 355.

29. Halpern addresses this issue in an analysis of Judges 4 and 5 in Baruch Halpern, "Doctrine by Misadventure: Between the Israelite Source and the Biblical Historian," in *The Poet and the Historian: Essays in Literary and Historical Biblical Criticism*, ed. Richard E. Friedman (Chico, CA: Scholars Press, 1983), 41–73; Halpern, "'Brisker Pipes Than Poetry': The Development of Israelite Monotheism," in *Judaic Perspectives on Ancient Israel*, ed. Jacob Neusner, Baruch A. Levine, and Ernest S. Frerichs (Philadelphia: Fortress Press, 1987), 77–115; Halpern, *The First Historians*, chap. 6.

ways—both of which are necessary to understanding the process of deuteronomistic historiography. Halpern focuses on the work of the Deuteronomist, understanding his process of selection, why he incorporates the sources he does, while Brettler focuses on the Chronicler, primarily because we have access to his sources (DtrH), and the choices of composition that he makes and how he adapts and rewrites his sources. In this book, I consider the approaches of both these scholars, taking into account both the compositional and selectional processes.

A third scholar who begins to bridge the gap between Halpern's work on antiquarian interest and Brettler's focus on theological and literary shaping is Gary Knoppers. In his two-volume work, *Two Nations under God*, Knoppers emphasizes the thematic elements present in DtrH, namely, the role of the unified monarchy in the entirety of the history.[30] Highlighting this theme and Jeroboam's literary role in the production of the history, Knoppers combines some of the main issues that Halpern, Brettler, and others have begun to explore, and applies them to the figures of Solomon and Jeroboam. Knoppers explicitly states that Dtr's "*modus operandi* is not so much to invent history as it is to shape history to conform to his own agenda."[31] In this way, Knoppers is attentive to the historian's use of his sources, as well as his intention to rewrite them for his own ideological purposes. He is among the first to consider the historiographical process for both its historical-critical and literary significance. My work is a direct extension of these three scholars and of work in historiographical theory in general.

---

30. Gary N. Knoppers, *Two Nations under God: The Deuteronomistic History of Solomon and the Dual Monarchies*, vol. 1, *The Reign of Solomon and the Rise of Jeroboam*, Harvard Semitic Monographs (Atlanta: Scholars Press, 1993); Knoppers, *Two Nations under God: The Deuteronomistic History of Solomon and the Dual Monarchies*, vol. 2, *The Reign of Jeroboam, the Fall of Israel, and the Reign of Josiah*, Harvard Semitic Monographs (Atlanta: Scholars Press, 1994).
31. Knoppers, *Reign of Jeroboam*, 182–83.

Poetics

Poetics, as defined by Meir Sternberg in his book *The Poetics of Biblical Narrative*, is what "the biblical narrator want[s] to accomplish, and under what conditions . . . he operate[s]."[32] Sternberg poses the following questions: "What goals does the biblical narrator set himself? What is it that he wants to communicate in this or that story, cycle, book?" Sternberg suggests that the reader approach biblical narrative as "oriented to an addressee and regulated by a purpose or a set of purposes involving the addressee. Hence our primary business as readers is to make purposive sense of it, so as to explain the *what's* and the *how's* in terms of the *why's* of communication."[33] This is my goal in dealing with the historiographical poetics of the preexilic Deuteronomist in Kings. I explore the ways in which Dtr writes his history, how he selects his sources, how he recrafts and integrates them into a comprehensive story that reflects the general history of the monarchy, and where he makes original compositions. A comprehensive analysis of this process is lacking in the prolific scholarship dealing with Kings specifically and DtrH generally. Greater understanding of the historiographical poetics of Dtr and his purposes in redaction and composition will greatly supplement the bevy of scholarship largely focused on redactional criticism and expand focus into literary composition. This work will advance the field so that once source and redactional lines have been drawn, it will be possible to understand Dtr's goals, explaining the whats, hows, and whys of his historiography.

The discussion of poetics is primarily a literary one, focused on the ways the author constructs his story, but the text need not be deemed fictional. The generic line between fiction and ancient

---

32. Sternberg, *Poetics of Biblical Narrative*, 2.
33. Ibid., 1.

historiography is complicated and blurry. Robert Alter adeptly describes the relationship the historian maintains to the story when he writes: "The biblical historian's drive to understand the political, moral, and psychological predicaments of the historical personages leads him to shape the events, amplifying what is known through shrewd literary elaboration, [but] there remain bothersome instances of invention plain and simple."[34] He also contends that "the writer could manipulate his inherited materials with sufficient freedom and sufficient firmness of authorial purpose to define motives, relations, and unfolding themes, even in a primeval history, with the kind of subtle cogency we associate with the conscious artistry of the narrative mode designated prose fiction."[35] Need this be categorized as fiction or can it be "interpretation"? Similarly, while the generic distinction between fiction and history can be endlessly debated, Hayden White, who has written influentially about historiography and historiographical theory, posits that generally "what distinguishes 'historical' from 'fictional' stories is first and foremost their content, rather than their form."[36] As such, historical and fictional narratives will appear similar, only distinguished by their subjects. According to White, the historical method requires the evaluation of documents (the content) in order to determine what is historical, followed by constructing the most plausible story (the form) from the evidence, not so much a product of the historian's poetic talents.[37] In putting together the story, the historian needs to follow the sequence of "facts" and "events," creating "content [that] may be thought to consist either of the factors linking events in chains of causes and effects or of the 'reasons' (or 'intentions') motivating the human

---

34. Alter, "Imagining History," 67.
35. *ABN* 32.
36. Hayden White, *The Content of the Form: Narrative Discourse and Historical Representation* (Baltimore: Johns Hopkins University Press, 1990), 27.
37. Ibid.

agents of the events in question."[38] The historian's vocation is "to translate knowing into telling," by creating a narrative (the form) as a solution "to the problem of fashioning human experience into a form assimilable to structures of meaning."[39] White's definition of history and the use of the historical method require us to consider both the author's intention and the way he used his sources. It is in this way that I focus on exploring Dtr's "poetics," attempting to understand Dtr's reasons and intentions for linking events, attributing cause, and in particular the development of form and style, how Dtr writes his story.

This endeavor is not only necessitated by the polarizing and divisive developments in biblical scholarship, but also by the development of postmodernist and new historicist theory. Terry Eagleton defines postmodernism as "the contemporary movement of thought which rejects totalities, universal values, grand historical narratives, solid foundations to human existence and the possibility of objective knowledge. Postmodernism is skeptical of truth, unity and progress, opposes what it sees as elitism in culture, tends towards cultural relativism, and celebrates pluralism, discontinuity and heterogeneity."[40] While the assumptions of postmodernism—rejection of the objective, erasing any distinction between the objective and the subjective, and maintaining the inexistence of a univocal, unambiguous meaning—are worthwhile guiding questions for the study of the Bible generally and of biblical historiography specifically, in the case of this subset of literature, we cannot and should not disregard the possibility of elucidating textual meanings.[41] It is especially the postmodernist critique of

---

38. Ibid., 41.
39. Ibid., 1.
40. Terry Eagleton, *After Theory* (New York: Basic Books, 2003), 13n1.
41. John J. Collins, *The Bible after Babel: Historical Criticism in a Postmodern Age* (Grand Rapids: Eerdmans, 2005), 27–28.

metanarratives that should be considered in the study of the Bible. My analysis makes clear that this literature was constructed using grand schemas to organize and interpret history.

While acknowledging the limits of our knowledge (the Halpern/ Brettler debate), and putting aside the fears of the doctrine of intentional fallacy, we can still claim some knowledge of the past, the historians' intentions, and the ways in which they used their sources.[42] This view reflects developments in new historicism, which considers "reality" in literary texts. This approach requires, when thinking about textuality, that one "recover in our literary criticism a confident conviction of reality, without giving up the power of literature to sidestep or evade the quotidian and without giving up a minimally sophisticated understanding that any text depends upon the absence of the bodies and voice that it represents."[43] In this way, "the real . . . to which the text implies, lies beyond the written word, outside its textual mode of being."[44] "The real" needs to be considered. In this way, Stephen Greenblatt states, "New historicist critics have tried to understand the intersecting circumstances not as a stable, prefabricated background against which the literary texts can be placed, but as a dense network of evolving and often contradictory social forces."[45] This suggests that all texts should be considered within their historical context and in respect to the social, political, and religious factors that contributed to the text's development. Just as the new historicists, focusing on texts themselves, see literature as a product of place and time, with the right tools we can derive some information about the history of ancient Israel from the text. This

---

42. Halpern, *The First Historians*, xxi.
43. Catherine Gallagher and Stephen Greenblatt, *Practicing New Historicism* (Chicago: University of Chicago Press, 2000), 31.
44. Ibid., 23.
45. Stephen Greenblatt, *Learning to Curse: Essays in Early Modern Culture* (New York: Routledge, 1990), 170.

is not to say that all of the text corresponds to fact or that we must completely deny the veracity of all those texts. We are informed by new historicism in recognizing the problematic boundaries between objective history, the things that happened, and subjective history, the narration of the things that happened.[46] As such, we must occupy a moderate middle ground between those who say we can never get to the intention of the authors (or that we would even want to) and those who assert that the history is wholly historical or ahistorical. We must identify what intent we can draw out of the text. We must employ the so-called historical-critical method, historical linguistics, redaction criticism, ancient Near Eastern analogies, in conjunction with the newer methods of literary and philosophical approaches, for a more complete interpretation of biblical historiography.[47] It is with this combination of approaches in mind that I will look seriously at Dtr's method as author and redactor.

The Deuteronomist

Since Spinoza in the late seventeenth century, scholarship of the DtrH has traditionally focused on the unity of the books of Deuteronomy through Kings and the role of the Deuteronomistic Historian. Since Noth, scholars have identified Dtr as an author and redactor. Noth acclaims a historian who "was not merely an editor but the author of a history which brought together material from highly varied traditions and arranged it according to a carefully conceived plan."[48] He insists that "Dtr. was the author of a comprehensive historical work, scrupulously taking over and quoting the existing tradition but at the same time arranging and articulating all the material independently, and making it clear and systematic

46. Hendel, "Culture, Memory, and History," 257.
47. White, *Content of the Form*, 185.
48. Noth, *Deuteronomistic History*, 26.

by composing summaries which anticipate and recapitulate."[49] While some scholars have relegated the inconsistencies within Dtr's text to the ineptitude of the scribe, Noth's theory allows that inconsistency comes from the historian's use of sources, which exonerates the redactor of incompetency.[50] Dtr had sources that he edited to form his narratives. He adds original material to them, sometimes only a few words or on occasion long narratives, creating a new work of history. In Kings, he presents a theological interpretation of the history of Israel and Judah.

My work further presents a theologically motivated historian, functioning as both author and redactor, who creates a complete, cohesive, and chronological historical document. He interprets his sources in light of his theology. The historical poetics I lay out in the following chapter will expand on the compositional and selectional method of Dtr. Dtr uses his sources, the prophetic tradition, and a system for organizing scenes while recrafting his work to promote the deuteronomistic program, attribute theological significance to historico-political events, and develop the portrait of his kings using a prototype strategy.

In this book, I will adopt a modified version of the Cross theory, which argues for a double redaction.[51] This is manifested in two versions of the Deuteronomistic History: the primary one written in the age of Josiah, whose goal was programmatic reform, and a

---

49. Ibid., 120.
50. Halpern, *The First Historians*, 117.
51. *CMHE* 274–89. Cross builds on Noth's deuteronomistic theory of viewing the books of Joshua to Kings as a single historical work of diverse sources that expresses the theological and historical slant of the editor, using a framework marked by speeches, patterned after Deuteronomy, characterized by a unique literary style. Cross opposes Noth's dating of the work to the exilic period, primarily based on the appropriateness of major themes to the historical context. While Noth saw the major theme of the history as doom, manifesting in a history of Israel that is a story of apostasy and idolatry, Cross sees a current of positive perspective running through the narrative. To Noth, this negative theme was most suitable to an exilic audience. In contrast, Cross identifies a positive outlook that he views as more fitting to a preexilic context and attributes the more negative themes to a second, exilic editor.

secondary revision that functioned as a sermon to the exiles. Cross names these two editors Dtr^1 and Dtr^2. In this way, the theme of hope in the original work is overwritten and contradicted in the second edition. Dtr^2 attempts to update the history in the postexilic world. This exilic edition preserves the work of the Josianic Deuteronomist (Dtr^1) and adds events and causalities without completing a stylistic revision.

I find this model and the arguments that support it to best fit with the evidence, although there remains considerable uncertainty about many details. The primary thematic and ideological concerns reflected in DtrH are most appropriate for the preexilic period. The hopefulness of the reign of Josiah and the unconditional Davidic promises, both as organizing frameworks and as historical events, lose their import and purpose if attributed to an exilic context. I agree with Gary Knoppers, who contends for a preexilic DtrH, wondering, "why would a Deuteronomist living during the Babylonian exile, write such an ambitious and laborious history, if his only message was a guarded expectation of divine compassion, predicated upon abject repentance?"[52] Also, it is possible to see within stylistic elements changes in the thematic concerns in exilic passages. This will be explored in chapter 6, with the counterexample of 2 Kings 21 demonstrating that only in the preexilic history does the Deuteronomist use a Davidic model for his kings.

At the same time, it is necessary to acknowledge that discussion of redactional layers and their themes and concerns are often built on circular arguments. Once the historical context of each Dtr's composition and redaction has been identified, by means of stylistic, thematic, or theological grounds, these elements then become "criteria" to further identify redaction and continue to derive

52. Knoppers, *Reign of Solomon*, 25.

identifiable criteria. Then, representative stylistic, thematic, and theological interests of a certain redactor are inferred when evaluating the texts previously assigned to those redactional levels.[53]

53. This is true for both the two prevailing redactional models of DtrH. The Cross/Harvard school focuses on the thematic interests of a preexilic and exilic Dtr, while the Smend/ Dietrich hypothesis–Göttingen school focuses on subject concerns of a historian, prophetic, and nomistic Dtr.

The alternative to Cross and the Harvard school's view of a double redaction theory, taken up by German scholars, agreeing with Noth, advocates for an exclusively exilic date. In 1971, Rudolf Smend, analyzing passages in Joshua and Judges, identifies contradictions in the conquest narratives, suggesting that many verses within these chapters were later additions. He views the narrative, which describes Joshua conquering the entire country and exterminating the ancient inhabitants, as the first edition of Dtr, but notes secondary passages illustrating a cohesive but contrary alternative narrative that describes an incomplete conquest, leaving many of the former inhabitants still living in the land. Smend suggests that this narrative be divided into two different redactional layers, yet both exilic. He identifies these two layers as DtrH (or DtrG, for the Deuteronomistic *Geschichtsschreiber*), the Deuteronomistic Historian who creates the first edition largely focused on presenting a historical account, and DtrN, a nomistic redactor who reedits DtrH, correcting it and adding other material according to the law (Rudolf Smend, "Das Gesetz Und Die Völker: Ein Beitrag Zur Deuteronomistischen Redaktionsgeschichte," in *Probleme Biblischer Theologie* (Munich: Kaiser, 1971), 494–509; Pury and Römer, "Deuteronomistic Historiography," 67–68).

Smend's student Walter Dietrich identifies a third layer of redaction that contains prophetic judgments, designating it DtrP. Dietrich's DtrP is an author and redactor who integrates the Deuteronomistic History with pre-Dtr material. History according to DtrP is the fulfillment of prophetic predictions. All three of these redactors are exilic; he specifically dates DtrH ending with 2 Kgs. 25:21 to around 580 BCE, DtrN ending with the rehabilitation of Jehoiachin around 560 BCE, and DtrP as somewhere in between, but located in Palestine, likely Jerusalem (Walter Dietrich, *Prophetie Und Geschichte Eine Redaktionsgeschichtliche Untersuchung Zum Deuteronomistischen Geschichtswerk*, FRLANT 108 [Göttingen: Vandenhoeck & Ruprecht, 1972]; Pury and Römer, "Deuteronomistic Historiography," 69).

Timo Veijola, another student of Smend, focuses on DtrN in Samuel and Kings. He evaluates the books from their theological perspectives, considering the attitude each redactor has of the institution of monarchy (Timo Veijola, *Die Ewige Dynastie: David Und Die Entstehung Seiner Dynastie Nach Der Deuteronomistischen Darstellung* [Helsinki: Suomalainen Tiedeakatemia, 1975]; Pury and Römer, "Deuteronomistic Historiography," 68–70; Martin Dietrich, "Martin Noth and the Future of the Deuteronomistic History," in *The History of Israel's Traditions: The Heritage of Martin Noth*, ed. Steven McKenzie and M. Patrick Graham [Sheffield: Sheffield Academic, 1994], 156).

There is a third collection of scholars who form something of a subgroup of the Harvard school. They argue for the first, primary, preexilic edition written in the time of or immediately following the reign of Hezekiah. This group includes Provan, Monroe, Barrick, Weippert, and Thomas, among others. Their arguments focus on the prevalence of the *bāmôt* theme leading up to Hezekiah's account and the absence of it following. Iain Provan, *Hezekiah and the Books of Kings: A Contribution to the Debate About the Composition of the Deuteronomistic History* (Berlin: de Gruyter, 1988); Lauren A. S. Monroe, *Josiah's Reform and the Dynamics of Defilement: Israelite Rites of Violence and the Making of a Biblical Text* (New York: Oxford University Press, 2011);

Linguistic grounds are the most reliable indicators, although they also are not absolute.

A major methodological problem arises out of these conflicts—how do we differentiate between the voices that reflect various layers of redactions and the voices of the component sources? How do we differentiate between the perspectives of a redactor and the perspectives represented in older traditions and later activity? And how can we characterize the extent of the work of an author/redactor? Should an extensive composition be considered the same act of creation as the insertion of a scribal gloss?[54] This complexity should not scare us away from identifying redactions and themes, but requires self-awareness of the pitfalls of this endeavor.

While recognizing these inherent challenges, we must still attempt to identify redactional layers. The value of the redactional assessments made in the following chapters are crucial to understanding the historiographical poetics of the preexilic Deuteronomist. In order to properly assess the ways in which the Deuteronomist (or Deuteronomists) work, it is essential to make clear which texts are indeed a part of a specific level of redaction and composition. Only then can they be evaluated for style. By first dividing the texts into their historical contexts, it is possible to use the thematic concerns to derive stylistic choices. Accordingly, each example given in the subsequent chapters will also include a redactional assessment of the pericope. The historiographical poetics can also offer more solid "principles" on which to make redactional decisions.

W. Boyd Barrick, *The King and the Cemeteries: Toward a New Understanding of Josiah's Reform*, VTSup (Leiden: Brill, 2002); Helga Weippert, "Die Deuteronomistischen Beurteilungen Der Könige von Israel Und Juda Und Das Problem Der Redaktion Der Königsbücher," *Biblica* 53 (1972): 301–39; Benjamin D. Thomas, *Hezekiah and the Compositional History of the Book of Kings* (Tübingen: Mohr Siebeck, 2014). Many thanks to Benjamin Thomas for sharing his manuscript with me before it was published.

54. Halpern, *The First Historians*, 112, 116.

Furthermore, recognition of stylistic differences in the competing thematic perspectives highlights the differences in the origins of composition. This will be particularly important in discovering the underlying historiographical concerns in these texts. The historiographical method will also be a location in which the seams of redaction can be uncovered. Accepting the Cross theory of a primarily preexilic Josianic redaction has a great impact on historiographical concerns. The theological function of the history, an attempt to promote the deuteronomistic program and the reform at the time of Josiah, is an essential guide to the construction of history. The persona of Josiah himself contributes to the portrait of the kings, good and bad, through the creation of a specific literary prototype, focused on David and based on Josiah, that was first established in the account of the reign of Solomon. This prototype is used to evaluate the kings and convey a didactic message to the people of Judah of the proper form of Yahwistic worship. This prototype, along with other stylistic elements on both selectional and compositional levels, illustrates a systematic, stylistic narrative framework imposed by Dtr on the majority of the history. Unlike the Smend-Dietrich theory (see n52), the unity of the narrative constructed is of utmost importance to the understanding and function of the history.

Portrait of the Kings

This work will systematically lay out the historiographical method the preexilic Deuteronomist uses in Kings. I suggest that his work operates on two different axes. The first is the axis of selection, which includes the methodological priorities that guide Dtr in his choice and redaction of sources. These priorities are threefold: Dtr attempts to find balance among (1) reporting the historical events that occurred and staying true to the sources that he possesses describing those events, likely those from the royal archives (Halpern's antiquarian interest,[55] a commitment to a source tradition); (2) loyalty to the prophetic tradition; and (3) the organizational strategies used for incorporating these sources, through the ordering of episodes.

The second axis is one of composition, rhetoric, and formation. The following compositional strategies are used: (1) promoting the deuteronomistic programmatic agenda, (2) attribution of historico-political events to theological causes, and (3) the use of a prototype strategy. Chapter 2 systematically lays out the historiographical poetics of the preexilic Deuteronomist. The exploration of this historiographical poetics is followed by the application of these priorities in a test case of 1 Kings 11 in order to further illustrate the ways this method functions.

The subsequent chapters will consider the narrative accounts of a few specific kings, and these priorities will be explored in each narrative. Those texts will be mined for understanding how Dtr as author and redactor works in constructing these narratives. Chapters 3–6 each have as their subject a different king. Chapter 3 begins with considering the criteria for being a good king, one who does הישר בעיני יהוה, "what is right in Yahweh's eyes." Few kings receive any praise from Dtr, but even fewer are compared to David. The remainder of the chapter continues to analyze the portrait of David in Kings and how this portrait is constructed as the model for other kings, a strategy of a royal prototype. The depiction of David is very different from the one we see in the book of Samuel.

This prototype is based on a literary picture of David in which he is the exemplum of covenant fidelity. He is the model of the deuteronomistically adherent king, the one whom all subsequent kings are required to emulate. Dtr uses David as the royal

---

55. Ibid., 76–99.

comparandum to construct the portrait of both good and bad kings. The good kings are those who are like David, while the bad kings are those who are not. Although the history of the monarchy spans half a millennium, only those kings who contribute to Dtr's metanarrative are constructed using this prototype. It is in the portrait of the kings that Dtr highlights that we can most clearly see his poetics and the expression of his theological concerns.

The following chapters consider a few select kings, Jeroboam, Josiah, and Manasseh, in respect to the application of the Davidic prototype explored in chapter 3. They examine how each king fits into the prototype, and they demonstrate the historiographical poetics in process, crafting the portrait of the kings. Chapter 4 considers the portrait of Jeroboam depicted in 1 Kings 11–14. The use of the Davidic prototype is strongly applied in constructing the portrait of Jeroboam. He is first presented as a second David, one who is given the opportunity to be heir to the Davidic promise. He is assured a secure dynasty and the majority of the kingdom if only he would be like David, remaining faithful to the covenant. Inevitably, Jeroboam is unable to live up to the model set by David. Instead of embodying the Davidic prototype, Jeroboam becomes its antithesis. He is the anti-David, one who not only does not keep Yahweh's laws and commandments, but who also inaugurates an uncentralized countercult that drags the entire people of Israel down with him. Opposed as he is to the Davidic prototype, Jeroboam becomes the prototype of the evil king. Jeroboam's sin is the sin of Israel and the primary theological justification for Israel's downfall and exile by Assyria. Dtr rhetoricizes the cult and its founder as idolatrous. The prototype strategy is an integral tool in portraying Jeroboam's cult sites as foreign rather than merely uncentralized.

Chapter 5 focuses on the portrait of Josiah, which similarly uses the Davidic prototype as its measure. In contrast to Jeroboam, who is developed as the anti-David, Josiah is constructed as a true second David, one who even surpasses the model of David. Josiah is the paradigm of covenant fidelity. Not only does he keep the laws and commandments, but he also institutes a major reform harmonizing the people of Judah and the national cult with the scroll of the law found in the temple. The account of Josiah's reign (2 Kings 22–23) is intertextually linked with all of the important events and figures in the history of the monarchy. Josiah is seen as the only king who can reverse the sins of the bad kings, restoring Israel to the unified Davidic kingdom, and as surpassing all of the good kings, outdoing the reform measures of even the reformers. These connections solidify the importance of these chapters to the entirety of the history and the literary intentions of Dtr in crafting the whole narrative. In this way, Josiah is the greatest of all kings, both those who precede and those who succeed him. The entire history has been building to prepare for the coming of Josiah. The account of his reign demonstrates a last attempt for Judah to escape the fate of Israel.

In contrast, chapter 6 takes as a counterexample the account of King Manasseh in 2 Kings 21, a royal portrait produced by an exilic redactor (Dtr²). In this narrative, it is possible to see how preexilic deuteronomistic historiographical priorities are recalibrated in an exilic setting. There are two major but interrelated differences in this example of exilic historiography. Rather than being concerned with syncretistic and decentralized worship, the exilic Deuteronomist is focused on eliminating the worship of foreign gods from Israelite practice. This concern manifests itself in a shift in the prototype strategy. Instead of casting Manasseh in the mold of the anti-David, Jeroboam, Manasseh is modeled after Ahab. The change conveys the different concerns of an exilic redactor: namely, the worship of Baal and other foreign gods. Despite this difference, the Manasseh narrative and the use of the prototype strategy are clear examples of how essential the historiographical method of Dtr^1 was to the deuteronomistic school and to Dtr^2. The impulse for the use of the prototype strategy is so strong that in Dtr^2's exilic rewrite of the Manasseh account, Dtr^2 attempts to use this method, taking the account of ordinary bad king Manasseh found in the preexilic history and reshaping the reign of Manasseh to appear as the worst of all kings, creating a suitable scapegoat on whom to blame the destruction of Judah and the Babylonian exile.

The analysis of the accounts of the reigns of these specific kings highlights the historiographical poetics at play in the construction of the accounts. Each example demonstrates how the selectional and compositional strategies used by Dtr create an effective account of the king's reign and the portrait of that king in order to contribute to Dtr's goals in promoting deuteronomistic theology. This approach produces greater understanding of Dtr's historiographical method, leading to a greater understanding of the book of Kings. The preexilic historian uses the prototype strategy to guide his telling of the history of the monarchy, highlighting only those kings who fit into the prototype. This strategy illustrates a grand narrative scheme in which the most important players in his history are connected, not only in their roles in history and their influence over the kingdoms of Israel and Judah, but also in their literary construction. By identifying Dtr's literary and historiographical style, it helps us to make redactional decisions, on grounds beyond thematic justifications. In this way, the historiographical poetics becomes a tool of textual analysis.

While textual criticism plays an important role in biblical interpretation and contributes to greater objectivity in redactional decisions, this volume will focus on the earliest achievable edition of Kings, which is most closely represented by the Masoretic Text (MT).[56] Accepting the primacy of the MT over the Septuagint (LXX) as closest to the original edition does not preclude me from adopting retroversions in the text based on LXX evidence. While the MT preserves the earlier version, many individual readings and details are best preserved by other witnesses. While the complete narrative version may be secondary, it is possible for me to use the LXX as a better witness to the proto-MT *Vorlage* that may have been corrupted in the process of transmission. The LXX often preserves the best reading. The texts explored in the subsequent chapters, especially the Jeroboam narrative, have some significant variations between MT and LXX, but my analysis will focus on the poetics of the historiography found in the MT edition.

The majority of Septuagint scholars fall into two camps: those who believe the LXX version is a midrash of sorts on the MT; and those who believe the LXX is based on an earlier stage in the literary development of the text.[57] I am convinced by the first group of scholars. There is also significant debate about the deuteronomistic influence on the

---

56. Sidnie White Crawford, Jan Joosten, and Eugene Charles Ulrich, "Sample Editions of the Oxford Hebrew Bible: Deuteronomy 32:1-9, 1 Kings 11:1-8, and Jeremiah 27:1-10 (34 G)," *VT* 58, no. 3 (2008): 359.

57. For more on this discussion, see: P. S. F. van Keulen, *Two Versions of the Solomon Narrative: An Inquiry into the Relationship Between MT 1 Kgs. 2–11 and LXX 3 Reg. 2–11*, VTSup 104 (Leiden: Brill, 2005), 4; Zipora Talshir, *The Alternative Story of the Division of the Kingdom: 3 Kingdoms 12:24a-z* (Jerusalem: Simor, 1993); Julio C. Trebolle, "Samuel/Kings and Chronicles: Book Divisions and Textual Composition," in *Studies in the Hebrew Bible, Qumran, and the Septuagint Presented to Eugene Ulrich*, ed. Eugene Charles Ulrich et al. (Leiden: Brill, 2006), 96–108; Trebolle, "Kings (MT/LXX) and Chronicles: The Double and Triple Textual Traditions," in *Reflection and Refraction: Studies in Biblical Historiography in Honour of A. Graeme Auld*, ed. Robert Rezetko, Timothy H. Lim, and W. Brian Aucker (Leiden: Brill, 2006), 483–501; Trebolle, "The Text-Critical Use of the Septuagint in the Books of Kings," *Seventh Congress of the International Organization for Septuagint and Cognate Studies, Leuven 1989*, ed. Claude E. Cox (Atlanta: Scholars Press, 1991), 285–99; Trebolle, "Redaction, Recension and Midrash in the Books of Kings," *Bulletin of the International Organization for Septuagint and Cognate Studies* 15 (1982): 12–35; Emanuel Tov, *The Text-Critical Use of the Septuagint in Biblical Research* (Jerusalem: Simor, 1981); Marvin A. Sweeney, "A Reassessment of the Masoretic and Septuagint Versions of the Jeroboam Narratives in 1 Kings/3 Kingdoms 11-14," *Journal for the Study of Judaism in the Persian, Hellenistic and Roman Period* 38, no. 2 (2007): 165–95; Crawford, Joosten, and Ulrich, "Sample Editions of the Oxford Hebrew Bible," 352–66; T. Michael Law, "How Not to Use 3 Reigns: A Plea to Scholars of the Books of Kings," *VT* 61, no. 2 (2011): 280–97.

LXX and its *Vorlage*. This is especially true when a passage parallel to one in MT Kings lacks deuteronomistic elements found in MT. Is this a sign of a proto-Dtr text, or does it reflect a text that has been emptied of its deuteronomistic rhetoric? This debate is outside the scope of this project. I am exclusively focused on the historiographical poetics of Dtr as depicted in the original edition of Kings, for which MT is our best source, since I view it as the original edition and the LXX as secondary.

Also, while this work is primarily focused on literary concerns and deriving the historiographical poetics, redaction criticism will play an essential role in determining which parts of texts are indeed a product of the preexilic Deuteronomist and therefore contribute to my analysis. Yet this will be a redactional critique with a more nuanced approach. Kings will not be viewed as a source of history; instead, it will be seen as the product of a redactor(s) constructing a history on a "grand schema." Postmodern cautions against viewing history this way are most certainly at play. As John Collins describes in his volume about historical criticism in a postmodern age, "Grand schemas are inherently ideological, and inevitably privilege some perspectives to the exclusion of others." Similarly, "it is common experience in history writing that stubborn facts resist and subvert the metanarratives of the historian. The paradigm shifts that occur with some regularity in the field testify not only to the changing interests of historians, but also, at least sometimes, to data that cannot be accommodated in the old paradigm."[58] My view of the historiographical poetics of the Deuteronomist is focused on identifying the schema of ideological privilege and considering where the data fits and does not fit with this ideology.

---

58. Collins, *The Bible after Babel*, 28, 29.

This volume builds on the scholarly perspectives presented over the past two hundred years. Conceiving of historiographical poetics relies on the work of Noth and the idea of a competent redactor who used sources to craft his history as well as inserted his own material at critical junctures. While I do not hold wholly to Noth's redactional theories, the concepts of unity in DtrH and Dtr's role in reshaping his sources into a theologically meaningful narrative are crucial components to the poetics I lay out. Although Noth and others assert that Dtr does indeed use sources, integrating and recrafting them, there has not yet been any comprehensive assessment of the methodology with which Dtr does so. This is the aim of my historiographical poetics.

I advance scholarship in this field in three ways. First, I take issues of literary style seriously. Bringing into play the method of the newer literary critics of the Bible, I consider the process of historiography, not just for its presentation of the past, but also for the ways in which the historian crafts his history in order to present the past, evaluating and cataloging the literary style and techniques that he uses to make his history successful. Second, I build on the redaction scholarship, demonstrating the various selectional techniques Dtr uses to make choices of what to include of the record of the past in his historical narrative and how to include it.[59] Previous scholarship has tended not to consider the ways in which earlier traditions are integrated into the text as well as why a specific Deuteronomist makes the choices he does. These two impulses make up the historiographical poetics that I outline in chapter 2 and will apply in the following chapters. And third, I highlight the importance and role of the prototype strategy in the intentional crafting of the portrait of the kings. That strategy

---

59. It is interesting to notice that despite the various redactional theories that scholars propound, they are often debating the same critical chapters and verses as the crucial evidence to their theory and the overall goals of the primary version of the history.

functions both in evaluating the kings of Israel and Judah similarly through deuteronomistic standards and in comparing the literary portraits of the kings.

2

The Historiographical Poetics of the
Preexilic Deuteronomist

Since the work of Benedict Spinoza in the late seventeenth century,[1] biblical critics have discussed the connection between the book of Deuteronomy and the historical books of the Former Prophets. For almost four centuries, scholars have considered the issues relating to the Deuteronomistic History along the lines of three topics: the identity and dating of the author(s), the process and date of the formation of the books, and the coherence of the books to each other and their connection with Deuteronomy.[2] Depending where scholars fall on the first two sets of issues usually determines how they view

---

1. Benedict Spinoza, *Tractatus Theologico-Politicus* (Amsterdam: Hamburgi, 1670).
2. De Pury and Römer highlight these as the issues that eighteenth-century scholars addressed. Albert de Pury and Thomas Römer, "Deuteronomistic Historiography (DH): History of Research and Debated Issues," in *Israel Constructs Its History: Deuteronomistic Historiography in Recent Research* (Sheffield: Sheffield Academic, 2000), 32. Benjamin Thomas also offers a comprehensive summary of the historical and recent work on the theories of composition and redaction in Kings: *Hezekiah and the Compositional History of the Book of Kings* (Tübingen: Mohr Siebeck, 2014), 1–45.

the unity of the books. More recently, there have been scholars who suggest an ultimate lack of consistency among the books and have disavowed the existence of a Deuteronomistic History. These issues come together in understanding the role of Dtr in the compilation of the history and are essential to consider in the discussion of Dtr's historiographical poetics.

W. M. L. de Wette, at the turn of the nineteenth century, is the first to use the term "deuteronomic" to describe the historical books. The books of Joshua, Judges, Samuel, and Kings reveal, more or less, an ideology that values and alludes to (explicitly and implicitly) the law of Deuteronomy. The debate over the (dis)unity of these books has a long historical precedent, focused on theological connections. In this work, I will provide a historiographical assessment of the book of Kings. Before diving into this conversation, it is necessary to clarify when the historian is situated, addressing two major concerns: the dating and extent of redactional levels and Dtr's historiographical process. Over the past two centuries since de Wette, several redaction theories have developed.

While scholars certainly dealt with these issues during the intervening century since de Wette, the contemporary history of the scholarship on the Deuteronomistic History primarily takes as its starting point the work of Martin Noth.[3] Although scholars may agree, disagree, or tweak Noth's theses, they all contend with him. Building on the established work of de Wette, Heinrich Ewald, Abraham Kuenen, Julius Wellhausen, and others, Noth looks beyond the layers of redaction and attempts to derive a description of the historiography of the Deuteronomistic History.[4] He addresses the

---

3. Martin Noth, *Überlieferungsgeschichtliche Studien. Die Sammelnden Und Bearbeitenden Geschischtswerke Im Alten Testement* (Tübingen: Max Niemeyer, 1957); Noth, *The Deuteronomistic History* (Sheffield: JSOT Press, 1981).

4. Abraham Kuenen, *Historisch-Kritisch Onderzoek Naar Het Ontstaan En de Verzmeling van de Boeken Des Ouden Verbonds*, 3 vols. (Leiden: Engels, 1861); Kuenen, *An Historico-Critical*

questions about the coherence and consistency of the history, laying out an organizational literary plan for the work of Dtr. Noth includes authorial artistry and narrative intentions in the conversation about the concept of "deuteronomism," and identifies the use of vocabulary and phrases uncommon to the Tetrateuch. Noth sees Dtr as an author, with a singular perspective and characteristic linguistic usage.

Noth derives a structure that focuses on the literary unity of the history, the framework that Dtr used to organize and bring together the disparate traditions.[5] He presents a Dtr who is involved with compilation and composition, creating an intentional unity within the history. In no uncertain terms, Noth declares that "Dtr. was not merely an editor but the author of a history which brought together material from highly varied traditions and arranged it according to a carefully conceived plan."[6] This also leads to the integration of the ideology of Deuteronomy and the question of the consistency of the books. In this way, Noth's Dtr incorporated deuteronomic law and then added other sources, organizing and shaping them, and including his own evaluations (often through speeches by major characters) at important points in the history. Noth appeals to Dtr as author and redactor, asserting a unity of composition. Yet he acknowledges that inconsistencies in perspective exist within the

---

Inquiry into the Origin and Composition of the Hexateuch (Pentateuch and Book of Joshua), trans. Philip H. Wicksteed (London: Macmillan, 1886); Heinrich Ewald, *Geschichte Des Volkes Israel*, 6 vols. (Göttingen: Dieterichs Buchhandlung, 1843); Ewald, *The History of Israel*, trans. R. Martineau, 3 vols. (London: Longmans, Green, 1869). Julius Wellhausen, *Prolegomena zur Geschichte Israels* (Berlin: Reimer, 1883); Wellhausen, *Prolegomena to the History of Israel*, ed. Douglas Knight (Atlanta: Scholars Press, 1994); Wellhausen, *Die Composition Des Hexateuchs Und Der Historischen Bücher Des Alten Testaments* (Berlin: Georg Reimer, 1889).

5. Noth's foundational evidence centered on the following: (1) Structural organization—at the important points in the course of history bringing in speeches of the important people (Noth, *Deuteronomistic History*, 18, 24); (2) smooth transitions between books (ibid., 24); (3) diversity between the old traditional material and the coherent uniformity of the deuteronomistic parts (ibid., 25); (4) a date of 480 years from the exodus to the dedication of the temple based on calculations found in DtrH (ibid., 43–44).

6. Ibid., 26.

history, which he attributes to Dtr's original source document. But he also contends that unity exists for Dtr as author in shaping and composing the history according to his own design.

I accept several of Noth's arguments. I view Dtr as an intentional author and redactor, one who seriously considered the use of his sources and the older traditions they reflected, while also (re)interpreting them within his unique theological perspective.[7] Where I differ from Noth, most specifically, is in the dating of his Dtr. Noth describes the work of a single historian, writing and redacting following the fall of Judah. This historical situation influences a history of Israel that is thoroughly negative. Instead, I see a two-stage redaction (similar to Frank Moore Cross's theory) in which these redactors worked. And while I do not deny Noth's emphasis on the use of speeches as Dtr's mode of interpreting history,[8] I derive a historiographical method that is more complex in substance and form. This chapter will describe the historiographical process of the preexilic Deuteronomist in Kings. Following that

---

7. John Van Seters in his book *The Edited Bible: The Curious History of the "Editor" in Biblical Criticism* (Winona Lake, IN: Eisenbrauns, 2006) argues against the use of the terms *redactor* and *editor* to describe the work of the biblical authors/compilers, suggesting that the modern idea of the editor is a medieval formulation "invented as a mode of literary analysis" and that such a vocation did not exist in antiquity (1). He concludes "that there never was in antiquity anything like 'editions' of literary works that were the result of an 'editorial' process, the work of editors or redactors. It is a figment of scholarly imagination that had its origins in an anachronistic analogy based on the supposition that the scribes and scholars of antiquity were engaged in the same kind of activity that occupied European scholars of the Renaissance" (ibid., 398). Instead, Van Seters suggests that DtrH is produced on a model similar to that of ancient Greek historiography; just as Herodotus was "both a compiler of a great quantity of traditional, folkloristic material and 'historical' sources, as well as a consummate storyteller," so too is the biblical historian (ibid., 400). While Van Seters's point and caution against adopting a nonnative and anachronistic category of activity should be acknowledged, much of the argument is semantic. My view of the activity of Dtr is as he describes the ancient historian, compiling ancient sources while telling his own story. In keeping with conventional scholarship, and in particular the work of Noth, I will continue to describe Dtr as author/redactor, defining his work of redaction in compiling, integrating, and rewriting his sources.

8. According to Noth, Dtr constructs his history by bringing "forward the leading personages with a speech, long or short, which looks forward and backward in an attempt to interpret the course of events, and draws the relevant practical conclusions about what people should do." This technique is not used outside DtrH (Noth, *Deuteronomistic History*, 18).

description, I will apply the method to a case study in 1 Kings 11. This analysis provides important insight into the questions of composition and selection, highlighting the theological and literary priorities of the historian. The historiographical poetics integrates many of the ideas of the vast and long scholarship on DtrH and presents it in a systematic and prescriptive way.

The Historiographical Poetics of the Deuteronomist

The work of the preexilic Deuteronomist in Kings functions on two different axes. The first is the axis of selection, which includes the methodological priorities that guide Dtr in his choice and redaction of sources. These priorities are threefold: Dtr attempts to find balance among (1) reporting the historical events that occurred and staying true to the sources that he possesses describing those events, likely those from the royal archives (this is a commitment to a source tradition); (2) loyalty to the prophetic tradition; and (3) the organizational strategies used for incorporating these sources, through the ordering of episodes.

The second axis is one of composition, rhetoric, and formation. The following compositional strategies are used: (1) promoting the deuteronomistic programmatic agenda, (2) attribution of historico-political events to theological causes, and (3) the use of a Davidic prototype strategy. The subsequent chapters will consider the narrative accounts of a few specific kings, and these priorities will be explored in each narrative. Those texts will be mined for understanding how Dtr as author and redactor worked in constructing these narratives.

The Axis of Selection

Scholarly Commitment to His Sources

Dtr has a "scholarly" approach to his sources or, as Baruch Halpern describes it, an "antiquarian" interest.[9] Similarly, Noth calls Dtr an "honest broker," one who "had no intention of fabricating the history of the Israelite people. He wished to . . . base it upon the material to which he had access."[10] Dtr consults his sources and reports what he finds in them, even adopting them wholesale and integrating them into his larger account. He will include accounts and events even when they are in conflict, because he is committed to preserving them.

In Halpern's discussions of the ways in which Dtr uses his sources, he suggests that while they were likely influenced by ideological, theological, and political views, the ancient authors had "authentic intentions. They meant to furnish fair and accurate representations of Israelite antiquity."[11] It was with this in mind that the historians attempted to give an account of a coherent sequence of past events. Halpern offers the example of the relationship between Judges 4 and 5 to demonstrate this "antiquarian interest" and how Dtr uses his sources.[12] Halpern illustrates that in his attempt to be as precise and accurate as possible in his interpretation of his source, Dtr misreads the poetic parallelism in Judges 5 and instead of seeing two parallel images interprets them as two disparate objects (e.g., Judg. 5:26, "She

9. Baruch Halpern, *The First Historians: The Hebrew Bible and History* (San Francisco: Harper & Row, 1988), 3.

10. Noth, *Deuteronomistic History*, 128.

11. Halpern, *The First Historians*, 3.

12. Baruch Halpern, "Doctrine by Misadventure: Between the Israelite Source and the Biblical Historian," in *The Poet and the Historian: Essays in Literary and Historical Biblical Criticism*, ed. Richard E. Friedman (Chico, CA: Scholars Press, 1983), 41–73; Halpern, "The Resourceful Israelite Historian: The Song of Deborah and Israelite Historiography," *HTR* 76, no. 4 (1983): 379–401; Halpern, *The First Historians*, 76–99.

put her hand to the tent peg and her right hand to the workmen's mallet" is misinterpreted in the prose version in 4:21 as two separate items).[13] This misinterpretation of biblical figurative language is demonstrative of the great pains to which the Deuteronomistic Historian (the author/redactor of the Judges 4 and 5 pericope) went in order to accurately render the information in his sources.

Dtr attempts to compose a history based on sources, whether those are the ones that he cites, for example, the annals of the kings, or others. Halpern describes this process as "imagination based on evidence."[14] I agree with Halpern, who contends that the history writer's intention is to "lead the reader to believe that the work is a valid representation of the past."[15] This does not necessarily mean that the past represented in any given account is an accurate historical portrayal, but that the author intends to present the information as true and that the reader believes that it is legitimate. This strategy is essential to the success of the history and its goal of religious inculcation; in order to promote his deuteronomistic agenda, the historian must make his reader believe the accuracy of the historical account. This is true for the writing and function of all history. Historian Johan Huizinga, in an essay on the philosophy of history, states that "history gives no more than a particular representation of a particular past, an intelligible picture of a portion of the past."[16] Historiography, as an intellectual activity, is the attempt to impose form and interpret what happens in the world. Similarly, in a helpful

---

13. This type of parallelism is typical of biblical poetry, in which the second part of a verse expands on the first, often using a less common word of a higher register. See Robert Alter, *The Art of Biblical Poetry* (New York: Basic Books, 1985), 3–26.

14. Baruch Halpern, *David's Secret Demons: Messiah, Murderer, Traitor, King* (Grand Rapids: Eerdmans, 2001), 101.

15. Halpern, *The First Historians*, xxiii.

16. Johan Huizinga, "A Definition of the Concept of History," in *Philosophy and History: Essays Presented to Ernst Cassirer*, ed. Raymond Klibansky and Herbert James Paton (New York: Harper & Row, 1963), 5.

and rarely addressed way, John Van Seters deals with the issue of the quest for historical writing in *In Search of History*.[17]

In Kings, the imperative to represent the history of Israel accurately is often at odds with the other priorities of Dtr's historiographical goals, but he does not omit events or characters that complicate those aims.[18] For example, had Dtr not possessed texts depicting a positive picture of Jeroboam would he have included an initially positive view? It is particularly interesting to consider this historiographical priority in contrast to those of the Chronicler. For example, in Chronicles, the David account is wholly positive and the northern kingdom is never acknowledged as legitimate. The Chronicler is not beholden to his historical sources to the same degree as the Deuteronomist and omits narratives or pieces of information that are not helpful or that are even detrimental to his overall goals in writing his narrative.

Despite this commitment to his sources, reflecting the thoroughness of a historian, there are countervailing forces at work in the process of selection. On the one hand, it seems, in some instances, as if Dtr does not quite have a choice in selection—everything must be included, therefore this is not really a process of selection at all. On the other hand, we do know that Dtr does not include in his narrative everything he possesses of the historical record. A common refrain is the deuteronomistic formulaic closing to the reigns of the kings, "And the remainder of the deeds of King *x* . . . , is it not in the writings of the books of the deeds of King *x*/kings of Israel/Judah?"[19]

---

17. John Van Seters, *In Search of History: Historiography in the Ancient World and the Origins of Biblical History* (Winona Lake, IN: Eisenbrauns, 1997).

18. Noth, *Deuteronomistic History*, 128.

19. See Solomon, 1 Kgs. 11:41; Jeroboam, 1 Kgs. 14:19; Rehoboam, 1 Kgs. 14:29; Abijam, 1 Kgs. 15:7; Asa, 1 Kgs. 15:23; Nadab, 1 Kgs. 15:25; Baasha, 1 Kgs. 16:5; Elah, 1 Kgs. 16:14; Zimri, 1 Kgs. 16:20; Omri, 1 Kgs. 16:27; Ahab, 1 Kgs. 22:39; Jehoshaphat, 1 Kgs. 22:45; Ahaziah, 2 Kgs. 1:18; Joram, 2 Kgs. 8:23; Jehu, 2 Kgs. 10:34; Joash, 2 Kgs. 12:19; Jehoahaz, 2 Kgs. 13:8; Joash, 2 Kgs. 13:12; Jehoash, 2 Kgs. 14:15; Jeroboam II, 2 Kgs. 14:28; Azariah, 2 Kgs. 15:6; Pekah, 2

This formula, in its essential nature, testifies to that fact that there are events in the reign of each king that were part of the archival record, but Dtr chooses to omit them.[20] Dtr seems to include those things that are of interest to him and to promote his agendas.

The kings who are not part of the construction of his story get slight mention and exist as not much more than temporal place markers. One has to assume that a king who reigned for, say, fifty-two years, like King Azariah (2 Kgs. 15:1-7), had some significant events occur during his reign that deserve to be included in a historical narrative, but Dtr reports Azariah's reign in only seven verses: he ascends the throne, does what was right in Yahweh's eyes, but does not take down the high places, contracts leprosy, and dies. Another historiographical impulse exists here, when, as in the cases of kings with almost no space allotted them, Dtr allows himself to leave things out. He banishes the remainder of the acts to the annals, omitting what he considers not important to him as a historian, yet a chronicler may have reported them more explicitly. The political and religious agenda of the court of Josiah is the strongest factor in determining who gets space, leading to the question: Does such-and-such a king contribute to the overall goals of the narrative? The kings who get the more extensive stories, Solomon, Jeroboam, Ahab, Hezekiah, Josiah, are all crucially linked to the deuteronomistic theological program, positively and negatively. While they too have the rest of their acts documented in the annals of the kings, their accounts seem to be semicomplete, and even include elements that undermine the religious program. The process of selection, as a historiographical methodology, is quite complex in that Dtr seems to play some role in selection, but is limited in how selective he may

Kgs. 15:31; Jotham, 2 Kgs. 15:36; Ahaz, 2 Kgs. 16:19, Manasseh, 2 Kgs. 21:17; Amon, 2 Kgs. 21:25; Josiah, 2 Kgs. 23:28.

20. Cf. Yairah Amit, *History and Ideology: An Introduction to Historiography in the Hebrew Bible* (Sheffield: Sheffield Academic, 1999), 56.

be. This impulse also adds to another literary strategy to be discussed below—the use of prototypes. Dtr develops the reigns of certain kings because of the way they contribute to his prototype construction and the ways in which that prototype augments the overall goals of the history.

Loyalty to the Prophetic Tradition

The second redactional priority is the use of prophetic tradition. This is done in two specific ways. The first is content based. Dtr uses a somewhat comprehensive prophetic source or record and disperses it into the larger narrative of his history. The second is structural; the use of prophetic sources creates a prophecy-fulfillment framework prominent throughout the history. This schema contributes to the greater theological messages of the history; prophets speak and warn, and the kings and people must heed their messages or they will be punished.

The use of prophetic material has been widely acknowledged.[21] Even within his single-author theory, Noth prominently mentions the use of the prophetical stories in the history: "Dtr. has made extensive use of stories about the prophets . . . [who] appear chiefly as opponents to the kings." These stories "stress the intervention of a prophet in domestic or foreign affairs."[22] Also, Anthony Campbell outlines the existence of a "prophetic record," an early, northern, prophetic document circulating at the end of the ninth century.[23] He

---

21. Antony F. Campbell, *Of Prophets and Kings: A Late Ninth Century Document (1 Samuel 1–2 Kings 10)*, Catholic Biblical Quarterly Monograph Series 17 (Washington, DC: Catholic Biblical Association of America, 1986); Alexander Rofé, *The Prophetical Stories: The Narratives about the Prophets in the Hebrew Bible, Their Literary Types and History* (Jerusalem: Magnes, 1988), 97; Mordechai Cogan, *1 Kings: A New Translation with Introduction and Commentary*, AB (New York: Doubleday, 2001), 92–94; Ehud Ben Zvi, "History and Prophetic Texts," in *History and Interpretation* (Sheffield: JSOT Press, 1993), 106–20; Ben Zvi, "Prophets and Prophecy in the Compositional and Redactional Notes in I–II Kings," *ZAW* 105, no. 3 (1994): 331–51.

22. Noth, *Deuteronomistic History*, 107.

looks to the books of Samuel and Kings as evidence of this source, highlighting the prophetic record present in 1 Kings 3–2 Kings 10.[24] As early as Ewald in the mid-nineteenth century, scholars have talked of a "Prophetical Narrator."[25] Similarly, Alexander Rofé describes the beginning of a new literary genre, "prophetic historiography," that developed as prophets gained influential political positions, and the writers of history fell under the influence of prophets.[26]

This prophetic source has a northern provenance. From the beginning of Kings until 2 Kings 18, all the prophets (except the man of God from Judah, 1 Kings 13) are Israelite. The use of this source accounts for the presence of northern editing in an otherwise southern history.[27] P. Kyle McCarter in his commentaries on 1 and 2 Samuel also speaks of a prophetic source used by Dtr in Samuel, a middle stage of predeuteronomistic redaction in which the stories were already in some basic order.[28] He suggests that "the first Book of Samuel derives its basic shape from a prophetic history of the origin of the monarchy that was intended to present the advent of kingship in Israel as a concession to a wanton demand of the people." In this way, the king would be the head of the government, but he is subject to the instruction and admonition of the prophet.[29] While I am unsure whether the prophetic tradition used in Kings is as complete and comprehensive as Campbell lays out, it is clear that pre-Dtr prophetic texts are certainly integrated into the history. Similarly, Ehud Ben Zvi suggests that the book of Kings incorporates

23. Campbell, *Of Prophets and Kings*, 1.
24. Ibid., 2, 14.
25. Ewald, *History of Israel*, 158.
26. Rofé, *Prophetical Stories*, 78–79.
27. Campbell, *Of Prophets and Kings*, 113.
28. P. Kyle McCarter, "Introduction," in *1 Samuel: A New Translation with Introduction, Notes and Commentary*, AB 8 (Garden City, NY: Doubleday, 1984), 18.
29. McCarter also pinpoints 1 Kgs. 11:29-39; 14:1-16; 16:1-4; 2 Kgs. 9:1-10 as deriving from this source (ibid., 21).

preexistent prophetic stories about prophets interacting with kings, both as a testament to the "real" history included in the work (the word of the true prophet was always fulfilled) and to incorporate the audience's own traditions in order to persuade them of the historian's perspective.[30] Ben Zvi and other proponents of the strata model identify an entire level of redaction (DtrP) as relating to prophetic texts.[31]

The second way the prophetic tradition influences the history is in its structure. The effect of the use of the prophetic texts is, as Gerhard von Rad describes, that prophecy and its fulfillment becomes an objective "framework schema" of the history.[32] Prophecy-fulfillment is "the theological structure of the Deuteronomistic historical work within the Books of Kings."[33] The prophet speaks and Yahweh's word is fulfilled in the course of history, defining deuteronomistic theology.[34] In this way, as Campbell similarly describes, "the Prophetic Record has imposed an ordered conceptual structure, with a unified picture of God's guidance in these events, and a clear sense of causation in the understanding of the role played by sin in the downfall of kings."[35] Also, the major verdicts handed down to kings and the people are frequently presented by the prophets, demonstrating the integration of the prophetic tradition and

---

30. Ben Zvi, "Prophets and Prophecy," 339, 346.
31. Reinhard G. Kratz, *Composition of the Narrative Books of the Old Testament*, trans. John Bowden (London: T&T Clark, 2005), 170; Kratz, *Die Komposition Der Erzählenden Bücher Des Alten Testaments: Grundwissen Der Bibelkritik* (Göttingen: Vandenhoeck & Ruprecht, 2000); Walter Dietrich, *Prophetie Und Geschichte Eine Redaktionsgeschichtliche Untersuchung Zum Deuteronomistischen Geschichtswerk*, FRLANT 108 (Göttingen: Vandenhoeck & Ruprecht, 1972); Dietrich, "Martin Noth and the Future of the Deuteronomistic History," in *The History of Israel's Traditions: The Heritage of Martin Noth*, ed. Steven McKenzie and M. Patrick Graham (Sheffield: Sheffield Academic, 1994), 153–75.
32. Gerhard von Rad, *Deuteronomium-Studien* (Göttingen: Vandenhoeck & Ruprecht, 1947); Rad, "The Deuteronomistic Theology of History in the Books of Kings," in *Studies in Deuteronomy*, trans. David Stalker (London: SCM, 1953), 78.
33. Rad, "Deuteronomistic Theology," 81.
34. Ibid., 83.
35. Campbell, *Of Prophets and Kings*, 111.

deuteronomistic theology. Similarly for Rofé, prophetic historiography attributes the cause of events to the prophetic word.[36] God's word never goes unfulfilled, and all Israelite history is presented as "a sequence of prophetic realizations."[37]

Furthermore, the prophet is acknowledged by deuteronomistic theology. In Deut. 18:14–22, the role of the prophet in Israelite society is outlined. Yahweh assures Israel that in each generation he will raise up a prophet to deliver his message. The words of Yahweh's true prophets will always come to fruition, and this will be the test for determining true prophets. By then applying this concept to the interpretation of history, it offers the historians additional authority. According to Ben Zvi, "These stories 'prove' that the position of the writers is correct . . . [and they] do that by referring to cherished prophets whose authority was accepted by received tradition."[38]

The value of the prophetic evaluation in this way and the influence of the prophetic text, even beyond Campbell's defined Prophetic Record, are pervasive throughout the entirety of the history. This prophetic text is not only the source for many prophetic passages but also a redactional influence for Dtr. Even when this particular source document is complete, Dtr finds other prophetic texts, many similar to those of the prophetic record, to weave into his history. This includes southern prophetic texts as well. The figure of the early prophets is influenced by the role of the prophets in the Prophetic Record. These prophets "are portrayed as central figures, exercising authority of king-maker and king-breaker in Israel."[39]

---

36. Rofé, *Prophetical Stories*, 79.
37. Ibid., 87.
38. Ben Zvi, "Prophets and Prophecy," 345.
39. Campbell, *Of Prophets and Kings*, 114.

The Ordering of Episodes

Once selectional choices have been made, there are two organizational principles used in the arrangement of multiple scenes in a given narrative. The first is the anachronistic renarrativization of sources and "historical" events, while the second is a juxtaposition of scenes that manifests itself in the piling up of episodes. Frequently, a narrative may reflect a chronological reorganization in order to highlight an ideological or artistic purpose over a historical one. David Glatt describes this as "chronological displacement," when "an author or editor intentionally transfers an episode from its original chronological context (of which he knew through general historical awareness or from another written source) into a different setting."[40]

Dtr also juxtaposes various scenes, collecting stories that have similarities and presenting them together. This is something akin to the rabbinic principle of סמיכות פרשיות, the juxtaposition of topics or proximity of issues. According to Yair Zakovitch, "The rabbis assumed that the textual proximity of different ideas may create an additional stratum of meaning."[41] סמיכות פרשיות is usually used as a hermeneutical tool that the rabbis employ to explain why two narratives, which superficially seem disparate, may be connected on a deeper level. An example of this is how the story of Judah

---

40. David A. Glatt, *Chronological Displacement in Biblical and Related Literatures* (Atlanta: Scholars Press, 1993), 1. In his book, Glatt develops a methodology for when we can see and evaluate chronological displacement, but he concentrates on episodes that have external comparisons (e.g., multiple accounts of Mesopotamian chronicles and biblical narratives with more than one account, namely Samuel-Kings and Chronicles), describing this as "empirical" evidence. He is less confident in his discussion of "chronological displacements inferred from internal evidence." Yet, while these narratives may not have the same external evidence, internal clues may exist that can give us a reasonable level of certainty. This topic constitutes chapter 4 of his book (ibid., 149–87).

41. Yair Zakovitch, "Juxtaposition in the Abraham Cycle," in *Pomegranates and Golden Bells: Studies in Biblical, Jewish, and Near Eastern Ritual, Law, and Literature in Honor of Jacob Milgrom*, ed. David P. Wright, David Noel Freedman, and Avi Hurvitz (Winona Lake, IN: Eisenbrauns, 1995), 510.

and Tamar in Genesis 38 interrupts the Joseph story. Readers have wondered why this story interpolates the larger Joseph narrative, and it has been explained by the use of סמיכות פרשיות, that the appearance of the words הכר נא and the theme of recognition are the impetus for bringing the two stories together. While this concept has largely been developed as a hermeneutical tool, it can also be viewed as a compositional and redactional strategy. Separate stories or sources may attract others based on similar words, themes, and so on, the same way they are evaluated from a hermeneutical perspective. Zakovitch considers the juxtaposition of two units as a mode of "inner-biblical interpretation" in which "one story is intended to influence our reading of another."[42] In this way, we need to ask, What were the redactor's intentions in bringing these stories together? Zakovitch contends that "in a cycle of stories . . . every story, by being placed next to its neighbor, creates a juxtaposition pregnant with meaning. Through these juxtapositions we are taught a lesson in the ideas and beliefs of the biblical editor, as well as in the Bible's own evaluation of some characters."[43]

Both of these principles greatly influence the formation of the final text. They are a way for Dtr to integrate the various sources and pieces of his record into a larger narrative, focused on achieving his historiographical goals and creating meaning within his narrative of the past.

The Axis of Composition

Once Dtr makes his choices in selection, he manipulates the sources to fit his ideological needs through three main compositional strategies.

---

42. Ibid.
43. Ibid., 511.

Promoting the Deuteronomistic Program

The single most important goal of DtrH is promoting the program of deuteronomistic theology. This theology is focused on centralization of the cult in Jerusalem, fidelity to the covenant, the eternity of the Davidic dynasty, and Jerusalem as the chosen city. Dtr uses the history as a didactic tool to teach proper worship and the necessity of compliance to the covenant. Similarly, the book of Kings is concentrated on establishing the proper (and improper) location and modes of worship of the Yahwistic cult. The correct forms of worship are often outlined through the evaluation of various kings and the fates of their kingdoms. It is through this theological lens that Dtr presents the events that take place in the history of Israel and the actors in this history. Those kings who keep the covenant are good and are (theoretically) rewarded with peaceful and prosperous reigns, and those who do not are punished.[44] This is also true for the collectivity of the people. The northern kingdom of Israel sinned by following the cult of Jeroboam, so they were destroyed and exiled. Dtr is particularly focused on his brand of the proper worship. Worship is only permitted in the temple in Jerusalem; previously accepted cult sites and iconography, such as Jeroboam's calves, 'ăšērîm, and maṣṣēbôt, were prohibited. In order to clearly identify these practices as forbidden, Dtr adopts a rhetoric of idolatry in which these previously acceptable Yahwistic and traditional practices are presented as foreign and idolatrous. Idolatry can be cataloged into three categories, in ascending order of impiety: wrong place, wrong symbols, and wrong deities.[45] The preexilic Dtr is primarily

---

44. Theologically this is how the length of reigns should be determined according to Dtr, as in 1 Kgs. 3:14, but historically this is not always the case. Two pertinent examples of when this theological principle is violated are the long reign of King Manasseh and King Josiah's death on the battlefield.

45. Thanks to Mark Smith for these categories (in conversation, December 12, 2011).

focused on the first two: place and symbol. These elements are often described as "syncretistic." While he does not condone worship of other deities, this concern does not appear as a primary focus of preexilic Dtr's theology and rhetoric. Similarly, Reinhard Kratz also highlights two levels of theological criteria for evaluation: the first is the unity of place of worship and deity, and the second is the oneness of Yahweh. He argues that both are related to the laws of Deuteronomy, but recognizes the unity of place and deity as original to Kings (that is, centralization and no worship of foreign objects), while the focus on the oneness of Yahweh belongs to a secondary redaction.[46] This corresponds with my assessment, although I do not agree with Kratz's compositional dating and redactional theory of the primary and secondary redactions.

By evaluating what happens to the players of history through the lens of deuteronomistic theology, Dtr attempts to make sense of history, particularly the bad things that have befallen Israel and Judah, and to inspire his audience to fidelity to that same theology. Dtr wants us to believe that if only the historical characters were faithful to the deuteronomistic covenant, their fates would have turned out differently. Likewise, the people of Judah should now get on board in the hopes that their future will conclude better. What is particularly interesting about Dtr's commitment to his religious theology as compared to other biblical writers is that he is driven by offering a view of the past that reflects his sources and the prophetic tradition. As such, he includes episodes that may undermine his overall programmatic goals (see the section "The Axis of Selection").

This unique brand of deuteronomistic theology emerges from the seventh-century-Jerusalem court of Josiah.[47] Many scholars locate

---

46. Kratz, *Composition*, 162–63.
47. Moshe Weinfeld, *Deuteronomy and the Deuteronomic School* (Winona Lake, IN: Eisenbrauns, 1992), 1, 7, 9.

the composition of DtrH to this moment in time. This contention is made largely because of accordance between the theology and the measures of Josiah's reform as outlined in 2 Kings 23, which specifically targets other cult sites and objects. (The focus on the found book of the law in 2 Kings 22 during the reign of Josiah and its connection to the book of Deuteronomy further contributes to this belief.)[48] Centralization of worship in Jerusalem and the removal of "traditional" and syncretistic cult symbols were a major break in Israelite religion and required the positive promotion of the Deuteronomistic Historian and his evaluation of history to disseminate his ideology and indoctrinate the people of Judah. This perspective takes into account a theory of double redaction, locating a primary edition of the history to the reign of Josiah and secondary additions made in the exile.

The Attribution of Historico-Political Events to Theological Causes

Throughout the history, Dtr attributes historical and political occurrences to religious, ideological, and theological causes. Yairah Amit, summarizing others, namely von Rad, Yehezkel Kaufmann, and Isaac Leo Seeligmann, describes this as the "dual causality principle," which attributes both historical and divine causality to

48. De Wette was the first to identify Deuteronomy with the found book in 2 Kings 22, highlighting that the unity of worship described in the book only appears historically for the first time during the reign of Josiah (Wilhelm Martin Leberecht de Wette, *Dissertatio Critico-exegetica Qua Deuteronomium a Prioribus Pentateuchi Libris Diversum, Alius Cuiusdam Recentioris Auctoris Opus Esse Monstratur* (Jena, 1805); de Wette, *A Critical and Historical Introduction to the Canonical Scriptures of the Old Testament*, trans. Theodore Parker [Boston: Charles C. Little and James Brown, 1850], 2:150). He points out that the religious practice in parts of Joshua, Judges, Samuel, and Kings does not match the picture of the Israelite cult in Exodus and Numbers, where sacrifices were offered at many local shrines, as well as wherever Israel gathered. Also, nonpriests sometimes played priestly roles (e.g., David when he brings the ark to Jerusalem). He therefore concludes that before the time of David and Solomon, Yahweh was worshiped at many holy places, and even after the building of the temple, worship continued at these places. It was only with the reign of Josiah that the freedom of religious worship came under attack (John W. Rogerson, *W. M. L. de Wette, Founder of Modern Biblical Criticism: An Intellectual Biography*, JSOTSup 126 [Sheffield: JSOT Press, 1992], 59–60).

events and occurrences.[49] Von Rad believes that during the period of the united monarchy a new kind of history emerged that showed a transition from the writing of miraculous episodes to that of a comprehensive historical work. These two methods represent the activity of God differently. This change in the perspective of Yahweh's role in history led to a new form of narrativity, in which Yahweh functions in the background of history while human action is in the foreground (as opposed to the prominent role of God in the use of miracles).[50] Kaufmann identifies this new narrativity as demonstrating the indirect governing of history by Yahweh. This is the dual aspect—causes are the result of both historical forces and divine providence. Amit sees a different manifestation of dual causality: the "shaping of plots, the portrayal of characters, the treatment of time and space, and finally the prominence of the place of God."[51] Amit offers two examples, that of Joseph's brothers (Genesis 37–45) and the story of Ehud (Judges 3). She explains that Joseph's brothers' jealousy develops as human action, but the characters and the reader learn later that it was all part of Yahweh's plan. The brothers' emotions and subsequent actions were guided by their own human psychology as well as by providence. With the example of Ehud, Amit suggests that many coincidences needed to occur in order for multiple points in the story to work out; without these coincidences, Ehud would not have been successful. For example, What if he had not been admitted to the privy chamber? If one of the guards had stopped him on the way out? If the guards had not waited as long to go up after Ehud left? All of these

49. Gerhard von Rad, *Theologie Des Alten Testaments*, vol. 1 (Munich, 1957); Rad, *Old Testament Theology* (London: SCM, 1962); Yehezkel Kaufmann, *The Book of Joshua* (Jerusalem: Ḳiryat-Sefer, 1959); Isaac Leo Seeligmann, "Menschliches Heldentum Und Göttliche Hilfe: Die Doppelte Kausalität Im Alttestamentlichen Geschichtsdenken," *TZ* 19, no. 6 (1963): 385–411.
50. Yairah Amit, "The Dual Causality Principle and its Effects on Biblical Literature," *VT* 37, no. 4 (1987): 387.
51. Ibid., 392.

coincidences were necessary in order to make Ehud successful. Amit describes this as "the elements of chance or surprise [that] may be joined together in a system of human reasoning; on the other hand, the manner of using them—in the very plots which apply the dual causality principle—is destined at one and the same time to signify the existence of a system of divine reasoning."[52]

While the attribution of double causes (divine and human) is at play in deuteronomistic composition (generally), the dual causality principle does not function in the same way in the more "history-like" narratives (as opposed to the more mythic accounts of Judges).[53] I am offering a more precise conception of how dual causality functions in the historical narratives. In Dtr's original compositions, there are often two causes for events. As in the example to be discussed below, the kingdom is divided because of Solomon's apostasy as described in 1 Kings 11 and Rehoboam's stubbornness against lessening the corvée obligations as described in 1 Kings 12. Although the split of the kingdom can be attributed to dual causes, this is different from what Amit discusses. In those stories, the dual causality principle is more integrated into the narrative. Without Yahweh's guidance, things might not have worked out (e.g., Ehud), or there would not be a good reason that events happen. (We must remember, especially in the more "mythic" narratives, that they are stories, told for specific purposes within the religious "corpus" of a nation.) Tales do not exist in isolation. The stories told and recorded have some national purpose. When we move to the more "historical" stories of DtrH, especially of Samuel and Kings, the divine causality is less integrated into the overall story because the narrative is based more or less on historical occurrences or remembrances of historical

---

52. Ibid., 394.
53. Note that the difference lies in passages of deuteronomistic composition. While Judges is part of DtrH, the voice of Dtr is not very prominent. He is merely the framer of earlier traditions, unlike in Kings, where he is an author of significant textual material.

occurrences. Divine causality is more constructed and less organic, as if a template of divine causality is imposed on historico-political causality, but the historico-political explanations often still (co)exist separately from the divine explanation. The divine reason does not seem to be the driving force but rather part of the organizing structure. In this way, it is possible to see that when Dtr applies the dual causality principle in the historical books, perhaps a narrative strategy he learned from the mythic oral and written stories, he does so in order to ascribe divine cause onto purely historico-political occurrences. The two causalities are not mutually dependent, as they are in the Joseph and Ehud stories; it is possible to pry them apart. And while they were inseparable in Dtr's worldview, it is possible for us to see the divine causality in Dtr as an ideological and theological attempt at understanding the historical events and ascribing divine meaning. This is an important element of the rhetorical method of Dtr. At almost every important stage in Israelite history, a political description (probably from a source document) is accompanied by a theological one, illustrating how all the major events in that history are the result of Yahweh working in history.

The Use of a Prototype Strategy in Constructing the Portrait of the Kings

A third strategy that is closely related to the use of juxtaposition is the smoothing of the narrative pieces through the application of what I will call a "prototype strategy." This process complies with the practice Hayden White calls "emplotment": "To 'emplot' a sequence of events and thereby transform what would otherwise be only a chronicle of events into a story is to effect a mediation between events and certain universally human 'experiences of temporality.' . . . The meaning of stories is given in their 'emplotment.'"[54] White discusses historiography as a process that requires interpretation. The historian has to interpret his material to construct some pattern. Sometimes he has more facts than he can include and has to exclude things, but at other times, he does not have enough information and has to fill in the gaps to offer plausible explanations.[55] White contends that historical facts are "selected" by the historian.[56] In this way, the historian chooses what he wants to include and refashions it through a narrative story line. White highlights "two levels of interpretation in every historical work: one in which the historian constitutes a story out of the chronicle of events and another in which . . . he progressively identifies the *kind of story* he is telling."[57] In this way, "a given historian is forced to emplot the whole set of stories making up his narrative in one comprehensive or *archetypal* story form."[58]

According to White, this process, of choosing the plot, occurs before telling the story. It is part of the interpretation of sources: "It can be argued that interpretation in history consists of the provisions of a plot-structure for a sequence of events so that their nature as a comprehensible process is revealed by their figuration as a *story of a particular kind*."[59] White supports his argument with historian R. G. Collingwood, who simultaneously "insisted that the constructive imagination was both *a priori* (which meant that it did not act capriciously) and *structural* (which meant that it was governed by notions of formal coherency in its constitution of possible objects of thought)."[60]

54. Hayden White, *The Content of the Form: Narrative Discourse and Historical Representation* (Baltimore: Johns Hopkins University Press, 1990), 172–73.
55. Hayden White, "Interpretation in History," *New Literary History* 4, no. 2 (1973): 281.
56. Ibid., 287–88.
57. Ibid., 292.
58. Hayden White, *Metahistory: The Historical Imagination in Nineteenth-Century Europe* (Baltimore: Johns Hopkins University Press, 1975), 8.
59. White, "Interpretation in History," 291.
60. Ibid., 293.

Similarly, in his focus on form, Marc Zvi Brettler highlights the use of typologies, a way in which the biblical historian puts events into patterns: "Events themselves do not typically occur in patterns. It is the historian who sees patterns in events or in traditions concerning events, and writes a historical account that reflects these perceived patterns."[61] This is one of the major tasks of a historian.

I am suggesting that White's theory of emplotment is at play in biblical historiography. Dtr uses a specific form of typology: a royal prototype strategy that he employs to construct the portrait of his kings. The prototype of the king is steeped in deuteronomistic language and concerns. Instead of being portrayed as a "real" person, each king is evaluated through the lens of the prototype to assess his fidelity to the covenant and his love of Yahweh. In Kings, Dtr uses a Davidic prototype (positively and negatively) to construct the portrait of his kings. Early on, von Rad, followed by Richard Nelson, made this observation, that the David of history (that is, David in the book of Samuel) is free of deuteronomistic additions.[62] Instead, David is used "as the prototype of a king who was well-pleasing to Jahweh."[63] In this way, David "is the king after the

---

61. Marc Zvi Brettler, *The Creation of History in Ancient Israel* (New York: Routledge, 1995), 34. Brettler suggests the use of typology as a reenactment, a prefiguration of events that conveys meaning. He offers the example of the wife-sister episode in Genesis 12 functioning as a preenactment of the exodus. For him, the most accurate way to view typology is through the use of vocabulary of another text (ibid., 52, 55). While themes and events in the content may be apparent, the use of a common vocabulary is a more certain indicator. This feature and the way in which Brettler describes the use of typology require that one text be the original against which the secondary text is reconstructed into a similar type. This is similar to the scholarly discussions about the use of typology in the New Testament.

62. John Van Seters offers an interesting, although unconvincing, explanation for this difference/problem. The flawed picture of David in the "Court History" is a later post-Dtr, postexilic addition to the history, because Dtr would never have let all the bad things about David get in unreworked. If Dtr "incorporated the Court History into his own work, how could he consistently maintain that David was the ideal ruler and the model that all the kings of Israel and Judah should follow?" (*In Search of History*, 278, 290).

63. Rad, "Deuteronomistic Theology," 86. Also, Richard D. Nelson, *The Double Redaction of the Deuteronomistic History* (Sheffield: JSOT Press, 1981), 119–28; Nelson, "Josiah in the Book of Joshua," *JBL* 100, no. 4 (1981): 531–40. Christof Hardmeier, "King Josiah in the Climax of

heart of the Deuteronomist. He is the prototype of the perfectly obedient anointed, and therefore the model for all succeeding kings in Jerusalem."[64] Similarly, Richard Nelson highlights "heroes and villains" as one of the themes in DtrH. The heroes include David as the prototype for the perfect king.[65] Furthermore, Ben Zvi argues for a pattern of thesis and antithesis, suggesting that the four kings Hezekiah and Josiah, Ahaz and Manasseh show an alternating pattern of the best and worst kings. Josiah's deeds are presented as the thesis and Manasseh's as the antithesis.[66] The result of this is "the existence of a literary pattern that unifies otherwise independent value judgments and turns them into one literary, and probably theological, discourse."[67]

While my argument for the use of a prototype strategy builds on these ideas, it takes into account further literary considerations. It is first necessary to consider what a literary prototype is, and how it functions in our historical narratives. Cognitive linguist George Lakoff defines prototypes as "cognitive reference points of various sorts [that] form the basis for inferences."[68] These inferences are part of the conceptual structure, in which prototypes have a "special cognitive status" of being a "best example."[69] Similarly, Ben Zvi suggests, "Connective features shared by characters in some group

the Deuteronomic History (2 Kings 22–23) and the Pre-Deuteronomic Document of a Cult Reform at the Place of Residence (23.4-15*): Criticism of Sources, Reconstruction of Literary Pre-stages and the Theology of History in 2 Kings 22–23*," in *Good Kings and Bad Kings: The Kingdom of Judah in the Seventh Century BCE*, ed. Lester L. Grabbe (New York: T&T Clark, 2005), 133; Ehud Ben Zvi, "The Account of the Reign of Manasseh in II Reg 21:1-18 and the Redactional History of the Book of Kings," *ZAW* 103, no. 3 (1991): 357–67; Ernest W. Nicholson, *Deuteronomy and Tradition* (Oxford: Blackwell, 1967).

64. Rad, "Deuteronomistic Theology," 88.
65. Nelson, *Double Redaction*, 125–26.
66. Ben Zvi, "The Reign of Manasseh," 359–60.
67. Ibid., 350.
68. George Lakoff, *Women, Fire, and Dangerous Things: What Categories Reveal about the Mind* (Chicago: University of Chicago Press, 1987), 45.
69. Ibid., 41.

(e.g., prophets, priests, etc.) created a web of attributes that reflected the implied understanding of the basic nature of the group, or one may say of a conceptual prototype of a 'generic' (nonindividualized) member of the group was (e.g., a prophet)."[70] In Kings, prototypes of individual kings (David as the model for the good king and an anti-David for the bad king) are laid out, allowing the reader to consider each king and his individual acts on micro and macro levels: What did this king do, and how does his character and reign fit into the larger history of Israel and Judah and reflect the way Yahweh works in history? Furthermore, the use of a prototype allows the reader to infer information about each king without the narrator supplying it because he is cast in a mold that the audience already recognizes.

The royal prototype strategy is a key element to Dtr's historiographical process. It is one of the major organizing structures employed throughout Kings. Dtr focuses on the royal portrait as a literary vehicle to convey his theological program. It is a way he can categorize the kings into two groups: those who do what is right and those who do what is evil in the eyes of Yahweh. Among those kings, Dtr highlights a few specific kings to make clear what behavior is to be tolerated and praised. The prototype of the king is steeped in deuteronomistic language and concerns. Instead of being portrayed as a "real" person, each king is evaluated through the lens of the prototype to assess his fidelity to the covenant and his love of Yahweh.

In Kings, Dtr uses a Davidic prototype (positively and negatively) to construct the portrait of his kings. This prototype is based on a literary picture of David as the exemplum of covenant fidelity. He is the model of the deuteronomistically adherent king, the one whom

---

70. Ehud Ben Zvi, "Prophetic Memories in the Deuteronomistic Historical and the Prophetic Collections of Books," in *Israelite Prophecy and the Deuteronomistic History: Portrait, Reality and the Formation of a History*, ed. Mignon Jacobs and Raymond Person (Atlanta: Society of Biblical Literature, 2013), 76.

all subsequent kings are required to emulate. Dtr uses David as the royal comparative to construct the portrait of both good and bad kings. The good kings are those who are like David, while the bad kings are those who are not.

Throughout this work, the portraits of the individual kings will be considered specifically for their role in this prototype strategy and the ways in which the use of the prototype strategy is a primary compositional tool of the Deuteronomist's method. Chapter 3 will lay out the way in which the Davidic prototype is constructed, and the remainder of this book will deal with the ways in which the prototype strategy is applied in the depiction of the other kings.

1 Kings 11: A Case Study

In the quest to describe the process of the Deuteronomistic Historian's historiography, it is fruitful to begin laying out his method with a clear example. First Kings 11 describes the fall of King Solomon followed by (or caused by) the rise of Jeroboam. The majority of scholars have long agreed that this chapter is made up of several discrete narratives that are reorganized into a more or less coherent plot.[71] The value of using this chapter as a paradigm also lies in the delineation between the voice of the Deuteronomist in his composition (which is quite clear) and the earlier sources.[72] This chapter consists of three main episodes: (1) the sin of Solomon with the foreign women and his punishment for covenantal disobedience (vv. 1-13); (2) the rise of two (or three) adversaries (vv. 14-27(28); and

---

71. Nadav Na'aman, "Sources and Composition in the History of Solomon," in *The Age of Solomon: Scholarship at the Turn of the Millennium*, ed. Lowell K. Handy (Leiden: Brill, 1997), 57–80. Gary N. Knoppers, *Two Nations under God: The Deuteronomistic History of Solomon and the Dual Monarchies*, vol. 1, *The Reign of Solomon and the Rise of Jeroboam*, Harvard Semitic Monographs (Atlanta: Scholars Press, 1993), 135–39; Knoppers, "Dynastic Oracle and Secession in 1 Kings 11," *Proceedings, Eastern Great Lakes and Midwest Biblical Societies* 7 1987 (1987): 160.

72. Dtr's composition is clear, especially in vv. 1-13, 32-39.

(3) the election of Jeroboam by Ahijah the prophet and the warning of fidelity to the covenant (vv. 29-39). The smooth integration of these three somewhat separate episodes comes together in a complete narrative account. The organization and melding together of each scene develops into a narrative context that combines the different story lines into one continuous plot. The goal of Dtr in writing together and organizing these stories is clear; it is an attempt to present Solomon at the end of his reign as being led astray by his foreign wives and the necessary punishment for this infidelity, while still maintaining the eternal dynastic Davidic promise. Deuteronomistic ideology is clearly the motivating factor in the weaving together of the stories. The macro story is smooth, but there are clear markers within the chapter that show the seams of reorganization. It is through these gaps that it is possible to ascertain some of the guiding principles of Dtr's historiographical methodology.[73]

1 Kings 11

(1) Now the King Solomon loved many foreign women along with the daughter of Pharaoh, Moabite and Ammonite, Edomite, Sidonian, and Hittite women. (2) **From the nations which Yahweh told the children of Israel, "Do not come among them and they will not come among you, they will surely turn your heart after their gods," Solomon clung to these**[74] **[gods] out of love.** (3) And he had

---

73. Deuteronomistic composition is designated by the bold font.
74. The referent of בהם is ambiguous. Does Solomon cling to the women? Although the preposition is a 3mp form, it would be grammatically justifiable to read this as women, especially since this is a response to Solomon's love, which has been established in verse 1 as for the women. Cogan translates in this way, making the referent explicit with the use of parentheses: "To such (women) Solomon held fast out of love" (Cogan, *1 Kings*, 325). בהם is also used twice in the first half of the verse, referring to the nations forbidden to Israel, so it could refer to the nations. "Solomon clung to the nations." Gray maintains the ambiguous "to them" and does not make his intention explicit (John Gray, *1 and 2 Kings: A Commentary*, 2nd ed., Old Testament Library [Philadelphia: Westminster, 1970], 272). Fritz implicitly seems to intend the gods, in using the proximal deictic pronoun "these" to refer to the most immediately preceding object (Volkmar Fritz, *1 and 2 Kings*, trans. Anselm Hagedorn,

700 hundred royal wives and 300 concubines. **And his wives turned away his heart.** (4) **And it happened in Solomon's old age [that] his wives turned away his heart after other gods, and his heart was not fully with Yahweh his God, as was the heart of David his father.** (5) **And Solomon went after Ashtaroth the god of the Sidonians, and after Milcom, the abomination of the Ammonites.** (6) **And Solomon did evil in the eyes of Yahweh and he was not fully behind Yahweh like David his father.**

(7) **Then Solomon built a high place to Chemosh, the abomination of Moab, on the mountain which is next to Jerusalem and for Molech the abomination of the Ammonites.** (8) **And thus he did for all his foreign wives who burned incense and sacrificed to their gods.** (9) **And Yahweh was angry**[75] **with Solomon** because he had turned his heart from Yahweh, God of Israel, the one who had appeared to him twice. (10) And he commanded him about this matter, to not go after other gods, but he did not keep that which Yahweh commanded.

(11) And Yahweh said to Solomon, "Because it was this way with you and you did not keep my covenant and my laws which I commanded you, I will surely rend the kingdom from you and give it to your servant. (12) But in your days I will not do it, for the sake of David your father, [but] I will rend it from the hand of your son. (13) But I will not tear [away] the whole kingdom, but one tribe I will give to your son for the sake of David my servant and for the sake of Jerusalem which I have chosen."

(14) **And Yahweh raised an adversary against Solomon,** Hadad the Edomite, from the line of the king of Edom. (15) And it was when David fought[76] Edom that Joab general of the army went up to bury the slain, having killed all the men of Edom. (16) For six months Joab

---

Continental Commentaries [Minneapolis: Fortress Press, 2003], 128). I make explicit "their gods" as the referent for two reasons. The first is that אלהיהם is the closest object in the syntax, immediately preceding בהם. The second is based on the general concern of the passage. This section of the chapter is focused on Solomon's apostasy of idolatry caused by his marriage to foreign women. The deuteronomistic theological perspective is pervasive throughout the whole account, and it is for this crime that Solomon is punished.

75. *'np appears in the *hip'il* only in Deuteronomy and Dtr (2 Kgs. 17:18). Elsewhere it appears in the *qal* (Cogan, *1 Kings*, 328.) It is a marker of deuteronomistic language.

76. This is corrected on the basis of LXX, בהכות for בהיות, as in 2 Sam. 8:16, the original report of this incident. This also makes sense within the syntax of the phrase. It is followed by את- אדום. The correction is a transitive verb and takes Edom as its direct object. היה is stative and therefore would not take an object.

and all of Israel dwelt there until they killed all the men of Edom. (17) Hadad and some of the Edomite men, servants of his father fled with him to Egypt and Hadad was a small child. (18) And they set out from Midian and came to Paran. They took with them men from Paran, then they came to Egypt to Pharaoh King of Egypt who gave him shelter and arranged for his sustenance, and gave him land.[77] (19) And Hadad found great favor in the eyes of Pharaoh, and he gave him as a wife the sister of his wife, the sister of Tahpenes the queen mother. (20) And the sister of Tahpenes bore him Genuvat his son and Tahpenes weaned him in the house of Pharaoh and Genuvat was in the house of Pharaoh among the children of Pharaoh. (21) But when Hadad heard from Egypt that David slept with his fathers and that Joab the general of the army died, and Hadad said to Pharaoh, "Send me away and I will go to my land." (22) And Pharaoh said to him, "But what are you lacking with me that you ask to go to your land?" and he said, "Nothing, but do let me leave."

(23) **And God[78] raised up an adversary against him.** Rezon son of Eliada who fled from Hadadezer king of Soba his lord. (24) And he gathered around him men and he was the leader of a band and David killed them, and they went to Damascus and dwelled there and ruled from Damascus. (25) And he was an adversary to Israel all the days of Solomon and [together] with the evil which Hadad [did], he despised Israel and ruled over Aram.

(26) Now Jeroboam son of Nebat the Ephramite, from the Zeredah and the name of his widowed mother was Zeruah, was a servant of Solomon and he raised his hand against the king. (27) And this is the account of raising his hand against the king. Solomon built the Millo, closed the breach in the city of David, his father. (28) Now the man Jeroboam was a capable man and Solomon saw how the young man did his work, so he put him in charge of all the corvée of the house of Joseph.

(29) And it happened at that time that Jeroboam went out of Jerusalem and the prophet Ahijah the Shilonite found him on the way. He covered himself with a new robe, and the two of them were alone in the field. (30) And Ahijah took hold of the new robe which was upon him and he tore it into twelve pieces. (31) And he said to Jeroboam, **"Take ten**

---

77. This is absent in LXX and is likely a gloss.
78. It is interesting to note that while the sentiments seem to be the same, the subject of the verb ויקם in vv. 14 and 23 is different. In v. 14, the text says that "Yahweh raised an adversary against Solomon, Hadad the Edomite," while v. 23 says, "God raised up an adversary against him, Rezon son of Eliada." This may indicate that the Rezon account was added later and the redactor paraphrased v. 14, switching *Elohim* for Yahweh.

pieces for yourself, for thus says Yahweh, the God of Israel. I am about to tear the kingdom from the hand of Solomon and I will give you ten of the tribes. (32) But the one tribe will be for him, for the sake of my servant David and for the sake of Jerusalem, the city which I chose from all the tribes of Israel. (33) Because [he] left me and [he] bowed to Astarte, god of the Sidonians, to Chemosh, god of Moab, and to Milcom, god of the Ammonites and [he] did not walk in my way, to do right in my eyes, and [to keep] my laws and ordinances as David his father. (34) But I will not take the entire kingdom from his hand for I will position him as *nāsî* all the days of his life, for the sake of David my servant, whom I chose, who kept my commandments and my laws. (35) And I will take the kingdom for his son and give it to you, the ten tribes. (36) But to his son I will give one tribe in order to be a lamp for David my servant all the days before me in Jerusalem the city which I chose for myself to establish my name there. (37) But it is you I will take and you will be king over all you desire and you will be king over Israel.[79]

(38) "Thus it will be if you heed all that I will command you and you will walk in my way and do what is right in my eyes, to keep my law and commandments, which David my servant did, then I will be with you and I will build for you a lasting dynasty as I built for David, and I will give to you Israel. (39) And I will humble the seed of David, but not forever."

(40) And Solomon attempted the murder of Jeroboam. Then Jeroboam got up and fled to Egypt to Shishak, king of Egypt, and he was in Egypt until the death of Solomon.

(41) And the remainder of the deeds of Solomon and all he did and his wisdom, is it not in the writings of the book of the deeds of Solomon? (42) And the days that Solomon was king in Jerusalem and over all Israel were forty years. (43) And Solomon slept with his fathers and he was buried in the city of David his father, and Rehoboam his son became king in his place.

---

79. Many scholars consider varying parts of vv. 36-39 as part of the northern original source, including Noth (vv. 36abα-37); Weippert (vv. 37, 38bαβ); Campbell (vv. 37-38b); Vanoni (vv. 36abα, 37) in Knoppers, *Reign of Solomon*, 191–96. The thematic content and phraseology are too deuteronomistic to attribute it to an earlier source.

The Axis of Selection

Scholarly Commitment to His Sources

In 1 Kings 11, the most remarkable sources that have been included but are unnecessary, and perhaps even undermine Dtr's construction of his metanarrative, are the stories of Hadad and Rezon, since they indicate a less-than-peaceful reign for Solomon. These scenes must have been part of the collection of sources that Dtr inherited. The accounts of these enemies do not quite fit into the overall narrative, as well as within their chronological sequence. Instead of leaving these episodes out of the historical record, Dtr attaches them onto the end of the narrative of Solomon. The way Dtr uses these "tacked-on" sources will be discussed further below as part of Dtr's organizational strategies, but it is important to recognize that Dtr's methodological commitment to his sources does not allow him to omit entirely these stories that challenge Solomon's long and peaceful reign.

This is also seen in the inclusion of the split of the kingdom. In his attempt to present what he deemed an accurate historical portrait, Dtr must include the split of the kingdom, even though the destruction of the unified Davidic kingdom is threatening to Dtr's theological program. This is unlike the Chronicler, who does not have the same historiographical commitment and does not report the split and the two-century existence of the divided kingdom. Dtr must include these historical occurrences, and he deals with his allotted history by recasting it.

The rejection of Solomon calls into question the deuteronomistic program mandating the unconditional eternity of the Davidic dynasty, as the first king to succeed David, his son Solomon, loses control over the entire country. Dtr transforms the historical fact of the split of the kingdom into an "educational moment" to teach kings (and the audience of the history) the importance of fidelity to the deuteronomistic covenant. Solomon was not faithful to Yahweh, and therefore he is punished, yet Yahweh's promise to David will still stand because one tribe will remain in the hands of the Davidic king. Here, both programmatic issues are addressed: the cult must be practiced in the deuteronomistic way (i.e., no syncretism and worship of other gods and foreign symbols), and the Davidic promise is maintained.

Loyalty to the Prophetic Tradition

First Kings 11 includes of the narrative of Ahijah the prophet. This was likely a northern, pre-Dtr prophetic tradition that Dtr integrates into his narrative and adapts to his evaluation of Solomon and the appointing of Jeroboam. While the passage is highly rewritten by Dtr, particularly verses 32-39, the beginning part of the story reflects an earlier kernel of a northern tradition.[80]

Dtr takes the core elements of the story, the prophet Ahijah putting aside King Solomon and designating Jeroboam king in his place, and inserts more deuteronomistic elements, found in verses 32-38. At the same time, it must be noted that the "first" mention of the divided kingdom appears in the words to Solomon. The interaction between Ahijah and Jeroboam follows the divine proclamation made by the narrator to Solomon. Ahijah's speech also mirrors those words.[81] The

---

80. Anthony Campbell attributes vv. 30, 31, 37 and 38b to an earlier prophetic source from the end of the ninth century BCE. He highlights the texts associated with the anointing of Saul, David, and Jehu and those designating and rejecting Jeroboam, Ahab, and Jehu as belonging to this source. He describes narratives from this source with several characteristic elements, which the story of Jeroboam and Ahijah share. Campbell describes the characteristic elements as (1) the tearing away of the kingdom from the present king; (2) designation of another king; (3) evil prophecy against the present king or his house; (4) the destruction of the royal house; (5) the cutting off of every male; (6) reference to the fate of the house of Jeroboam; (7) the fate of those who die in the city or the country. Ahijah's speech in the designation of Jeroboam includes the first two elements, the tearing away of the kingdom and designation of another as king, and the rest occur in the oracle to Jeroboam's wife in 1 Kgs. 14:7-16 (Campbell, *Of Prophets and Kings*, 24, 25).

81. Ben Zvi, "Prophets and Prophecy," 340.

story of Ahijah gives the punishment of Solomon and the subsequent split of the kingdom further authority. Still, Dtr maintains the general narrative integrity of the original prophetic source. The story of Ahijah fits well with the idea of prophets as "kingmakers" and may be an indicator of its origin from a northern prophetic record, an earlier tradition that Dtr incorporates into his narrative.[82] The narrative of Jeroboam's investiture will be discussed further in chapter 4 in the analysis of the portrait of Jeroboam.

The Ordering of Episodes

Once Dtr makes his selection of sources, here the stories of the foreign adversaries and Ahijah's prophecy, he uses his organizational methods to craft them into a coherent narrative. Several time markers in 1 Kings 11 show a reorganization of events. In the first section of the chapter, about Solomon's sin, verse 4 begins with ויהי לעת זקנת שלמה, "and it happened in Solomon's old age."[83] This definitively sets the scene at the end of his life, and presumably at the end of his reign; it is an unambiguous time marker that attempts to cast the infidelity late into his reign, demonstrating a break from his faithfulness as a young man, evident in his wisdom and the general success and prosperity of the greater part of his reign.[84] While scholars may disagree as to when the negative critique of Solomon begins,[85]

---

82. Campbell, *Of Prophets and Kings*, 114.

83. It is interesting to note that LXX makes it further explicit that the idolatry was isolated to late in Solomon's reign. In the reorganization of MT vv. 1–3, LXX attaches 3b (that the women turned Solomon's heart) at the end of v. 4. Verse 4 says that Solomon's heart was not completely with Yahweh in his old age and LXX continues that "the foreign women turned his heart back after their gods" (Marvin A. Sweeney, "A Reassessment of the Masoretic and Septuagint Versions of the Jeroboam Narratives in 1 Kings/3 Kingdoms 11–14," *Journal for the Study of Judaism in the Persian, Hellenistic and Roman Period* 38, no. 2 [2007]: 180).

84. This break is made clear in the disjunctive syntax of the first verse. First Kings 11 begins with the fronting of the subject, והמלך שלמה אהב נשים נכריות רבות creating a disjunctive sequence and a complete break with the narrative that precedes it.

85. J. Daniel Hays, "Has the Narrator Come to Praise Solomon or to Bury Him? Narrative Subtlety in 1 Kings 1–11," *JSOT* 28, no. 2 (2003): 149–74; Marc Zvi Brettler, "The Structure of 1 Kings

the general treatment of Solomon and what happens to him makes a sharp turn at this juncture; even the grammar suggests it.

The punishment for Solomon's sin described in verses 11-13 manifests itself in the raising up of adversaries, first Hadad and Rezon, and then, we are led by the organization of the chapter to believe, Jeroboam. It is through Dtr's reconstruction of these narratives that the adversaries are set up as vehicles of punishment and are banished to the periphery of the Solomon account, the last acts at the end of his life and reign. Yet it is possible to see through several temporal clues that the stories of Hadad and Rezon were removed from their original chronological place in the events of the reign of Solomon (and David) and reset at the end of his story.[86] Verse 14 begins with the raising up of Hadad the Edomite as an adversary of Solomon.[87]

Hadad is an enemy acquired from the time of David. Verse 15 continues with another temporal marker, ויהי בהכות דוד את אדום, "and it was when David fought Edom." Young Hadad flees to Egypt from David and Joab's annihilation of Edom. Hadad remains in Egypt, living in the court of Pharaoh, even marrying Pharaoh's sister-in-law, until the death of David, when he requests to return to his land.[88] The temporal markers in the specific narrative of Hadad the

---

1-11," *JSOT* 16, no. 49 (1991): 89; Kim Ian Parker, "Repetition as a Structuring Device in 1 Kings 1-11," *JSOT* 13, no. 42 (1988): 19-27.

86. Glatt, *Chronological Displacement*, 163; James A. Montgomery, *A Critical and Exegetical Commentary on the Books of Kings*, ed. Henry Snyder Gehman, International Critical Commentary (New York: Scribner's, 1951), 241.

87. The verse begins with a *wāw*-consecutive verb, ויקם continuing the sequence of actions from v. 11. There Yahweh speaks (ויאמר) to Solomon declaring the king's infidelity and pronouncing the verdict that the kingdom will be torn away from him. The next action begins with ויקם in v. 14, presumably that after Yahweh spoke to Solomon he raised the adversary against Solomon. The consecutive action shown by the syntax demonstrates the relationship between the two acts, the pronouncing and raising up of the enemy. The temporal context of v. 4 wants us to read this act as the continuation of the previous section, leading us to understand that the ויקם of v. 14 occurs similarly during the period of the old age of Solomon. Yet as the narrative continues, it is made clear that Hadad is an adversary of Solomon's early reign.

88. In v. 21, we are given the indication of the passage of time that links us to the new historical context. Verse 21 begins with disjunctive syntax, fronting the subject, emphasizing Hadad: והדד שמע במצרים שכב דוד עם אבתיו וכי מת יואב "But when Hadad heard from Egypt that

Edomite demonstrate a different chronology from that of the larger frame of the chapter, setting Hadad as a divinely raised adversary at the end of Solomon's reign rather than the beginning.

The anachronistic renarrativizing of the episodes in the chapter continues with the raising up of a further adversary, Rezon son of Eliada. While the account of Rezon lacks many of the details of that of Hadad, Rezon is presented similarly as a second adversary whose group was also killed by David and fled his land. Verse 25 says, ויהי שטן לישראל כל ימי שלמה, "And he was an adversary to Israel during all the days of Solomon." Like Hadad, Rezon does not appear to be an adversary who emerges in Solomon's old age, toward the end of his reign, as verse 4 would like to establish. Instead, Rezon was an adversary throughout the life (and reign) of Solomon. The explicit temporal markers in the two accounts of the adversaries demonstrate that these textual snippets and the "historical" events they describe were rechronologized to fit into the greater goals of the frame story of the chapter. The two enemies from the beginning and throughout the duration of Solomon's reign are renarrativized by Dtr to appear when summoned. They are adversaries raised up by Yahweh in Solomon's old age to punish him for his sins of infidelity to Yahweh and the covenant. They appear only at the end of Solomon's story to further highlight the "change" in Solomon's behavior at this time from earlier in his reign.[89] In this way, the enemies of Solomon are portrayed as participating in a causal relationship of the sin and its subsequent punishment, supporting the deuteronomistic program of covenant obedience.

David slept with his fathers and that Joab had died. . . ." It is at that time that Hadad petitions Pharaoh to return to Edom. While we do not have any account of what happens to Hadad after that request, we may presume that he returns to the land, rid of the tyrant who decimated his people, and takes the offensive against Solomon. This would set the temporal context for having become an adversary to Solomon at the beginning of Solomon's reign (more precisely, at the death of David).

89. Glatt, *Chronological Displacement*, 164.

Similarly, these events come together in a juxtaposition of episodes; there is a piling up of "adversary" stories. Diana Edelman sees them as a trio of "bad guys," functioning in a folkloric pattern of repetition of threes.[90] First presented is the story of Hadad, as discussed above. This story is followed by a second adversary, Rezon. Almost the same words are used to introduce the appearance of these two adversaries.[91]

The narrative continues to a possible third enemy. Because of the connection of the first two adversaries, when Jeroboam is introduced, although not as an "adversary" per se, rather as one who raises his hand against the king (v. 26), he automatically falls into the category of the third "adversary." This is the effect of the juxtaposition; the separate stories are juxtaposed and their meaning is enhanced by the literary connection. Solomon's punishment is twofold. It is not only the tearing away of the kingdom from Solomon's son, as pronounced in verses 11-13, but also the raising up of two (three) adversaries who will torment Solomon in his old age (or throughout his reign). Dtr brings these three stories together because of their commonalities. This is also a testament to Dtr's attempt to represent his sources (both written and oral). Dtr is committed to maintaining the stories and finding a way to work them into his overall narrative.

---

90. Diana Edelman, "Solomon's Adversaries Hadad, Rezon and Jeroboam: A Trio of 'Bad Guy' Characters Illustrating the Theology of Immediate Retribution," in *The Pitcher Is Broken: Memorial Essays for Gösta W. Ahlström*, ed. Steven W. Holloway and Lowell K. Handy, JSOTSup 190 (Sheffield: Sheffield Academic, 1995), 168.

91. The Hadad story may have been the original because of its level of detail, and the Rezon story is later added to it. We are given information about the life of Hadad in Egypt that is superfluous to the context of Hadad being an enemy of Solomon and the means of exacting punishment. It is unclear whether these stories were collected and juxtaposed by Dtr or whether they had previously circulated together in Dtr's *Vorlage*. It is clear in the way LXX rewrites and further combines these independent stories that they were already connected in the LXX *Vorlage*. In the MT, the separate originals can be detected, but in LXX the rewriting erases the existence of separate origins. LXX reflects the deuteronomistic addition of ויקם in the introduction of the adversaries, but combines the introduction of Hadad and Rezon with a *wāw*-conjunction and only one ויקם: Καὶ ἤγειρεν κύριος σαταν τῷ Σαλωμων τὸν Αδερ τὸν Ιδουμαῖον καὶ τὸν Εσρωμ υιον Ελιαδαε (v. 14); equivalent to the Hebrew, ויקם יהוה שטן לשלמה את הדד האדמי ואת רזון בן אלידע.

The effect of the juxtaposition is also heightened when the pattern of juxtaposition is broken. Dtr sets up a sequence of adversaries raised by Yahweh in the case of Hadad and Rezon, and while the juxtaposition clearly allies Jeroboam with them as a third adversary, the difference in his introduction (lacking the announcement of an adversary) highlights his importance and uniqueness, directing the reader to take him more seriously than the others. The breaking of the pattern signals a new phase in the history.[92] This contrast is also made in the use of the verbs announcing each adversary. Hadad and Rezon are both introduced as follows: "Yahweh/*Elohim* raised up an adversary against Solomon," וַיָּקֶם, the *hip'il* of √קום. In contrast, Jeroboam "raised his hand against the king," וַיָּרֶם, the *hip'il* of √רום. Jeroboam takes action, while Hadad and Rezon are the vehicles of punishment.[93]

---

92. Robert L. Cohn, "Literary Technique in the Jeroboam Narrative," *ZAW* 97 (1985): 26.

93. The verb used for Jeroboam's rebellion is also a verb of ascension, parallel to וַיָּקֶם. This (1 Kgs. 11:26-27) is the only context in which √רום + יד means rebel. There are many other verbs for rebellion (including פשע, מרה, מרד that are used by Dtr), but this is the only instance where this expression is used. The parallel verbs further connect Jeroboam to the others, yet the contrast of the verbs, representing Hadad and Rezon as passive objects and Jeroboam as an active agent, further highlight the importance of Jeroboam among the adversaries. Also, we need to ask what Jeroboam does to "raise his hand against the king." Is the act of וַיָּרֶם יד developed from finding a parallel verb? There is no report of rebellious behavior. This comment is closely followed by the report that Solomon saw Jeroboam as capable and set him over the house of Joseph (v. 28). This also precedes the secret meeting with Ahijah. Is accepting the interaction with Ahijah considered rebellion? The juxtaposition to the previous adversaries colors our reading of v. 26, creating a rebellious figure who sets out against Solomon, as do Hadad and Rezon. Thanks to Jeffrey Tigay (in conversation) for this question. Similarly, Halpern presupposes the resistance of a rebellion, naming "Jeroboam's putative revolt" as "boast[ing] prophetic support as its religious motive force" (Baruch Halpern, "Levitic Participation in the Reform Cult of Jeroboam I," *JBL* 95 [1976]: 526). Robert Cohn suggests that the interruption of the Jeroboam and Solomon narrative by Ahijah's prophecy, placing it before the notice that Solomon wants to kill Jeroboam: "The author supplies a reason for Solomon's anger. He implies that Solomon acts before the prophecy and compounds his sin by attempting to defy the divine will" (Cohn, "Literary Technique," 27).

The Axis of Composition

Promoting the Deuteronomistic Program

The theological stance of Dtr is most prominent in the first part of 1 Kings 11. Verses 1, 3a, and 8 are from Dtr's source, while the majority of verses 1–13 are a clear deuteronomistic composition. As discussed above, this chapter may reflect an earlier tradition (written or oral) in which Solomon had one thousand wives (certainly an exaggerated number), many (if not all) of whom were foreign, and for whom he built various things, including religious sites. The passage is so reworked by Dtr, illustrating deuteronomistic themes, ideology, and phraseology, that it is no longer possible to peel back the deuteronomistic layer and reveal earlier sources. Dtr highlights that through Solomon's acquisition of the foreign women, he was tempted by them and led away from Yahweh into worship of the gods of the foreign women. He is unlike his father David, the paradigm of deuteronomistic theology, and his heart is not completely dedicated to Yahweh.[94]

The centrality of the covenant is clearly seen in the punishment. Solomon is punished because he is not faithful to the covenant, while the promise to David is still upheld. For the sake of David and Jerusalem, Yahweh will only take ten of the tribes from Solomon's dynasty, and not during Solomon's lifetime. While the final form of the narrative corresponds to deuteronomistic theology, it also reflects Dtr's struggle with the actual historical occurrences. The historical separation of the kingdom did not take place during Solomon's reign,

---

94. It is interesting to note the concept of אהבה previously committed to the dedication of Yahweh (e.g., Deuteronomy 5, 6, 7, 10, 11) is now directed to the women and their gods (v. 2). The verb אהב is covenantal, deuteronomic language. While אהב in relation to Solomon's women is employed in the secular sense of the word, it is still significant that it is used, echoing its theological sense, so important to Dtr, alluding to a turning away of religious love and loyalty and transferring it to the foreign women and by extension, their gods.

and Dtr must account for that. Also, a complete break with the Davidic dynasty would undermine the Davidic promise; therefore, some of the kingdom must remain in Davidic hands, with a promise for a future return. All of these elements are theologically essential to Dtr reworking the original story.

Additionally, the phraseology is clearly deuteronomistic.[95] Dtr talks about Jerusalem as the chosen city, David as the ultimate servant, and Solomon's apostasy as a turning of his heart away from Yahweh, again connected with the language of love. It is here, with David's successor, that Dtr sets the standard for the measure of a good king—one whose heart is fully with Yahweh and who is like David. (This will be explored further in chapter 3.) The comparison with David (either like him or, more commonly, not like him) continues in the evaluation of the subsequent kings. The concern of being fully with Yahweh makes clear that syncretistic worship is not acceptable. Likely this is the charge against Solomon, not that he gives up all Yahwistic worship, but that he is also worshiping, sacrificing, and offering incense to the gods of the foreign women. This is also common to Dtr's strategy of pursuing his theological goals—placing all worship that he does not deem appropriate into a category of idolatry. Here, syncretism is utterly forbidden and should be treated as a complete forsaking of Yahweh and Yahwistic worship.

The Attribution of Historico-Political Events to Theological Causes

First Kings 11 is based on the description of several historical events. First and foremost is the split of the northern and southern kingdoms, which occurs after the death of Solomon. The second is the uprising of Hadad and Rezon as foreign enemies. And the third is the rise of Jeroboam to the position of king over the North. As discussed

---

95. For deuteronomistic phraseology, see Weinfeld, *Deuteronomy and the Deuteronomic School*, esp. appendix A, 320–65.

previously, foreign adversaries Hadad and Rezon are framed as a means of punishment for Solomon's sin. This connection is made explicit through the consecutive syntax of the verses. Both episodes begin with ויקם (vv. 14, 23), the *wāw*-consecutive, highlighting the connection of these events with what precedes them, namely, the sin and doom pronouncement on Solomon. Yet within the text there is an implicit indication of a more political cause. Joab, general of the army under David, slaughtered all the men of Edom (v. 15), forcing Hadad to flee. Similarly, Rezon son of Eliada fled David's massacre of his band and lived in exile in Damascus (v. 24). Both Hadad and Rezon wait until the death of David to return, presumably plotting their revenge.

Furthermore, the split of the kingdom, which occurs in 1 Kings 12, when Rehoboam travels to Shechem, is attributed to political reasons. The men of the North request relief from their heavy corvée, but instead of lessening the burden, Rehoboam increases it. In response, the people separate from the Judean king, declaring Jeroboam their king in his place. Instead of a political reason for the separation, Dtr constructs a theological one, as is described in the beginning of chapter 11. Yahweh's direct speech in verses 11-13 makes clear that the kingdom will be torn away from Solomon because he did not keep Yahweh's covenant and laws. While this split is the consequence of Solomon's behavior, the historical "reality" demands that this occurs during the reign of Rehoboam and not that of Solomon, and the Davidic dynasty, though diminished, will continue. Dtr must contend with this fact and covering his bases addresses this issue with theological reasons.

The third historical occurrence is the rise of Jeroboam as king of Israel. There are two versions of the choosing of Jeroboam. The first is by the prophet Ahijah, setting Jeroboam up as the vehicle for Solomon's punishment. It also follows a trope of prophetically elected kings (similar to Saul and David).[96] The second version appears in 1 Kgs. 12:1-24, describing the historical account and Rehoboam's unwillingness to lighten the corvée of the North. First Kings 12:1-19 likely preserves a historical report, bearing what Carl Evans argues is "the clear stamp of reliability."[97] While the conversations between Rehoboam and his two sets of advisors are imagined, the political and economic situations they reflect could likely be historical and may represent an earlier royal source reporting the reasons and/or justification for the split of the kingdom.

By combining these two accounts, Dtr takes this arguably historical account and puts his own deuteronomistic spin on it, attributing the cause of the split to Solomon's apostasy (1 Kings 11) and including the story of the prophet Ahijah as kingmaker to execute Yahweh's desire for a split in the kingdom with Jeroboam as the king. While it may have been difficult for Dtr to contemplate the breach in the united monarchy, the rise of a non-Davidic king over Israel, and what appeared to be an abandonment of the Davidic promise (key elements of deuteronomistic ideology), he cannot deny the split of the kingdoms. His historiographical commitments do not allow him to erase history, but he can rewrite and interpret it.

Similarly, the vilification of Jeroboam, the Israelite kings, and the people of Israel is a drawn-out attempt to ascribe theological meaning to the destruction of the northern kingdom by Assyria. The negative treatment of the North is frequently part of the agenda to promote the deuteronomistic program. According to Dtr, Jeroboam rises to power in an act of divine providence. The split of the kingdom is

---

96. Mark Leuchter, "Jeroboam the Ephratite," *JBL* 125, no. 1 (2006): 51–72; Cohn, "Literary Technique," 26.
97. Carl D. Evans, "Naram-Sin and Jeroboam: The Archetypal *Unheilsherrscher* in Mesopotamian and Biblical Historiography," in *Scripture in Context II: More Essays on the Comparative Method*, ed. William W. Hallo, James C. Moyer, and Leo G. Perdue (Winona Lake, IN: Eisenbrauns, 1983), 115.

explained theologically; the kingdom is divided because of Solomon's apostasy rather than the socioeconomic conflict between the North and South over Rehoboam's corvée. By blaming Solomon, and not Rehoboam or the northern representatives, for the downfall of the united kingdom, Dtr makes the split about centralization and apostasy, not economic oppression. Consequently, according to Knoppers, "Solomon's construction of high places and his worship of other gods is more foundational than the division between Judah and Israel. And if infidelity lies at the root of disunion, then requiting such infidelity can mend the rift between northern and southern tribes"—as such, Josiah can reunite all of Yahweh's people theologically, even though the northern kingdom no longer exists.[98] In this way, the infidelity of Israel is correctable by Dtr's hero, Josiah. Even in the report of the split of the kingdom so early in the history of the monarchy, Dtr is cognizant of the larger picture. The history is written from the perspective of the Josianic court, and the coming of Josiah and his reform are the high point of the history of the monarchy. Similarly, Solomon's apostasy legitimates the division of the kingdom. In Chronicles, Solomon never sins; it is not literarily necessary, as the Chronicler views the northern kingdom as illegitimate. He does not need to justify its formation; instead, he ignores it. In Kings, Solomon builds a high place that Dtr and Josiah cast as foreign, giving Dtr the opportunity to further the deuteronomistic program and elevate Josiah as hero. Solomon's act sets up Josiah's reform as a way to reunite the kingdom.[99] In this way, the rise of Jeroboam, the rejection of the Davidic king (theologically Solomon and politically Rehoboam), the split of its kingdom, and its eventual reunion by Josiah are clearly constructed by Dtr's casting these events with theological causation.

98. Knoppers, *Reign of Solomon*, 158–59.
99. Halpern, *The First Historians*, 154, 155.

The Use of a Prototype Strategy

In 1 Kings 11, the prototype strategy is used prominently in the construction of Jeroboam. He is set up to be a second David. The words of Ahijah's annunciation of Jeroboam clearly link Jeroboam's position both to the words of Solomon's punishment in verses 11-13 and David's words to Solomon in 1 Kgs. 2:3, describing how to be a good king. Dtr uses the anointing of Jeroboam to make these connections, demonstrating Jeroboam as the inheritor of the Davidic tradition. Jeroboam has the opportunity to be a good, even great, king like David. The role of Ahijah's prophecy (1 Kgs. 11:29-39) in establishing Jeroboam in the Davidic prototype will also be explored in detail in chapter 4.

The casting of Jeroboam in the Davidic prototype is a strategy that continues in the portrait of the kings most important to Dtr. Beginning with Jeroboam, Dtr uses a Davidic prototype to portray his kings. The ways the Davidic prototype is created and applied will be address in chapter 3. In the case of Jeroboam, he is given the opportunity to be Davidic, but he cannot live up to this expectation. Instead, in Ahijah's second prophecy in 1 Kings 14, Jeroboam is established as an anti-David. The use of the prototype strategy in the portrayal of Jeroboam in 1 Kings 11 sets the stage for the use of this methodological technique, critical to Dtr's historiographical poetics, throughout the remainder of his history.

Through the analysis of 1 Kings 11, it is possible to see the historiographical method of the preexilic Dtr functioning on both the selectional and compositional axes. This mode of analysis makes clear the strategies that Dtr employees in order to craft his history. These priorities describe the ways Dtr chooses (or does not choose) his sources, how he adapts them to suit his purposes, and how he writes new material to further his goals and tie together his sources.

This method is encapsulated in the use of the prototype strategy, influencing which kings Dtr focuses on and how he portrays them. The Davidic prototype is used to construct the portraits of the kings, evaluate their cultic behavior, create a cohesive chronological narrative of the history of the monarchy, and compare the kings to each other and, ultimately, to David and Josiah. The remainder of this volume will focus on exploring the prototype strategy and how it is used by the preexilic Dtr, while making reference to the other priorities of the two axes throughout.

This analysis contributes to the scholarly discussion of the method of historiography of the Deuteronomistic Historian, building on theories espousing the competency of the author/redactor, Dtr's use of predeuteronomistic sources both from the royal archives and the prophetic tradition, and the ways in which Dtr integrates and rewrites those sources. Dtr functions in the history as both author and redactor and pays careful attention to a select group of kings whose portrayal he crafts using the Davidic prototype strategy.

3

David, "Who Observed My Commandments and Who Followed Me with All His Heart, Doing Only What Was Right in My Eyes"

The historiographical poetics as laid out in chapter 2 demonstrate that the preexilic Deuteronomist maintained specific selectional and compositional priorities in constructing his history. The most prominent of them is the use of a prototype strategy based on the literary portrait of David in Kings. Throughout the history of the monarchy, kings are evaluated in two ways; the bad kings are said to do what is "evil in the eyes of Yahweh," and are compared to Jeroboam and Ahab, and often to each king's father if his father acted similarly. The good kings are those who do what is "right in the eyes of Yahweh," and are compared to their own fathers, if they were also good. Only three kings, Asa, Hezekiah, and Josiah, are compared to David, who is set up as the prototype of the good king. This raises the question, What does it mean to be like David? Is there some set of criteria that can be derived from the narrative of Kings that would qualify a certain king to be like or unlike David? Furthermore, would David, as represented in Samuel, be "like David" as constructed in Kings, or is David, as the standard for good kings, exclusively a deuteronomistic construct and typological tool?[1]

Through the analysis of the individual regnal formulae of the good kings, it is possible to answer some of these questions. Once the model has been established, it can be used to reflect back on the character of David, exploring whether David is actually like his literary alter ego. Establishing the range of this prototype and its antithesis gives us a deeper look at the Deuteronomist's historiographical poetics and the literary methods used in constructing the portrait of his kings. This portrait of David is very different from that found in Samuel.

My analysis is directed at the heart of the debate about the relationship between Kings and the rest of the Deuteronomistic History, considering the role of the redactor/author in Kings and DtrH as well as determining the strata of composition and redaction. The prototype strategy provides linguistic criteria for establishing a distinct redactional layer, directing the reader to view the historian's literary use of the narratives of the individual kings to promote his theological program. Focus on the Davidic prototype highlights the literary value of Dtr's composition and redaction, providing a view into the author's intentional method. It also combats Konrad Schmid's critique that the common use of the proof of language is deceptive, that there are deuteronomistic-sounding texts that contain undeuteronomistic content. "Linguistic usage is not a sufficient characteristic for identifying Deuteronomistic texts, which must

---

1. Also see my article for extended treatment of this subject, "Who Is Like David? Was David Like David?: Good Kings in the Book of Kings," *CBQ* 77 (2015): 20–41.

instead be conceptually demonstrable as such."[2] The prototype strategy offers such additional criteria.

While my argument for the use of a prototype strategy builds on linguistic commonalities, it takes into account further literary considerations. Cognitive linguistics contributes to our understanding of a literary prototype and how it functions in our historical narratives. I return to the literary definition laid out in chapter 2 by linguist George Lakoff. Prototypes are "cognitive reference points of various sorts [that] form the basis for inferences."[3] These inferences are part of the conceptual structure, in which prototypes have a "special cognitive status" of being a "best example."[4] In Kings, prototypes of individual kings (David as the model for the good king and an anti-David for the bad king) are laid out, allowing the reader to consider each king and his individual acts on micro and macro levels: what did this king do, and how do his character and reign fit into the larger history of Israel and Judah and reflect the way Yahweh works in history? Furthermore, the use of a prototype allows the reader to infer information about each king without the narrator supplying it because he is cast in a literary convention that the audience already recognizes.

Establishing the Prototype through the Regnal Formula

The regnal formula has long been seen by scholars as an unequivocal site of deuteronomistic evaluation. At the start of the account of each king, Dtr includes a formulaic introduction that gives details about the king's background and reign as well as contains an evaluation measuring the king by deuteronomistic standards. The regnal

2. Konrad Schmid, *The Old Testament: A Literary History*, trans. Linda M. Maloney (Minneapolis: Fortress Press, 2012), 74.
3. George Lakoff, *Women, Fire, and Dangerous Things: What Categories Reveal about the Mind* (Chicago: University of Chicago Press, 1987), 45.
4. Ibid., 41.

formula is a narrative tool used by Dtr to synchronize the narratives about the kings of Israel and Judah, to make the chronology of events and reigns clear, to create segues and uniformity in the presentation of the information about each king, and most importantly, to put into application the major concepts of deuteronomistic theology through the judgment formulae. Dtr uses these formulae to interpret the narratives, employing them to frame and mold the story of each king. In this way, the formulae are intrinsically linked to the process of historiography. They created continuity between the narrative sources, as Van Seters describes: "The author has tied together blocks of material of uneven length by means of a number of unifying devices characteristic of the paratactic style. These include patterns and analogies, repetition of formulaic statements in a framework, prophecies and their fulfillment, and contrasts between major figures like David and Saul or David and Jeroboam."[5] The regnal formulae are also the place where the application of the Davidic prototype begins. While scholarship on these formulae has largely focused on synchronizing chronology between the two kingdoms and as indicating signs of different levels of redaction, the accession formulae deserve inquiry on their own merit, in addition to their use in the teasing out of redactional layers.[6]

---

5. John Van Seters, *In Search of History: Historiography in the Ancient World and the Origins of Biblical History* (Winona Lake, IN: Eisenbrauns, 1997), 321.

6. For recent work on the regnal formulae, see Richard D. Nelson, "The Regnal Formulae in Kings," in *The Double Redaction of the Deuteronomistic History* (Sheffield: JSOT Press, 1981), 29–42; Baruch Halpern and David S. Vanderhooft, "The Editions of Kings in the 7th–6th Centuries BCE," *HUCA* 62 (1991): 179–244; Iain Provan, "The Judgment Formulae of the Books of Kings," in *Hezekiah and the Books of Kings: A Contribution to the Debate about the Composition of the Deuteronomistic History* (Berlin: de Gruyter, 1988), 33–55; Antony F. Campbell, *Of Prophets and Kings: A Late Ninth Century Document (1 Samuel 1–2 Kings 10)*, Catholic Biblical Quarterly 17 (Washington, DC: Catholic Biblical Association of America, 1986); Erik Eynikel, *The Reform of King Josiah and the Composition of the Deuteronomistic History* (Leiden: Brill, 1995); Helga Weippert, "Die Deuteronomistischen Beurteilungen Der Könige von Israel Und Juda Und Das Problem Der Redaktion Der Königsbücher," *Biblica* 53 (1972): 301–39; W. Boyd Barrick, "On the Removal of the High-Places in 1–2 Kings," *Biblica* 55, no. 2 (1974): 257–59; Klaus-Peter Adam, "Warfare and Treaty Formulas in the Background

Many scholars have focused on the regnal formulae as important evidence for unity or multiplicity of authorship. According to Richard Nelson, "The historian's formulae, especially the verdicts upon the Judean kings, reflect a fascinating diversity, always made up of the same basic material of Deuteronomistic clichés and always with the same overall pattern, but never exactly alike. But the formulae of the exilic editor are carbon copies of each other with only the slightest differences, and even those were forced upon him by circumstances."[7] The advocates of a two-edition theory assert that the second editor must have copied the usage of the first. These formulae become less varied and more stereotyped.[8]

In the regnal formulae, I am most interested in the judgment evaluation and the explanations given for such evaluation. In this chapter, I will deal specifically with the regnal formulae of the "good" kings, Asa, Jehoshaphat, Jehoash, Amaziah, Azariah, Jotham, Hezekiah, and Josiah. All of these kings are said to do הישר בעיני יהוה, "what is right in the eyes of Yahweh."[9] I will consider the

of Kings," in *Soundings in Kings: Perspectives and Methods in Contemporary Scholarship*, ed. Mark Leuchter and Klaus-Peter Adam (Minneapolis: Fortress Press, 2010), 35–68; Benjamin D. Thomas, *Hezekiah and the Compositional History of the Book of Kings* (Tübingen: Mohr Siebeck, 2014), 62–177.

7. Nelson, *Double Redaction*, 42.

8. Ibid., 31.

9. Redactional conversations attempt to divide the individual formulae into patterns. Helga Weippert contends that there are as many as six different formula patterns, reflecting three levels of redaction (and a northern and southern version at each level). While there is disagreement on the provenance of various redactors, it is worthwhile to note that there is some consensus among scholars that most of the kings' formulae I am concerned with are identified as deriving from the same hand and part of the same pattern (Weippert's RIS1; Campbell's B pattern; Provan's Hezekian Redaction). Weippert includes Jehoshaphat, Jehoash, Amaziah, Azariah, Jotham, and Josiah in her RIS1 pattern (1st Redaction, southern kings, 1 for הישר, the negative assessments are 2). She identifies Asa, Hezekiah, and Josiah as part of RIIS (2nd southern redaction) ("Beurteilungen Der Könige," 308, 325, 335). Barrick wants to extend Weippert's designation of RI (Jehoshaphat to Ahaz) to include Asa and Hezekiah ("On the Removal," 258). Provan argues for their inclusion as well, asserting that it is impossible to attribute the David and *bāmôt* elements of the formulae to different authors (*Hezekiah and the Books of Kings*, 53). Provan and Campbell both exclude Josiah's formula from this pattern, Campbell because he sees Hezekiah as the last of his pre-Dtr "B" pattern, and Provan because he identifies a Hezekian provenance for the primary pre-exilic DtrH.

regnal formulae of these eight kings as part of the same pattern, even if the pattern is not verbatim. It is a product of the Josianic redactor. While some scholars exclude a few of the kings I have mentioned from this pattern, especially those who argue for a predeuteronomistic Hezekian history, even if they were the product of subsequent redactors, it does not affect the case for trying to understand what the Josianic author/redactor constructed in the figure of David.[10] And it is not my intention to argue whether there had been a Hezekian history that preceded the Josianic one.

These scholars also isolate a second pattern, a subset of those who do what is right: those also compared with David (Asa, Hezekiah, and Josiah). Despite these arguments, I will include the two patterns together on the grounds that either the Josianic redactor is responsible for both patterns or he inherited the earlier "like David" tradition, and then exploits it in his composition. Yet, while the regnal formulae simultaneously display diversity and unity, they seem to be constructed on the same model and from the same hand. In the evaluations of the "good" kings, there are three elements included in the designation "good": that the king does הישר בעיני יהוה, a paternal comparison (to David the ancestral father or to the literal father), and whether his לבב is with Yahweh.[11] By tracking these designations, I attempt to discover what it means to be a "good" king,

---

10. Halpern and Vanderhooft argue that the variations in the regnal evaluations are not reliable proof for the distinguishing of edition (Halpern and Vanderhooft, "Editions of Kings," 179–244).

11. It is interesting to note that those scholars who deal with parsing the various patterns of the regnal formulae do not identify לבב as a constituent element. Instead, they focus on the judgment, the comparison, and the במות theme. This may reflect scholarship that does not recognize the majority of these accession formulae as Dtr and לבב as an unequivocally deuteronomistic concept (Campbell, *Of Prophets and Kings*, 144–51; Provan, *Hezekiah*, 33–55; Weippert, "Beurteilungen Der Könige," 301–39). Only von Rad seems to acknowledge the use of לבב in constructing the prototype (Gerhard von Rad, "The Deuteronomistic Theology of History in the Books of Kings," in *Studies in Deuteronomy*, trans. David Stalker [London: SCM, 1953], 87–88).

even the best of kings, and whether David in Samuel stacks up to these standards.

הישר בעיני יהוה—What is Right in the Eyes of Yahweh?

Of the more than forty monarchs who reign over Israel and Judah, only eight are reported to have done what is right in Yahweh's eyes, הישר בעיני יהוה.[12] All of these are kings of Judah. The command to do what is right in the eyes of Yahweh is a deuteronomistic injunction, intrinsically linked with observing the commandments. This phrase is first used in Deut. 6:18, where the connection to the deuteronomistic covenant is made clear and defines how one does what is right: שמור תשמרון את מצות יהוה אלהיכם ועדתיו וחקיו אשר צוך. ועשית הישר והטוב בעיני יהוה, "Surely you shall keep the commandments of Yahweh your God, his testimonies and his statutes which he commanded you. And you shall do what is right and good in the eyes of Yahweh" (vv. 17-18; cf. Deut. 13:19). The kings who do what is right in Yahweh's eyes are those who are faithful to the deuteronomistic theology and covenant. Throughout DtrH, obedience to these commandments and statutes is repeated. Doing what is right is usually said to result in a long and peaceful life and reign (e.g., 1 Kgs. 3:14), although this is not always the case. Manasseh, Josiah, and others challenge this assumption.

כדוד אביו—Like David his Father

The designation of doing what is right is connected with being like David only four times in the evaluations of the good kings (Asa, Amaziah, Hezekiah, and Josiah), yet one of these connections is negative.[13] (Amaziah is explicitly not like David, but like his father

---

12. Asa (1 Kgs. 15:11), Jehoshaphat (1 Kgs. 22:43), Jehoash (2 Kgs. 12:3), Amaziah (2 Kgs. 14:3), Azariah (2 Kgs. 15:3), Jotham (2 Kgs. 15:34), Hezekiah (18:3), Josiah (2 Kgs. 22:2).

Joash, 2 Kgs. 14:3).[14] Due to the infrequency of the connection to David, it is difficult to understand what is deemed right or not right in Yahweh's eyes and what it means to be like or unlike David. If we take the formulaic assessments and the collection of information about the acts of each king in the subsequent narrative and use his deeds as evidence for designation, the evidence is contradictory. Also, while one may wonder why a comparison made so infrequently should be considered of utmost importance, the instructions given to Solomon as he becomes king make clear that being like David is essential for the proper behavior of kings.

It has long been argued that Josiah is the hero of DtrH, and many also include Hezekiah. Both Hezekiah and Josiah execute major religious reforms, carrying out the religious ideals of deuteronomistic theology. Hezekiah tears down the high places, removing an asherah and maṣṣēbôt, and takes down the bronze serpent, Nehustan, that Moses erected, because people are worshiping it. While Josiah, upon finding a law scroll in the temple, reaffirms the covenant, purges Israel and Judah of idolatrous practices—tearing down cult sites, removing objects from the temple, deposing idolatrous priests—and celebrates the Passover. The praise for these kings is unparalleled. They are both set up as kings of incomparability.[15] We are told about both Hezekiah and Josiah that there was never before or following someone like him. Hezekiah is not merely like David (as reported in the Asa account), but he does "all that David did," ככל אשר עשה דוד אביו (2 Kgs. 18:3). Even more impressive is Josiah's emulation of David: וילך בכל דרך דוד אביו ולא סר ימין ושמאול, "And he

---

13. Twice a bad king is said to not be like David (Abijam, 1 Kgs. 15:3; and Ahaz, 2 Kgs. 16:2). For this reason, Weippert includes them in her RI ("Beurteilungen Der Könige," 335).

14. Many scholars see this negative comparison to David as a secondary addition (Provan, *Hezekiah*, 93).

15. Hezekiah (2 Kgs. 18:5-6), Josiah (2 Kgs. 23:25).

walked in all the ways of David his father and did not stray to the right or left" (2 Kgs. 22:2).[16]

It is not surprising that Hezekiah and Josiah are both compared to David, but the designation of King Asa is less expected. The account begins, King Asa "did what was right in the eyes of Yahweh, like his father David" (1 Kgs. 15:11). He expelled the qĕdēšîm and removed the idols his ancestors made; he deposed his mother Maacah as queen mother because she made an asherah. He brought votive gifts to the temple, but later took gold and silver from the temple to make a treaty (rather more like a bribe) with Ben-Hadad against Baasha of Israel. Even though he did many things towards cultic reform, Asa did not remove the high places. Cogan describes these inconsistent actions as "deviations from cultic rigorism."[17] The quality of "rightness" of Asa's deeds is mixed—he got rid of idolatrous practices, but did not remove the high places; he brought offerings to the temple, but also took from it to promote his foreign policy. While he does not explicitly state it, Dtr would likely have viewed Asa's taking objects from the temple negatively.[18] Deuteronomistic notice of construction in the temple adds to the positive assessment in the routine formula, but taking the treasure to enlist foreigners against the northern kingdom is not positive.[19] Regardless of the mixed

---

16. The comment about Josiah is made in the concluding formula of his reign, while the others are in the accession formula. This may be significant in chronologizing the composition and the construction of this contention.

17. Mordechai Cogan, *1 Kings: A New Translation with Introduction and Commentary*, AB (New York: Doubleday, 2001), 398n14.

18. Ibid., 402.

19. Mordechai Cogan and Hayim Tadmor, *2 Kings: A New Translation*, AB 11 (Garden City, NY: Doubleday, 1988), 141. Klaus-Peter Adam in his discussion of the regnal formulae highlights three criteria for positive judgment: (1) above average term of office, (2) military success, and (3) religious impact ("Warfare and Treaty Formulas," 39). These are descriptive qualifications, derived from weighing the details given about each of the positively regarded kings. The second element, military success, is based on the example of Asa in 1 Kgs. 15:17-23, but in this context is not precedent-setting. This is the only example of military success, except for, as Adam states, Ahaz who partly has military success and has a partial positive judgment (39). Also,

deeds, Asa's acts earn him a triple praise designation: he does what is right; he is like David; and his heart was completely with Yahweh (לבב היה שלם, 1 Kgs. 15:14) all his days. Given the focus on the deuteronomistic purge of the cult of Yahweh from all "foreign" elements even if they had been traditional features of Israelite worship in the past, the inclusion of Asa, who does not remove the high places, is baffling. While the motivation for Dtr's addition of Asa to Hezekiah and Josiah is unclear, the designation is even more confusing when compared to the evaluation and deeds of Asa's son Jehoshaphat. Jehoshaphat is portrayed very similarly. It is even possible to view his actions as more praiseworthy than Asa's, yet he does not receive the same acclaim. Jehoshaphat "walked in all the ways of his father Asa, he did not stray from them, doing what was right in the eyes of Yahweh" (1 Kgs. 22:43). Like Asa, he did not remove the high places, but he made peace with Israel (v. 44), rather than taking from the temple to secure allies against Israel. (It is unclear whether peace or war with Israel is judged positively or negatively by Dtr, but regardless, Dtr did not likely approve of taking gold and silver from the temple).[20] Jehoshaphat removed the remnant of the qĕdēšîm who were left from the days of Asa (v. 46). This statement belies the fact that the act for which Asa receives the highest praise was incomplete, and Jehoshaphat has to rectify the situation.[21] Iain Provan reasons why Asa receives this acclaim: "While it is true that only Asa, Hezekiah and Josiah are compared positively to David, it is equally true that only these three kings

there is no evaluation of the military success against Israel given in the text, so it is not known whether the author regarded it positively.

20. Cogan, *1 Kings*, 402; contra Adam, "Warfare and Treaty Formulas."

21. This act is also seemingly incomplete as Josiah also removes the houses of the qĕdēšîm (2 Kgs. 23:7). Their existence perhaps is a persistent trope.

attempted reformation."[22] Does this mean that Jehoshaphat's purge of the *qĕdēšîm* is not a reform?

For these deeds, Jehoshaphat receives only one element of praise, that he did right in Yahweh's eyes. Instead of being compared to David, the ancestral father, Jehoshaphat is compared to his actual father, Asa, and nothing is said about his heart. One difference is that Jehoshaphat's act of removing the *qĕdēšîm* is only included in the closing formula, rather than in the introductory formula, as in Asa's case. But the reforms of Josiah are also not included in the introductory formula. After Josiah's introduction, the narrative continues with the finding of the scroll in the temple. Thus this difference may be inconsequential in determining why Asa is so praised.

Perhaps the account of Jehoshaphat is not the best test case, because his evaluation is constructed differently from the other seven kings who do what is right. Except for Jehoshaphat, the evaluation begins with ויעש הישר בעיני יהוה. In all but one case (Jehoash[23]), the verse then continues with a comparison: Asa, Hezekiah, and Josiah to David; and Amaziah (additionally, not like David), Azariah, and Jotham to their fathers. In the case of Jehoshaphat, the judgment begins with the comparison and is followed by the הישר בעיני יהוה phrase. In the table below, the anomaly of the construction of Jehoshaphat's evaluation is quite clear.

---

22. Provan, *Hezekiah*, 40.
23. Jehoash does not follow in the footsteps of his father Ahaziah, the son of Athaliah, the daughter of Omri, who walked in the ways of the house of Ahab (2 Kgs. 8:27). Instead, after being hidden away from his grandmother Athaliah by the priest Jehoiada, he follows the teaching of Jehoiada (2 Kgs. 12:3).

	Was like PN (esp. David), his father	Did what was right in the eyes of Yahweh
Asa (1 Kgs. 15:11)	כדוד אביו	ויעש אסא הישר בעיני יהוה
Hezekiah (2 Kgs. 18:3)	ככל אשר עשה דוד אביו	ויעש הישר בעיני יהוה
Josiah (2 Kgs. 22:2)	וילך בכל דרך דוד אביו ולא סר ימין ושמאול	ויעש הישר בעיני יהוה
Jehoshaphat (1 Kgs. 22:43)		וילך בכל דרך אסא אביו לא סר ממנו לעשות הישר בעיני יהוה
Amaziah (2 Kgs. 14:3)	רק לא כדוד אביו ככל אשר עשה יואש אביו עשה	ויעש הישר בעיני יהוה
Azariah (2 Kgs. 15:3)	ככל אשר עשה אמציהו אביו	ויעש הישר בעיני יהוה
Jotham (2 Kgs. 15:34)	ככל אשר עשה עזיהו אביו עשה	ויעש הישר בעיני יהוה
Jehoash (2 Kgs. 12:3)	אשר הורדו יהוידע הכהן	ויעש יהואש הישר בעיני יהוה כל ימיו

The comparison of this father and son, two of the few "good" kings, does not fully illustrate the defining criteria for praise. They both fail to carry out one of the key elements of deuteronomistic theology: removing the high places. Yet Asa receives the triple praise like Josiah and Hezekiah, who enact more thorough reforms, but Jehoshaphat does not. This is further confounded by considering the assessment of Amaziah. Amaziah did what was right in Yahweh's eyes, but "not like his ancestor David" (explicitly not like David, as opposed to Jehoshaphat, for whom all reference to David is omitted). Amaziah does all that his father Joash does (2 Kgs. 14:3); Jehoash (Joash) is also said to do what was right in Yahweh's eyes but does not remove the high places (2 Kgs. 10:31, to be discussed below). Amaziah's political acts include killing the servants who murdered his father, but not killing their children. Dtr seems to approve of this action, giving it divine sanction, connecting it to a proscription in the law of Moses (2 Kgs. 14:6). Amaziah also instigates a battle, in which he is defeated, with King Jehoash of Israel. He seems no worse than the other good kings. One difference in the indictment against Amaziah for not removing the high places, as compared to Asa, is that the narrator adds that the people continue to sacrifice at the high places, yet this is also true for Jehoshaphat, Jehoash, Azariah, and Jotham, who are all said to do what is right like their fathers. All references, positive or negative, to David are omitted in the judgment of these three kings.

	The people continued worshipping at the *bāmôt*	Did not remove *bāmôt*
Asa (1 Kgs. 15:14)	רק לבב אסא היה שלם עם יהוה כל ימיו	והבמות לא סרו
Jehoshaphat (1 Kgs. 22:44)	עוד העם מזבחים ומקטרים בבמות	אך הבמות לא סרו
Jehoash (2 Kgs. 12:4)	עוד העם מזבחים ומקטרים בבמות	רק הבמות לא סרו
Amaziah (2 Kgs. 14:4)	עוד העם מזבחים ומקטרים בבמות	רק הבמות לא סרו
Azariah (2 Kgs. 15:4)	עוד העם מזבחים ומקטרים בבמות	רק הבמות לא סרו
Jotham (2 Kgs. 15:35)	עוד העם מזבחים ומקטרים בבמות	רק הבמות לא סרו

Given the overwhelming praise of Josiah and Hezekiah, it seems that the designation of Asa as like David is anomalous. Separating Hezekiah and Josiah from the other good kings, the main differences in Asa's religious behavior, which according to Dtr is usually what warrants evaluative judgment, is that there is no explicit report of the people continuing to sacrifice at the high places.[24] Since Asa does not remove the high places, the verse continues with a restrictive clause: והבמות לא סרו רק לבב אסא היה שלם עם יהוה כל ימיו, "But the high places he did not remove, yet the heart of Asa was full with Yahweh all his days" (1 Kgs. 15:14). The verse begins with a disjunctive fronting of the object, emphasizing the high places themselves, as well as grammatically separating it from the preceding verses of Asa's praiseworthy behavior and of the things that he did indeed remove (סור/√): the idols (v. 12) and Maacah (v. 13). The second clause begins with רק, which introduces a restrictive clause, limiting the thrust of the first clause, and allowing the second clause to take on more importance, significance, and meaning, creating a contrast with the first phrase.[25] Even though he did not remove the high places, Asa's heart was fully with Yahweh. This is a grammatical difference from the other reports of the nonremoval of high places. Instead of the disjunctive fronting of the object, those clauses begin with the restrictive particle רק. It is unclear whether this is significant in measuring the "rightness" of acts or whether the author just wanted to vary his construction, not beginning both clauses in 1 Kgs. 15:11 with רק.[26]

---

24. Weippert argues that the differences are the result of two different layers of redaction. Her RI does not directly blame the individual kings, but rather the people, for their sins. This is true for the southern and northern reports of this redactor. For the northern kings who did not turn away from Jeroboam's sin, the blame is on Jeroboam, not the individual king. As such, Weippert designates the Asa report as a product of her second redactor, RII. She also includes 2 Kings 18–23 (the reports of the reigns of Hezekiah and Josiah) as originating from the same hand, while the other formulae derive from her RI (Provan, *Hezekiah*, 35–38). While her redactional schema is not well supported, it is interesting to note that her divisions deal with similar contradictory elements in the pattern as my argument: focusing on why Asa is singled out as like David and the difference in the culpability of Asa in not removing the high places.

25. Wilhelm Gesenius, *Gesenius' Hebrew Grammar*, ed. Arthur Ernest Cowley and Emil Friedrich Kautzsch, 2nd English ed. (Oxford: Clarendon, 1910), 153.

26. W. B. Barrick argues that the differences in the words proceeding the high places, ו (1 Kgs. 15:14), אך (2 Kgs. 22:44), and רק (2 Kgs. 12:4; 14:4; 15:4, 35), demonstrate a conscious attempt by the redactor to show a worsening situation. For this reason, he contends that Asa should be included with the work of RI ("On the Removal," 258). While this may reflect a decline in the behavior of the kings, the grammar does not support this. אך and רק as restrictive particles seem

רק, or in one instance אך (also a restrictive particle), is used to qualify some element of the regnal judgment. In the case of Asa, it is to restrict the degradation of his praiseworthiness and cultic commitments; although he did not remove the high places, his heart is fully with Yahweh (1 Kgs. 15:14). This same particle רק is used to introduce a restrictive clause in the evaluation formula of Amaziah, ויעש הישר בעיני יהוה רק לא כדוד אביו, "He did what was right in Yahweh's eyes, yet he was not like David his father" (2 Kgs. 14:3). Furthermore, the rightness of the other five good kings is restricted by רק or אך (in the case of Jehoshaphat) that they did not remove the high places.

It seems that to be like David means to enact some kind of cultic reform, which Asa, Hezekiah, and Josiah all do. But Jehoshaphat enacts reforms and is not said to be like David. Furthermore, the praise only few receive for doing what is right is qualified in the cases of those who do not remove the high places. There are five kings who did what was right in Yahweh's eyes and are not compared to David. They did not remove the high places and the people continued to worship there. Their acts lack cultic rigorism, and their virtue is somewhat diminished by this qualifier. This is not unexpected. It is surprising that Asa, who like those five does not remove the high places, is said to be like David. What makes Asa's judgment, as seen through both the grammatical construction and the triple praise, different from and more praiseworthy than the other five kings whose evaluations seem similar? If we can make any conclusion from the examples, those who are like David do some kind of reform, but not all reformers are like David. Also, to be like David does not require the removal of the high places. Evaluation

to have the same semantic range and restrictive force (Bruce K. Waltke and Michael Patrick O'Connor, *An Introduction to Biblical Hebrew Syntax* (Winona Lake, IN: Eisenbrauns, 1990), 39.3.5).

of the third element of praise heaped on David, לבב שלם may help clarify these designations.

לבב—Heart

The third component of praise for the good kings is the directing of one's לבב, "heart." The use of לבב in the book of Kings, as an evaluation of the kings, is related to cultic loyalty, a prominent deuteronomistic theme. The concept of "the love of God" in the book of Deuteronomy reflects political loyalty as seen in suzerain treaties of the ancient Near East. Weinfeld describes it as follows: "The suzerain demands the vassal's love of heart and soul or whole hearted love."[27] In deuteronomistic terms, loyalty is expressed through fidelity to the covenant.

The application of one's לבב, demonstrating loyalty, is connected with specific actions, as in Deut. 10:12-13. The rhetorical question, "What does Yahweh require of you?" defines this important behavior.

ועתה ישראל מה יהוה אלהיך שאל מעמך כי אם ליראה את יהוה
אלהיך ללכת בכל דרכיו ולאהבה אתו ולעבד את יהוה אלהיך בכל
לבבך ובכל נפשך. לשמר את מצות יהוה ואת חקתיו אשר אנכי מצוך
היום לטוב לך

And now, Israel, what does Yahweh your God ask of you? That you fear Yahweh your God, walk in all his ways and love him and serve Yahweh your God with all your heart and all your soul. Observe Yahweh's commandments and his laws, which I commanded you, for your well being.

The connection between loving Yahweh, בכל לבב, and observing the commandments is made clear.

While the concept of covenantal love and observance of the law is present in the book of Samuel (e.g., 1 Sam. 12:20, 24), it is never

---

27. Moshe Weinfeld, *Deuteronomy and the Deuteronomic School* (Winona Lake, IN: Eisenbrauns, 1992), 81.

applied to David in that narrative. Instead, it only relates to David in Kings, and first in the instructions to Solomon. In Kings, the concept of covenantal love and לבב is intrinsically connected with Dtr's evaluation of the religious behavior of the good kings.

As our topic at hand is the evaluation of the kings, I focus understanding of the definition of directing one's לבב as one of the elements of praise in the regnal formulae. Only the three kings who are likened to David—Asa, Hezekiah, and Josiah—have a positive remark made about their לבב. Asa's comment appears in the introductory regnal formula. Even though he did not remove the high places, Asa was wholeheartedly (לבב אסא היה שלם) with Yahweh (1 Kgs. 15:14). Josiah's comment appears in his closing formula and his statement of incomparability: "There was no king before him who turned with all his heart and all his soul and all his might [בכל לבבו ובכל נפשו ובכל מאדו] to all the teaching of Moses, and none like him arose after him" (2 Kgs. 23:25). Hezekiah's comment is in his own prayer (2 Kgs. 20:3). More commonly, לבב appears as a negative statement, of a king not directing his heart (e.g., Jeroboam, 1 Kgs. 14:8; Abijam, 1 Kgs. 15:3; Jehu, 2 Kgs. 10:31).

The application of the לבב is intrinsically connected to David, usually in the cases of kings who are not like him, or do not direct their hearts like him.

Was David Like David?

Thus far, the discussion has been focused on the following questions: What does it mean to be a good king? What does it mean to have a full heart and be wholeheartedly with Yahweh? And what does it mean to be like David? This final question requires further thought—Was David like David? The answer, it seems, is that David as royal comparative is a prototype construct that functions to evaluate the kings but does not reflect the presentation of David in Samuel, even within its deuteronomistically composed passages. Provan even divides the portrait of David into two different themes, the "comparative" and the "promissory."[28] And while he suggests that both of these Davids are present in Kings, I'd like to suggest that the David of Kings, in a typological sense, is effectively the "comparative," while the David of Samuel is the "promissory," the one to whom the promise of eternal dynasty is made. Also, rather than focusing on specific, individual verses, as Provan does to identify the two themes, I argue that the portrayal of the comparative David is pervasive throughout Kings and is a primary literary tool for the construction of the entire narrative history. Similarly, Auld recognizes "David as comparator."[29] It is clear, as von Rad says, that the picture of David "had a completely independent cycle of conceptions superimposed upon it, namely, that of the ideal, theocratic David, exemplary in obedience."[30] In Kings, Dtr projects his theology onto the preexisting portrait of David in Samuel. Van Seters states that there is a "contradiction between the behavior of David in the Court History and Dtr's judgment of David that he was the epitome of the just and righteous king who was completely obedient to Yahweh and who was the model for all subsequent kings."[31] Similarly, "cultic criterion is never directly applied to David."[32] The implications of this distinction between the David of Samuel and the David of Kings are twofold. First, it is another support for the theories of composition of Samuel (mentioned below) that the primary narrative and coherence of Samuel is

28. Provan, *Hezekiah*, 91–131.
29. A. Graeme Auld, *Kings without Privilege: David and Moses in the Story of the Bible's Kings* (Edinburgh: T&T Clark, 1994), 93.
30. Rad, "Deuteronomistic Theology," 88.
31. John Van Seters, "The Court History and DtrH: Conflicting Perspectives on the House of David," in *Sogenannte Thronfolgegeschichte Davids: Neue Einsichten und Anfragen*, ed. Albert de Pury and Thomas Römer, OBO 176 (Fribourg: Universitätsverlag; Göttingen: Vandenhoeck & Ruprecht, 2000), 71.
32. Ibid., 72.

predeuteronomistic. In this way, the composition and redaction of Kings is differentiated from that of Samuel. Second, Dtr creates a Davidic prototype that he uses to construct the portraits of subsequent kings. When creating this deuteronomistic view of David, Dtr has the other kings, especially Josiah, in mind. In this way, Dtr simultaneously constructs a literary model on which to base the portraits of the other kings while also portraying those kings. As such, Dtr takes the well-known figure of the great King David and constructs the David of Kings as a prototype to function as a literary tool to further promote his deuteronomistic theology as a paradigm of obedience.

The disparity between the two Davidic portraits is seen in several ways. In particular, the characteristic evaluations of the kings are missing from the David story. The phrase עשה הישר בעיני יהוה does not appear in Samuel.[33] This may be a result of the sparse deuteronomistic composition in the book. Even in 2 Sam. 5:4-5, where a somewhat typical regnal accession formula interrupts the David narrative, this common evaluation is missing: "David was thirty years old when he became king, he ruled forty years. In Hebron, he was king over Judah seven years and six months, and in Jerusalem he reigned thirty-three years over all Israel." Also significant, even in Moshe Weinfeld's discussion about the covenant at the plains of Moab, he begins a paragraph, "David's loyalty to God is couched in phrases that are even closer to the grant terminology" (meaning love and loyalty expressed through a לבב phrase), but Weinfeld follows this comment with four textual examples, all of which are from Kings.[34] David's covenant love and loyalty are not expressed in Samuel. This is a deuteronomistic addition in Kings.

---

33. Weinfeld, *Deuteronomy and the Deuteronomic School*, 335.
34. Ibid., 77.

There is some scholarly consensus that the narratives of Samuel are the product of earlier sources that Dtr lightly redacted together, adding few editorial comments. Since the work of Leonhard Rost (1926), the book has been seen as the amalgamation of several complete, independent narratives.[35] As a whole, Samuel ignores many of the major concerns of Dtr such as the fight against idolatry and centralization of the cult.[36] Dtr's compositional contribution to Samuel is minimal, while in Kings it is particularly strong.

As such, in Samuel deuteronomistic concerns are limited. While much of the book is focused on transgression and punishment, especially in the David narratives, it is not the straight sin-and-punishment theology of Deuteronomy. David is not evaluated for transgressions against the covenant; instead, he is criticized for his actions in the Bathsheba affair, and so on. David is praised for his zeal for Yahweh, but not his cultic activity. Despite the critique of David and the disputed effect it has on the overall focus of the book, the central deuteronomistic ideology expressed in Samuel is the unconditional validity of the eternal Davidic promise. This promise is expressed in Nathan's oracle in 2 Samuel 7, which many scholars have identified as deuteronomistic and a later addition to the independent narratives.[37] Second Samuel 7 emphasizes two major themes of DtrH: the Davidic promise and the temple. While the passage may be deuteronomistic and focused on proper worship of Yahweh, a place in Samuel where we might expect to see the same view of the good king as Kings, it is very different. Even here, the establishment of the temple in Jerusalem with Solomon as its builder lacks the emphasis

---

35. Leonhard Rost, *Die Überlieferung Von Der Thronnachfolge Davids* (Stuttgart: Kohlhammer, 1926); Rost, *The Succession to the Throne of David*, trans. Michael D. Rutter and David M. Gunn (Sheffield: Almond, 1982).

36. Moshe Garsiel, "The Book of Samuel: Its Composition, Structure and Significance as a Historiographical Source," *JHS* 10 (2010): 21.

37. P. Kyle McCarter, *2 Samuel*, AB 9 (Garden City, NY: Doubleday, 1984), 210.

on removing idolatry and fidelity to the covenant ever-present in Kings and linked to the evaluations of the good kings. And while the addition of this chapter to the pre-Dtr narratives of Samuel does direct the overall reading of the book, it does not transform its royal portrait into the theological perspective of Kings.

According to Weinfeld, in 2 Samuel 7, Dtr "attaches the promise of the perpetuation of the dynasty to the Davidic dynasty in particular . . . provided that the Davidic house observe the law."[38] Contra Weinfeld, while the Davidic connection to the eternity of the dynasty is made in 2 Samuel 7, the covenant in Nathan's oracle is mostly unconditional, emphasizing the relationship between father and son. Obedience to the law, as articulated in Kings, is not expressed here. This is completely different from the perspective of Kings, where the fate of the people and the king relies on the king's covenant fidelity. It is only in Kings that the conditions compelling the Davidic house to observe the law are made. While 2 Samuel 7 establishes the Davidic house, the characteristic language of obedience is missing. In a work where the language of covenant, *běrīt*, is so prevalent (Dtr uses *běrīt* more than any other author), the promise in 2 Samuel 7 is not constructed as a *běrīt*, which would entail reciprocal commitments by both parties: on the part of the king (and Israel) fidelity to the law. Dtr does not use *běrīt* except to talk about the covenant of the patriarchs and the Mosaic covenant, not in relation to the promise to David.[39]

It is significant that 2 Samuel 7, with its central role in deuteronomistic theology (establishing the eternity of the Davidic dynasty) and given the consensus that this is indeed a deuteronomistic passage (as early as Wellhausen, scholars have associated the composition of 2 Samuel 7 with Josiah's court), that the typical

38. Weinfeld, *Deuteronomy and the Deuteronomic School*, 5.
39. *CMHE* 260.

deuteronomistic phraseology is absent. There is no mention of the מצות, of the חקים ומשפטים, as usually found with deuteronomistic reward. Even though scholars like P. Kyle McCarter assert that the passage reflects the "themes from the larger history," this chapter stands in stark contrast to the portraits of the kings in Kings and especially to the depiction of David as the paradigm of deuteronomistic covenant behavior. [40]

The Davidic Prototype

The best picture we have of David's commitment to the covenant is retrospectively found as bookends to the Solomon story, where the portrait of David as the prototype of the good king is first developed. First, David is the exemplar for Solomon and then, at the end of his reign, the standard against which Solomon does not measure up. Solomon, given specific instructions of how to be a good king, helps us define what that role means. Solomon functions proleptically for all the kings, good and bad. Through the portrait of Solomon, the prototype of the comparative David is constructed, against which Solomon, the first good and bad king, and all subsequent kings can be measured. The concept of the good king, one who is faithful to the covenant, is first established in 1 Kgs. 2:3-4, David's charge to Solomon. Prosperity and dynastic continuity rely on the king following the laws and commandments, statutes and testimonies of the law of Moses.

Then, before instructing Solomon to do away with all of his enemies, David orders Solomon to keep the covenant in order to ensure that the promise Yahweh made to David of an eternal dynasty will be fulfilled. This is also the location at which we see the

---

40. McCarter, *2 Samuel*, 215.

beginning of the construction of the portrait of David in Kings as obedient to the deuteronomistic covenant:

ושמרת את משמרת יהוה אלהיך ללכת בדרכיו לשמר חקתיו מצותיו
ומשפטיו ועדותיו ככתוב בתורת משה למען תשכיל את כל אשר תעשה
ואת כל אשר תפנה שם. למען יקים יהוה את דברו אשר דבר עלי לאמר
אם ישמרו בניך את דרכם ללכת לפני באמת בכל לבבכם ובכל נפשם
לאמר לא יכרת לך איש מעל כסא ישראל

Keep the mandates of Yahweh your God, following his ways, keeping his statutes and commandments, laws and warnings, as is written in the instruction of Moses, so that you will be successful in whatever you do and to whatever you turn. In order that Yahweh will fulfill his word which he spoke to me, saying, if your sons are careful in their way to walk before me faithfully with all their heart and with all their soul, no one will be cut off from the throne of Israel. (1 Kgs. 2:3-4)

These verses express many of the most crucial concepts of deuteronomistic covenant theology.[41] Verse 3 describes the condition for success as linked to careful observance of Yahweh's laws, stipulated in the multiple terms of the עדות, משפטים, מצות, חקים, as repeated often throughout Kings. Verse 4 highlights the conditions for an eternal Davidic kingship as dependent on the faithfulness of David's sons, in the directing of בכל לבב ובכל נפש, which requires the application of the heart and soul as the way to observe the commandments and demonstrate loyalty, as in the suzerain treaties. While he does not explicitly say, "Just as I did," we presume that the David portrayed in this passage behaved in this way. These verses precede David giving Solomon instructions to do away with his enemies. The tone and content of these verses is very different from what follows in the rest of the chapter. It is clear that these initial theological instructions are added to the preexisting narrative by Dtr to begin the process of establishing the Davidic prototype. The

---

41. Weinfeld, *Deuteronomy and the Deuteronomic School,* 334.

portrait of David that begins to be depicted here is entirely different from that of the book of Samuel.

In his initial actions, Solomon follows the statutes of his father David (ויאהב שלמה את יהוה ללכת בחקות דוד אביו, 1 Kgs. 3:3). Also, at Gibeon, Solomon appeals to the image of David as Yahweh's servant: ויאמר שלמה אתה עשית עם עבדך דוד אבי חסד גדול כאשר הלך לפניך באמת ובצדקה ובישרת לבב עמך, "And Solomon said [to Yahweh], 'You showed great favor for your servant David, my father, because he walked before you in faithfulness and righteousness and the integrity [rightness] of his heart was with you'" (1 Kgs. 3:6). In Yahweh's response to Solomon's prayer at Gibeon, the connections between the David of the book of Samuel (the lover of Yahweh and recipient of Yahweh's favor) and the prototypical David constructed in Kings (the deuteronomistically adherent) are made. In granting Solomon's request for wisdom, Yahweh affirms that observance of the laws and commandments ensures long life and being like David: ואם תלך בדרכי לשמר חקי כאשר הלך דויד אביך והארכתי את ימיך, "And if you walk in my way, observing my laws and commandments, as David your father walked, I will lengthen your days" (1 Kgs. 3:14).

Similar to the events at Gibeon, the development of the David concept continues with another prayer-response sequence. The image of David is doubly affirmed through Solomon's prayer and Yahweh's response after the building and dedication of the temple. In 1 Kgs. 6:12, Yahweh says: הבית הזה אשר אתה בנה אם תלך בחקתי ואת משפטי תעשה ושמרת את כל מצותי ללכת בהם והקמתי את דברי אתך אשר דברתי אל דוד אביך, "This house which you have built, if you follow my laws and statutes, you shall do and observe all my commandments following them and I will establish this word with you as I spoke to David your father." It is unclear exactly what Yahweh promises Solomon. What is the "word"? Presumably it is the eternity of the Davidic dynasty, as seen in 2 Samuel 7, but the language of covenant loyalty as connected to observing the law is missing from the promise in 2 Samuel 7 (as discussed above). In fact, the conditional covenant established here with Solomon is wholly different from the unconditional one established with David. This sets the tone for the relationship between Yahweh and subsequent kings.

Solomon offers his prayer to Yahweh in 1 Kings 8, suggesting what it means to be wholeheartedly with Yahweh (1 Kgs. 8:61): Solomon directs Israel to set its heart to be fully with Yahweh, והיה לבבכם שלם עם יהוה אלהינו. In response, Yahweh reaffirms and elaborates on the promise of 6:12, further articulating how David behaved and what Solomon will receive if he emulates David.

ואתה אם תלך לפני כאשר הלך דוד אביך בתם לבב ובישר לעשות
ככל אשר צויתיך חקי ומשפטי תשמר. והקמתי את כסא ממלכתך על
ישראל לעלם כאשר דברתי על דוד אביך לאמר לא יכרת לך איש
מעל כסא ישראל.

And if you walk before me as David your father walked with a blameless heart and righteousness, doing all that I commanded you, my laws and statutes you will observe. And I will establish the throne of your kingship over Israel forever as I spoke to David your father, saying there will not be a man of yours cut off from the throne of Israel. (1 Kgs. 9:4-5)

These verses establish the conditional nature of the Davidic promise as expressed in Kings and include the three criteria for good kings like David.

The rise of Solomon and the development of the Davidic prototype heighten the impact of the fall of Solomon. These early chapters of Kings create a constructed character that is used to evaluate all the kings, but few have the ability to live up to the standard. Being a good king and maintaining the kingship requires fidelity to the covenant (1 Kgs. 2:3-4; 6:12; 9:4), being like David (1 Kgs. 3:3; 6:14; 9:4), and directing one's heart to Yahweh (1 Kgs. 9:4). At the end of the narrative in 1 Kings 11, Solomon is portrayed as a bad king; he is not like David. In his old age, Solomon literally has a change of heart: ולא היה לבבו שלם עם יהוה אלהיו כלבב דויד אביו, "And his heart was not fully with Yahweh his God, as was the heart of David his father" (v. 4). Also, in a judgment similar to the regnal formulae, Solomon's deeds are evaluated negatively in 1 Kgs. 11:6: ויעש שלמה הרע בעיני יהוה ולא מלא אחרי יהוה כדוד אביו, "And Solomon did what was evil in the eyes of Yahweh, and he was not fully behind Yahweh like David his father."

The creation of the prototype construction begins with the establishment of the kings who succeed David. Solomon is set up with conditions of how to be like David. He is to keep the laws and the statutes, walking in the way of Yahweh as David did (1 Kgs. 3:14; 6:12; 9:4-5). Both the potential buildup of how Solomon should be and the rebuke for the reality of his character highlight what it means to be like David.

The transition from the David of Samuel to the Davidic prototype of Kings begins with Dtr transforming the unconditional promise of 2 Samuel 7 into the Davidic comparative typology, with its conditional success, as depicted in Kings. Dtr reimagines the promise of a Davidic dynasty, taking on the themes of 2 Samuel 7 in which David is established as an essential character in the history of the monarchy, and exploits the importance of David in founding the dynasty. This role sets him up as fitting for the part of the prototype of the good king. It is then in Solomon's succession of David that Dtr makes apparent his covenantal requirements for the continuity of the dynasty.

In this way, the Deuteronomist creates a prototype of the good king, and the best of the good kings; one who is faithful to Yahweh and the covenant and initiates religious reform. Dtr retrospectively projects this image onto the known figure of King David, the eponymous ancestor of the Davidic dynasty. This convention is only used in Kings; even though Samuel chronicles the reign of David, the portrait of the cultically adherent king is missing. Given the establishment of the Davidic prototype of the measure of the good king, it is not surprising that only those kings of the Davidic dynasty, as opposed to the kings of Israel, might achieve praiseworthy status. While this literary application occurs, it is clear that the model of the good king is not based on the portrait of David in Samuel. It is much more likely that the prototypical David constructed in Kings is modeled on the figure of Josiah, the great reformer, the hero of the book of Kings, and out of whose court the history emerges.[42] We see in 2 Kings 22–23 how completely Josiah fulfills and even supersedes the Davidic prototype. More generally, although it is possible to see that while both end products show the mark of the Deuteronomist, Samuel and Kings had unique compositional and redactional paths. The predeuteronomistic source documents that make up the majority of the narrative of Samuel have different foci and narrate the story of a different David, while the portrait of David found in Kings is thoroughly deuteronomistic.

My analysis of the prototype strategy takes von Rad's argument for the use of a Davidic prototype and further develops it. This strategy can be explored in considering its literary value to the entirety of Kings. The Davidic prototype is used to construct the portrait of the kings. From the original portrayal of David in Kings, the prototype is employed to evaluate all subsequent kings, those who are like and unlike David. The kings, in whom Dtr is particularly interested and receive longer and fuller attention, are fleshed out through the use

42. Nelson, *Double Redaction*, 125.

of the prototype in order to establish their significant role in the history of Israel and Judah and to act as didactic figures to convey the importance of fidelity to the tenets of the deuteronomistic covenant theology. It is possible to see the application of the prototype most clearly in the portraits of Jeroboam and Josiah. Jeroboam is first established (1 Kings 11) as the realization of the Davidic prototype. He is initially set up as a potential second David. Ultimately, he does not maintain this role and is transformed into the anti-David, the antithesis to the Davidic prototype (especially 1 Kings 14). The bad kings, particularly those of the kingdom of Israel, are said to walk in the ways of Jeroboam. In contrast, Josiah is the only king to completely inhabit the literary model. Throughout the history of the monarchy, each king is held up against the Davidic prototype. These comparisons create a literary unity in the portraits of the kings as well as a characteristic marker of the level of redaction.

The use of the prototype strategy also further refines the themes outlined by Frank Moore Cross in his double redaction theory. Cross highlights two contrasting themes present in the preexilic history: the faithfulness of David and the sin of Jeroboam.[43] The use of the prototype strategy makes the discussion of the contrast of these themes more precise. This is not just a matter of the acts of the kings and the effects they have on the course of the history of the monarchy as Cross presents them; the contrast between David and Jeroboam, as the anti-David, is intrinsic to the literary construction of the portrait of these and the other kings. These kings are inherently connected to each other through their literary relationship to the prototype strategy and not just in the contrasting of themes. This is further developed in the portrait of Josiah, who is fashioned not only as the Davidic prototype, perhaps even surpassing his model,

43. *CMHE* 274–89.

but also as the antidote to the anti-David. Only Josiah, in his role as the next David, has the ability to overturn the sins of the anti-David Jeroboam. No other king, not even Hezekiah, has this potential, because of the absence of the Davidic model. In this way, the Davidic prototype becomes the primary literary convention in crafting the portrait of the kings, highlighting the major themes and promoting deuteronomistic theology, characteristic of the Josianic edition.

4

———

Jeroboam "Who Caused Israel to Sin"

Jeroboam is introduced as a second David, the first king presented to match the wholehearted devotion of Dtr's literary David. Jeroboam is constructed using the Davidic prototype strategy, but he is unable to live up to the literary expectations. He is depicted as deliberately rejecting his Davidic potential and then is established as the anti-David, the prototype of the evil king, based on an oppositional portrait to the Davidic prototype. Not only does Jeroboam come to embody the evil king, the standard against which the subsequent bad kings of Israel are measured, but also his blatant disregard for his literary potential ultimately leads to his own demise and that of his house and the entirety of his kingdom. The building of the Davidic potential only further emphasizes the depth to which Jeroboam will fall. This portrait is possible because of the use of the prototype strategy and the implementation of Dtr's historiographical poetics. Employing Jeroboam as the prototype of the evil king (as opposed to Ahab, the most evil king) highlights one of the major foci of the preexilic Dtr, railing against a system of decentralized worship. The

Jeroboam narrative is made up of several discrete episodes, preexisting passages that Dtr adopts and adapts for his greater purpose. In 1 Kings 11–14, the portrait of Jeroboam is initially positive, but it is Jeroboam's negative legacy that has long-term staying power. The narrative begins by introducing Jeroboam following the other adversaries of Solomon (1 Kgs. 11:26-28), as discussed in chapter 2. Ahijah stops Jeroboam on the road, tears his robe, gives ten pieces to Jeroboam, and tells him of Yahweh's plans to punish Solomon and make Jeroboam king of ten tribes (1 Kgs. 11:29-39). This interaction is followed by the assembly of Israel requesting that Rehoboam, Solomon's son, lighten their corvée. When Rehoboam refuses, Israel separates from the Davidic monarch and makes Jeroboam king over them (1 Kgs. 12:1-19). To shore up his political control of the kingdom, Jeroboam establishes countercult shrines to keep his subjects from returning to the temple in Jerusalem (1 Kgs. 12:25-33). At the dedication of the shrine at Bethel, the man of God from Judah proclaims the impending doom of Jeroboam's kingdom (1 Kgs. 13:1-10). This is followed by the man of God's journey and his interactions with the old prophet of Bethel (1 Kgs. 13:11-32). The Jeroboam narrative concludes with a second Ahijah oracle, pronouncing doom on the house of Jeroboam and the entire kingdom of Israel (1 Kings 14). The two Ahijah oracles function as an inclusio, framing the entire narrative, with the appearance of the man of God from Judah at its center. The two oracles highlight Jeroboam's great rise and deep fall. Through the full account of Jeroboam, the different historiographical priorities can be seen working in tandem, and while it is possible to tease out how each individual element is employed, they are so well integrated that their effect on the construction of the narrative is quite overlapping. For example, prophetic texts, prominent in this story that features no fewer than four prophetic interactions, are rewritten to be an integral part of defining the prototype strategy.[1] They develop Jeroboam as the next David with the first Ahijah oracle and as the anti-David with the second. These oracles also contribute theological meaning to the rise of Jeroboam, seemingly a political and historical event. The prophecies, especially the condemnation of Jeroboam in Ahijah's second oracle and by the man of God from Judah, are essential in the promotion of the deuteronomistic program denigrating the religious cult of Jeroboam, a theme prominent throughout the history of the kingdom of Israel and DtrH as a whole. The entirety of the Jeroboam narrative in these four chapters is purposeful and displays comprehensiveness and completeness. While Dtr uses many sources, including earlier prophetic legends, he orders them and smooths them into a full narrative. Here, Dtr is clearly working as both creative author and thoughtful and intentional editor.[2] The movement of Dtr's plot is an integrated literary whole that sets the narrative of the entire history into motion. Through Ahijah's oracles, we see Jeroboam's rise and fall, and at the height of the narrative, the prophecy of the man of God from Judah pronounces the ultimate destruction of Jeroboam's cult, setting it up as a cult of idolatry, and looking forward to the coming of Josiah.[3] It is in this way that the literary intentions and power of Dtr's historiographical process can be seen. The Davidic prototype is applied to Jeroboam and is further expanded on. The focus on Jeroboam as the anti-David sets at the center of the history the battle against decentralized worship.

---

1. Lissa Wray Beal rightly argues that the four prophetic scenes must be read as a "bounded set" ("Jeroboam and the Prophets in 1 Kings 11-14: Prophetic Word for Two Kingdoms," in *Prophets, Prophecy, and Ancient Israelite Historiography*, ed. Mark J. Boda and Lissa M. Wray Beal [Winona Lake, IN: Eisenbrauns, 2013], 105–24.)

2. Steven L. McKenzie, *The Trouble with Kings: The Composition of the Book of Kings in the Deuteronomistic History*, VTSup 42 (Leiden: Brill, 1991), 80.

3. Robert L. Cohn, "Literary Technique in the Jeroboam Narrative," *ZAW* 97 (1985): 35. Cross describes this as the work of an "overenthusiastic" Dtr, "preparing the reader's mind for the coming climax" of DtrH (*CMHE* 279–80).

The Davidic Prototype in the Jeroboam Narrative

Jeroboam is initially cast in the mold of David by the first Ahijah oracle in 1 Kgs. 11:29-40 but is then turned into the anti-David and the prototype of the evil king, the standard against which the kings of Israel are measured. Just as the Davidic prototype was developed through the regnal formulae of the good kings of Judah, so too is the antitype constructed through the regnal formulae of the kings of Israel (see more below). In this way, the portraits of the kings—good and bad, northern and southern—are literarily consistent throughout the history, demonstrating a unified style characteristic of Dtr[1]. They are judged by the same theological standards and compared to the same literary prototype.

Jeroboam as the Second David: Ahijah's First Oracle

After Jeroboam's introduction as an adversary to Solomon (see chap. 2), Jeroboam is met by the prophet Ahijah, who, tearing his robe into twelve pieces and giving ten to Jeroboam, raises Jeroboam to the position of king. This presentation is accompanied by conveying the desires of Yahweh in splitting the kingdom and appointing Jeroboam as king of the North. Jeroboam is presented as a potential David, in both word and symbol.[4]

> And it happened at that time that Jeroboam went out of Jerusalem and the prophet Ahijah the Shilonite found him on the way. He covered himself with a new robe, and the two of them were alone in the field. (30) And Ahijah took hold of the new robe which was upon him, and he tore it into twelve pieces. (31) **And he said to Jeroboam, "Take ten pieces for yourself, for thus says Yahweh the God of Israel, I am about to tear the kingdom from the hand of Solomon and I will give you ten of the tribes. (32) But the one tribe will be for him, for the sake of my servant David and for the sake of Jerusalem,**

4. The bold text marks deuteronomistic composition. The plain text may be Dtr's source.

the city which I chose from all the tribes of Israel. (33) "Because [he] left me and [he] bowed[5] to Astarte, god of the Sidonians, to Chemosh, god of Moab, and to Milcom, god of the Ammonites and [he] did not walk in my way, to do right in my eyes, and [to keep] my laws and ordinances as David his father. (34) But I will not take the entire kingdom from his hand for I will position him as *nāśîʾ* all the days of his life, for the sake of David my servant, whom I chose, who kept my commandments and my laws. (35) And I will take the kingdom from his son and give it to you, the ten tribes. (36) But to his son I will give one tribe in order to be a lamp for David my servant all the days before me in Jerusalem, the city which I chose for myself to establish my name there. (37) But it is you I will take and you will be king over all you desire and you will be king over Israel. (38) "Thus it will be if you heed all that I will command you and you will walk in my way and do what is right in my eyes, to keep my law and commandments which David my servant did, then I will be with you and I will build for you a lasting dynasty as I built for David, and I will give to you Israel. (39) And I will humble the seed of David but not forever." (40) And Solomon attempted the murder of Jeroboam. Then Jeroboam got up and fled to Egypt to Shishak, king of Egypt, and he was in Egypt until the death of Solomon. (1 Kgs. 11:29–40)

The investiture presents Jeroboam in the model of David, Yahweh's (and the Deuteronomist's) beloved king. The denunciation of Jeroboam becomes even more formidable when he is rejected for not being David-like. Similarly, Paul Ash describes this phenomenon: "David and Jeroboam become opposites. Jeroboam becomes the anti-David, the cause of Israel's fall and a *negative* standard of comparison for future kings."[6] In the last chapter, the Davidic prototype was established using the regnal formula. The explicit Davidic comparison coupled with the portrait of Solomon in 1 Kings 1–10

---

5. The MT has these two verbs as plural, but a plural subject does not make sense in this context. I read along with the LXX, Syriac, and manuscripts of the Vulgate, which have singular verbs; Solomon is their subject.

6. Paul S. Ash, "Jeroboam I and the Deuteronomistic Historian's Ideology of the Founder," *CBQ* 60 (1998): 19.

highlight several criteria for being like David. The best of kings are those who do הישר בעיני יהוה, whose לבב is with Yahweh, and are like David. When applied to Solomon, these criteria are fleshed out, demonstrating that doing הישר meant fidelity to the deuteronomic covenant. Solomon is unable to achieve the Davidic ideal. The charges against Solomon associate him with the worst kings, initiating the model for how to evaluate bad kings—those who are not like David. The connection between Jeroboam and Solomon in the construction of the prototype strategy is deeply rooted in many literary elements of the chapter. The first and most obvious is Jeroboam as the replacement of Solomon, both literally as king of ten tribes and prototypically as the next David and then the model of the bad king. Similar to the words spoken by David to Solomon, Jeroboam is chosen and installed as king by Ahijah.

והיה אם תשמע את כל אשר אצוך והלכת בדרכי ועשית הישר בעיני
לשמור חקותי ומצותי כאשר עשה דוד עבדי והייתה עמך ובניתי לך
בית נאמן כאשר בניתי לדוד ונתתי לך את ישראל

If only he will heed all that I will command you and you will walk in my way and do what is right in my eyes, to keep my law and commandments which David my servant did, then I will be with you and I will build for you a lasting dynasty as I built for David, and I will give to you Israel. (1 Kgs. 11:38)

This instruction echoes the words spoken to Solomon by David in 1 Kgs. 2:3-4, as discussed in the previous chapter:

ושמרת את משמרת יהוה אלהיך ללכת בדרכיו לשמר חקתיו מצותיו
ומשפטיו ועדותיו ככתוב בתורת משה למען תשכיל את כל אשר תעשה
ואת כל אשר תפנה שם. למען יקים יהוה את דברו אשר דבר עלי לאמר
אם ישמרו בניך את דרכם ללכת לפני באמת בכל לבבכם ובכל נפשם
לאמר לא יכרת לך איש מעל כסא ישראל

Keep the mandates of Yahweh your God, following his ways, keeping his statutes and commandments, laws and warnings, as is written in the instruction of Moses, so that you will be successful in whatever you do and to whatever you turn. In order that Yahweh will fulfill his word which he spoke to me, saying, if your sons are careful in their way to walk before me faithfully with all their heart and with all their soul, no one will be cut off from the throne of Israel.

While not quite as verbose as David's words to Solomon, Ahijah's injunction to Jeroboam demonstrates similar sentiments. Ahijah charges him to do הישר בעיני יהוה, one of the characteristic elements of the regnal formula, by following Yahweh's way, obeying his commandments and law. These terms (הלך בדרך, עשה הישר, חקות, מצות, משפטים, עדות) function as *Leitwörter* in Kings. The comparison to David is made explicit—do these things, just as David "my servant" did. Being like David will merit Jeroboam David's reward; Yahweh will be with him and will build him a lasting dynasty. It is significant to note that the royal concept of בית נאמן is only mentioned in relation to David (1 Sam. 25:28) and Jeroboam. (A third instance of בית נאמן also appears in 1 Sam. 2:35 in respect to a priestly house that will replace the Elides.) While the examples in 1 Samuel may be predeuteronomistic,[7] the concept is revised by Dtr and applied to the Jeroboam story. Ahijah's words clearly set Jeroboam up to be the next David. If he keeps the covenant, as David did, he will be like David, the father of a בית נאמן. In both the punishment of Solomon and in the installation of Jeroboam, the text focuses on the importance of fidelity to deuteronomistic theology. Despite building the temple and the promise to David, Solomon is unable to hold on to the entire kingdom because of his gross violation of the covenant. Solomon, in worshiping Astarte, Chemosh, and Milcom (1 Kgs. 11:33), does the opposite of fulfilling the criteria of the Davidic prototype. He is unfaithful to the covenant, so he must be

---

7. Antony F. Campbell, *Of Prophets and Kings: A Late Ninth Century Document (1 Samuel 1–2 Kings 10)*, Catholic Biblical Quarterly Monograph Series 17 (Washington, DC: Catholic Biblical Association of America, 1986), 29.

punished for his infidelity. Jeroboam, by no merit of his own, is the vehicle for that punishment. He is explicitly set up as king because Solomon did not follow Yahweh's commands and statutes. Yahweh's words of punishment to Solomon in verses 11-13 are mirrored in Ahijah's words of investiture to Jeroboam. In deuteronomistic style, Dtr repeats almost verbatim the conditions of the division of the kingdom, just as Yahweh speaks to Solomon:

> Because it was this way with you and you did not keep my covenant and my laws which I commanded you [ולא שמרת בריתי וחקתי אשר צויתי עליך], I will surely rend the kingdom from you and give it to your servant. (12) But in your days I will not do it, for the sake of David your father, [but] I will rend it from the hand of your son. (13) But I will not tear [away] the whole kingdom, but one tribe I will give to your son for the sake of David my servant and for the sake of Jerusalem which I have chosen. (1 Kgs. 11:11-13)

Ahijah speaks the following words to Jeroboam: "But the one tribe will be for him, for the sake of my servant David and for the sake of Jerusalem, the city which I chose from all the tribes of Israel" (1 Kgs. 11:32). The similar language used in these two speeches intrinsically connects Jeroboam's "reward" with Solomon's punishment. The words of Solomon's injunction (1 Kgs. 2:3-4) repeated to Jeroboam (1 Kgs. 11:38) are used contrastively to condemn Solomon: ולא הלכו בדרכי לעשות הישר בעיני וחקתי ומשפטי כדוד אביו, Solomon "did not walk in my way, to do right in my eyes and, [to keep] my laws and statutes as David his father" (1 Kgs. 11:33). This language (similar to that of the regnal evaluations) explicitly connects the literary portraiture of David, Solomon, and now Jeroboam. Additionally, the prototype connections between Jeroboam and David continue with many implicit allusions. One such similarity is the circumstance in which they both become king. David and Jeroboam are raised up as king as a form of punishment for the current king. After Saul's disobedience in his failure to kill Agag and the best of the sheep and cattle, David is selected to replace him (1 Samuel 15). Likewise, Jeroboam is put into office to punish Solomon. Another allusion, and even foreshadowing of Jeroboam not being like David, is Jeroboam's "rebellion." Jeroboam "raises his hands" against Solomon (although we do not really know what Jeroboam actually does to rebel; see chap. 2), while David refuses to "put forth his hand against Saul" (1 Sam. 24:7; 26:9, 11, 23). Although the parallel is not exact as Jeroboam הרים יד while David does not לשלח יד (in all examples), the sense is similar. The circumstances of Jeroboam's appointment also further the David connection. He is one of only four kings specifically appointed by Yahweh; the others are Saul, David, and Jehu—all are initiators of dynasties and the first of their kind.[8] Like David, Jeroboam has been singled out by divine providence. Jeroboam is promised a secure kingdom if he observes Yahweh's covenant like David. Also, they are both designated by a Shilonite (Ahijah and Samuel). Weippert calls this genre *Legitimationslegende*, which supports usurper kings who do not have a hereditary claim to the throne.[9] As both David and Jeroboam can be considered something of usurper kings (although neither seeks out the kingship), this leads to a tense relationship between the new king and the old king. Saul seeks to kill David (1 Sam. 19:2; also 18:21), as Solomon does Jeroboam (1 Kgs. 11:40). Both David and Jeroboam are chosen and elevated by prophets in a common prophetic motif of "prophets as king makers."[10] Samuel in 1 Samuel 16 approaches Jesse and his sons and according to the word of Yahweh picks out David from among his brothers. This story uses two standard topoi of

8. Eva Danelius, "Sins of Jeroboam ben-Nabat, Part I," *JQR* 58 (1967): 95–114; Danelius, "Sins of Jeroboam ben-Nabat, Part II," *JQR* 58 (1968): 100.
9. Weippert in McKenzie, *The Trouble with Kings*, 45n15.
10. Campbell, *Of Prophets and Kings*, 114.

prophetic tales, described by Robert Cohn as "the secluded meeting between the prophet and the future king at which the king secretly announces his kingship (cf. I Sam. 9, 27-10, 1; II Reg 9, 1-10); and second, the tearing of the prophet's robe to symbolize the loss of the kingdom (cf. I Sam. 15, 27-28)."[11] Like David, Jeroboam is in the king's service, has to flee, and is chosen by Yahweh, in the deuteronomistic style, without seeking out and initiating anointing. Unlike any other king, in Israel or Judah, Jeroboam begins his career as *David Redivivus*.[12] With these parallels in place, the reader has high hopes for Jeroboam and the success of the northern kingdom. In this way, both explicitly and implicitly, using the prototype strategy Jeroboam is set up to be a second David, one who is loyal to the covenant and whose actions promote the deuteronomistic program. These similarities between David and Jeroboam are no accident of history, but rather an intentional literary strategy to wed the portraits of David and Jeroboam.

Contrasting Josiah: The Man of God from Judah

Following Ahijah's investiture of Jeroboam and a historico-political report of the northern leadership's rejection of Rehoboam and the appointing of Jeroboam as king over them (1 Kings 12), the overturning of the Davidic prototype begins with the appearance of the man of God from Judah who proclaims the arrival of Josiah as a religious savior from Jeroboam's cult (1 Kgs. 13:1-10). While Jeroboam is cast in the Davidic prototype in Ahijah's first oracle, the remainder of the Jeroboam narrative works to destroy this portrait as well as construct the prototype of the evil king, an anti-David. Jeroboam begins to shore up his kingdom politically and religiously. After ascending the throne, Jeroboam initiates several building

---

11. Cohn, "Literary Technique in the Jeroboam Narrative," 26.
12. Ash, "Ideology of the Founder," 18.

projects: fortifying Shechem and Penuel (1 Kgs. 12:25). It was common behavior in the ancient Near East for the new king to embark on major building programs of both religious and political, strategic buildings.[13] In this way, Jeroboam is able to fortify his kingdom politically, but the central shrine of Yahweh remains in Jerusalem, part of the kingdom of Judah. Jeroboam is concerned that it will challenge the political loyalty of pious Israelites who are faithful to Yahweh. After Jeroboam dedicates his shrines in 1 Kgs. 12:28-33, the man of God from Judah arrives to condemn them. As is common in DtrH, the prophetic oracle makes explicit Dtr's negative judgment of the king and demonstrates the prophet's and Yahweh's intervention in domestic and foreign affairs.[14] Through the fulfillment of the prophetic oracle, Yahweh's role in history is clearly articulated and Dtr's and Yahweh's judgments expressed and enacted. It is also through this oracle that Dtr connects the story of Jeroboam with that of Josiah, setting the stage for the continuation of the Davidic prototype strategy. Implicitly and explicitly, Dtr works to promote his programmatic agenda. Here, a southern prophet denounces the king and his shrines, invalidating the entirety of the northern kingdom, its monarch, and its cult. This prophecy derives from a different source from the other oracles. Not only does it reflect a southern perspective, but it also has a definitively later provenance with its reference to the coming of Josiah and the condemnation of Jeroboam's uncentralized cult. The story of the man of God from Judah is at the earliest Josianic or as other scholars, including Van Seters, have identified postdeuteronomistic.[15] Knoppers argues, and

---

13. Gary N. Knoppers, *Two Nations under God: The Deuteronomistic History of Solomon and the Dual Monarchies*, vol. 2, *The Reign of Jeroboam, the Fall of Israel, and the Reign of Josiah*, Harvard Semitic Monographs (Atlanta: Scholars Press, 1994), 35.

14. Martin Noth, *The Deuteronomistic History* (Sheffield: JSOT Press, 1981), 107; Gerhard von Rad, "The Deuteronomistic Theology of History in the Books of Kings," in *Studies in Deuteronomy*, trans. David Stalker (London: SCM, 1953), 78.

I concur, that "at least part of 1 Kgs. 13:1-2 and part of 1 Kgs. 13:32 are deuteronomistic."[16] Those verses connect directly to Josiah and setting up Josiah as the history's hero. The condemnation of Jeroboam and his shrines is extremely subtle. Rather than rejecting the shrines on their own grounds, as locations of decentralized worship and competitors (as they were intended) of Solomon's temple, the man of God's oracle (as well as the "factual" report in 1 Kgs. 12:28-33; see more below) casts Jeroboam's cult as idolatry. While the political report may allow for the permissibility of these shrines, the prophecy of the man of God from Judah makes the condemnation against Jeroboam overt. Dtr uses the man of God's speech to articulate his opinion and establish sequences of prophecy and fulfillment.

And behold a man of God came from Judah to Bethel by the word of Yahweh. And Jeroboam was standing on the altar to make an offering. (2) And he [the man of God] called out against the altar by the word of Yahweh. And he said: "O Altar, Altar, thus says Yahweh, 'Behold, a son will be born to the house of David, Josiah by name, and he will sacrifice upon you the priests of the high places, the ones offering sacrifices upon you, and human bones will be burned upon you.'" (3) And on that day he gave a portent,[17] saying, "This is the portent that Yahweh has spoken, 'Behold, the altar will break apart and the ashes upon it will be spilled.'" (4) When the king heard the word of the man of God that he called out against the altar at Bethel, Jeroboam stretched out his hand from the altar, saying: "Seize him!" But the hand that he stretched out withered,

---

15. John Van Seters, "On Reading the Story of the Man of God from Judah in 1 Kings 13," in *The Labour of Reading: Desire, Alienation, and Biblical Interpretation*, ed. Fiona Black, Roland T. Boer, and Erin Runions (Atlanta: Society of Biblical Literature, 1999), 225–34.

16. Knoppers, *Reign of Jeroboam*, 52.

17. Uriel Simon makes a distinction between an אות ("sign") and מופת ("portent," in his translation), which frequently appear together. Simon differentiates "portent" as a miraculous act "which lends credibility to the prophet and truth to his utterance." He defines "sign" as a symbolic act (or word) "which serves to concretize and further strengthen the word of the Lord through an actual deed or powerful symbolism," like the tearing of Ahijah's robe. Here the withering and restoring of the hand serves as a "portent." The man of God's prohibitions and their violation in the second half of the chapter are "signs." Simon's distinction is justified (Uriel Simon, "I Kings 13: A Prophetic Sign—Denial and Persistence," *HUCA* 47 [1976]: 86).

and he was not able to draw it back to himself. (5) And the altar broke apart and the fatty ashes spilled from the altar, in accordance with the sign that the man of God gave by the word of Yahweh. (1 Kgs. 13:1-5)

In this passage, a southern prophet corrects the word of the northern prophet Ahijah. This story is strategically included after the first Ahijah oracle raising Jeroboam as king and charging him with deuteronomistic fidelity, but before Ahijah's condemnation of Jeroboam. Reaching far into the future (although contemporaneous with the deuteronomistic composition), the man of God looks to Josiah as the future king to truly be cast in the mold of the Davidic prototype, setting aside the ruined potential David in Jeroboam. Even though Jeroboam is convinced of the legitimacy of the man of God as prophet, as seen by his request to be healed by the man (1 Kgs. 13:6), Jeroboam does not denounce and close his shrines. Dtr makes this point explicit in his conclusion to the episode: "After this [אחר הדבר הזה], Jeroboam did not turn from his evil path" (1 Kgs. 13:33). Instead, he consecrates "any people who wanted to be priests," and all of Israel continue to worship at the site (1 Kgs. 13:33-34).[18] Literarily, Dtr tries (and succeeds) to delegitimize the cult. It seems illogical that Jeroboam would embrace the power of the prophet yet blatantly deny the message of his prophecy, especially since he seems to attempt to be faithful to Yahweh. This is another clue that the acts and oracle of the man of God are the product of Dtr's reimagining of the older prophetic story. The oracle is a literary tactic constructed by the Deuteronomist in order to convict Jeroboam, continually painting Jeroboam in a negative light, even in respect

---

18. One way Dtr does this, as Halpern argues, is the inclusion of non-Levitical priests. Halpern views these alleged non-Levitical priests as an invention of Dtr in "an attempt . . . to denigrate the northern cult." He suggests the priests at Jeroboam's shrines likely would have been still Levites (perhaps Mushites over Aaronides, but Levites nonetheless) (Baruch Halpern, "Levitic Participation in the Reform Cult of Jeroboam I," *JBL* 95 [1976]: 32). If Halpern's contention is correct, this would just be one more example of Dtr's rhetorical rewrite of history in order to delegitimize Jeroboam's cult and further the deuteronomistic program.

to reasonable behavior. Van Seters points to this inconsistency: why would Jeroboam affirm the validity of the prophet and continue to practice the "condemned" cult, and why would Jeroboam act so amicably, inviting him back to the palace, when the man of God destroyed his newly dedicated altar? Van Seters points to these inconsistencies as justification for a postdeuteronomistic composition, arguing that they and others (sixteen in total) are uncharacteristic of Dtr's style.[19] While Van Seters's list of textual difficulties is compelling, it does not necessarily mean the passage must be postdeuteronomistic. There are two specific compositional and redactional impulses at play that contribute to the inconsistencies. Dtr is simultaneously integrating a source document into his narrative, reframing it to suit his purposes, as is characteristic of Dtr,[20] and connecting it to the activity of Josiah's reform. Rather than attributing the entire story of the man of God to a very late editor lacking in literary skill, as Van Seters does,[21] we should see it as Dtr's redaction because of the integral (rather than secondary) role it plays in Dtr's overall narrative. Marvin Sweeney argues how well it serves the agenda of Dtr: "It condemns Jeroboam, the altar at Beth El, and even the city itself as the home of a lying prophet. The present narrative serves the Josianic DtrH by pointing to Josiah as the figure who will eventually destroy the Beth El altar, ridding the land of Jeroboam's sins."[22] The man of God's appearance has a compounded effect: he denounces the cult of Jeroboam and its priesthood, predicting a day on which it will be destroyed and its priests burned; he introduces and predicts the coming of the

19. Van Seters, "On Reading."
20. "The Deuteronomist seems to have largely integrated the prophetic legends into his narrative by rewriting their introduction (vv 1-3) and conclusion (v 32) and by adding his own commentary on their significance (vv 33-34)" (Knoppers, *Reign of Jeroboam*, 55).
21. Van Seters, "On Reading," 233.
22. Marvin A. Sweeney, *First and Second Kings: A Commentary*, Old Testament Library (Louisville: Westminster John Knox, 2007), 179.

deuteronomistic savior, Josiah, who will rescue Israel from its illegitimate and nondeuteronomistic modes of worship. Josiah, unlike Jeroboam, will be the true second David. The man's ability to perform the "magic act" of paralyzing the king's arm legitimizes his status as divine messenger, reminiscent of Moses' demonstrations of power in the court of Pharaoh.[23] The announcement of Josiah prefigures the Josianic reform, in deed and word. Josiah will do these things, and they will happen exactly as they have been enumerated here. The language of the report in 2 Kgs. 23:15-16 makes clear the connection and the prophecy fulfillment.[24] Josiah's centralization of the cult will overthrow the cult of Jeroboam. Jeroboam is the foil for Josiah; each is mentioned in the other's narrative. Both are compared to David, the exemplar and prototype. "What Jeroboam does, Josiah undoes."[25] The literary opposition of these two characters is developed through the prototype strategy. Jeroboam is established as the antitype, the anti-David and the anti-Josiah.

From Hero to Villain: Ahijah's Second Oracle

While Ahijah's first oracle sets Jeroboam up as a second David, the second oracle pronounces his doom. This is the final episode in the Jeroboam saga, following the initiation of his cult. Ahijah's second oracle, in 1 Kgs. 14:7-16, is spoken at Yahweh's behest to Jeroboam's wife. In a twist on the motif of consultation oracles (frequently a sick king seeking an oracle) Jeroboam sends his disguised wife to inquire

---

23. Van Seters, "On Reading," 230.
24. "And also, the altar at Bethel, the high place that Jeroboam son of Nabat made, who caused Israel to sin—he pulled down that altar along with the high place. He burned the high place, crushing it to dust; he also burned the Asherah. And Josiah turned, he saw the tombs there on the hill; and he sent and took the bones out of the tombs, and burned them on the altar, and defiled it, according to the word of Yahweh which the man of God proclaimed these things" (2 Kgs. 23:15-16).
25. D. W. Van Winkle, "1 Kings XII 25–XIII 34: Jeroboam's Cultic Innovations and the Man of God from Judah," *VT* 46 (1996): 111.

about Jeroboam's sick son.[26] Yahweh alerts Ahijah that she is coming and he "recognizes" her based on Yahweh's tip-off, despite the fact that his eyes "had grown dim with old age" (1 Kgs. 14:4). Although he is blind, he has the ability "to see" what Jeroboam and Israel cannot—the sinful nature of Jeroboam's cult. Following the words of the man of God from Judah, condemnation by a northern prophet (1 Kings 14), especially the one who originally raises Jeroboam as king, is particularly pregnant with meaning. Even a blind northern prophet can see the error of the establishment of the northern kingdom, its founding monarch, and its national cult. The following is Ahijah's second oracle:[27]

> When Ahijah heard the sound of her footsteps as she came in the doorway, he said, "Come, wife of Jeroboam. Why do you make yourself unrecognizable? I have been sent with a hard message for you. **(7) Go, say to Jeroboam, "Thus says Yahweh, God of Israel, 'because I raised you up from among the people and I made you a *nāgîd* over my nation Israel. (8) And I tore the kingdom from the house of David and I gave it to you,** but you have not been like my servant

---

26. Knoppers, *Reign of Jeroboam*, 77–78; see also McKenzie, *Trouble with Kings*, 62.

27. Italics indicates the earlier doom prophecy, while bold designates deuteronomistic composition. The plain type may be the remnant of Dtr's original source. Ahijah's oracle in vv. 6–16 incorporates earlier sources, a prophetic account that uses the sick-king motif as well as a doom prophecy on the house of Jeroboam. While much of the language (esp. vv. 8–9, 15–16) is characteristically deuteronomistic, the content of the oracle is more graphic than is typical for Dtr. Carl Evans suggests that the oracle was originally a doom prophecy on the house of Jeroboam alone, with language uncharacteristic of Dtr (although this language is repeated in the report of the fall of the northern kingdom in 2 Kings 17 and in the oracles against the houses of Baasha and Ahab, demonstrating how completely it has been adopted and adapted by Dtr) (Carl D. Evans, "Naram-Sin and Jeroboam: The Archetypal *Unheilsherrscher* in Mesopotamian and Biblical Historiography," in *Scripture in Context II: More Essays on the Comparative Method*, ed. William W. Hallo, James C. Moyer, and Leo G. Perdue [Winona Lake, IN: Eisenbrauns, 1983], 118). Similarly, McKenzie suggests that Dtr may have "used an older treaty curse as the basis for the judgment oracle. But he completely changes the *Sitz im Leben* of the curse to refer to the demise of the Northern royal house. Dtr may have had a prophetic legend about the consultation of Ahijah for Jeroboam's sick son that he used as the setting for his oracle" (McKenzie, *Trouble with Kings*, 63). While the original oracle from a preexisting Ahijah tradition referred to the house of Jeroboam alone, Dtr reenvisions this to apply to the northern kingdom as a whole. The blame for the destruction of Israel is on its first king, Jeroboam (Evans, "Naram-Sin and Jeroboam," 120).

David, who observed my commandments and who followed me with all his heart, doing only what was right in my eyes. (9) You have done worse than all who came before you. You have gone and made for yourself other gods and molten images to anger me, and me you cast off behind your back. (10) *"Therefore, I am ready to bring evil onto the house of Jeroboam and I will cut off every male[28] belonging to Jeroboam, even the restricted and abandoned of Israel. And I will sweep away the house of Jeroboam, as one burns dung completely. (11) Those of Jeroboam who die in the city, the dogs will eat, and those who die in the field, the birds of the sky will eat' for Yahweh has spoken. (12) As for you, get up and go to your house, when your foot comes to the city, the child will die. (13) And all Israel will lament him and bury him, for he alone of Jeroboam['s kin] will come to the grave, for in him among the house of Jeroboam some good has been found by Yahweh, God of Israel. (14) Then Yahweh will raise up for himself a king over Israel, who will destroy the house of Jeroboam, this day and even right now.* (15) Yahweh will strike Israel like a reed that sways in the water and drive out Israel from upon this good land, which he gave to their ancestors. He will scatter them across the river because they made 'ăšērîm, angering Yahweh. (16) And he will give over Israel because of the sins of Jeroboam which he committed and because he caused Israel to sin. (1 Kgs. 14:6-16)

The initial charge against Jeroboam is a reprise of the injunction to Jeroboam and Solomon, recalling the elements of the regnal formulae: "You have not been like my servant David, who observed my commandments and who followed me with all his heart, doing only what was right in my eyes" (1 Kgs. 14:8). Jeroboam does not do הישר, his לבב is not with Yahweh, and he is not like David. Because of this, he will be punished. The creation of Jeroboam in the anti-Davidic prototype is solidified with this verse. The primary claim against Jeroboam is that he is not like David. (The sins of his cult are only how he is not like David.)[29] He is set up with the opportunity and constructed according to the literary prototype, but he does not

---

28. Literally, "the one urinating against the wall."
29. Ash, "Ideology of the Founder," 19.

live up to the expectations. Instead of being like the paradigm of the good king, he becomes the prototype of the bad king. He has "done worse than all who came before [him]" (1 Kgs. 14:9). This contention cannot possibly be literal, as Jeroboam is the first king of the North. This reflects the standard Dtr comparative formula used in relation to the other kings, but there is no one to whom Jeroboam can be compared. He is the first, yet this statement belies his status as a comparative figure. Knoppers convincingly argues against scholars who claim this comparative is "anachronistic." Instead, he suggests that since the "negative incomparability formula" is only applied to a few kings—Jeroboam, Omri, Ahab, and Manasseh—in making the statement of incomparability, they are recognized for "their unparalleled apostasy."[30] Dtr further qualifies what Jeroboam has done: "You have gone and made for yourself other gods and molten images to anger me [√כעס], and me you cast off behind your back" (1 Kgs. 14:9b). Jeroboam has not been faithful to the deuteronomistic covenant. The house of Jeroboam will be destroyed and Israel will be exiled. Yahweh "will scatter them across the river because they made 'ăšērîm, angering Yahweh. And he will give over Israel because of the sins of Jeroboam which he committed and because he caused Israel to sin" (1 Kgs. 14:15-16). This final line of Ahijah's oracle becomes the common refrain for the fate of Israel. Jeroboam inhabits the prototype of the evil king, or the *Unheilsherrscher*, the "ill-fated, hapless" ruler, a typology used in other ancient Near Eastern historiographical texts, in which, according to Evans, "the king's religious offenses bring condemnation on himself and ruin to his family and nation."[31] Jeroboam becomes the standard of the evil king, against which the remainder of the kings of Israel will be measured. [32] And he is the cause of the sins of the entire

30. Knoppers, *Reign of Jeroboam*, 106.
31. Evans, "Naram-Sin and Jeroboam," 99, 118.

kingdom of Israel. These two elements, being like Jeroboam and having caused Israel to sin, become the constituent elements of the regnal formulae of the kings of Israel.

Establishing the Davidic Antitype through the Regnal Formulae

As with the comparative David, Jeroboam as the prototype of the evil king is established and propagated through the regnal formulae. Similar to the Judean kings, as discussed in chapter 3, the kings of Israel are also evaluated through stereotyped judgment formulae that introduce and conclude the reigns of each king. These formulae not only evaluate each king, but also structure the entire history, juxtaposing and synchronizing the kings of both kingdoms. In contrasting the accounts of the kings of Israel and Judah, Dtr can compare the kings and kingdoms literarily and theologically while separated politically; the kingdoms and their kings are both judged by deuteronomistic theology.[33] More specifically, the Davidic prototype developed for constructing the narrative of the kings of Judah also applies to the kings of Israel. Jeroboam, as discussed above, is presented in the mold of the Davidic prototype. Similarly, it is through these judgment formulae that the two prototypes of good and bad kings are thoroughly established. Jeroboam becomes the prototype of northern sin; despite this, he is the only northern king compared (albeit negatively) to David.[34] Like the regnal formulae of the Judean kings, the regnal formulae of the Israelite kings are crucial components in evaluating the kings and advancing the Davidic

---

32. Benjamin Thomas further highlights that "without David, Solomon, Asa, Jehoshaphat, or Hezekiah, there is no positive, counter-protagonist (*Heilsherrscher*) to set up the contrast with the northern *Unheilsherrscher*, a role played by Jeroboam (and Ahab)" (*Hezekiah and the Compositional History of the Book of Kings* [Tübingen: Mohr Siebeck, 2014], 160). This is the effect of the use of the prototype strategy.

33. E. Theodore Mullen, "The Sins of Jeroboam: A Redactional Assessment," *CBQ* 49 (1987): 215.

34. Mark Leuchter, "Jeroboam the Ephratite," *JBL* 125, no. 1 (2006): 59.

antitype. The comparative Jeroboam prototype strategy is pervasive throughout the reported reigns of all the kings of Israel. Similar to those of Judah, the first constituent element of the northern regnal formulae is the evaluation that they did הרע בעיני יהוה, what was "evil in the eyes of Yahweh." Not one northern king receives a thoroughly positive assessment. Only Jehu has a chance, but he still continues in the sin of Jeroboam. This is certainly the effect of the Judean writer's perspective, never missing an opportunity to denigrate the northern kingdom. The patterns of evaluation are pervasive throughout, as fifteen of the nineteen kings of Israel who succeed Jeroboam are said to do הרע בעיני יהוה. Three others, Elah, Tibni, and Shallum, have no regnal formula.[35] Only Jehu (2 Kgs. 9:1—10:36) is said to do הישר because of how he followed Yahweh's instructions to wipe out the house of Ahab (10:31), yet the praise for Jehu is tempered because he does not abandon the sins of Jeroboam (10:29). This is a sign that he did not follow Yahweh with all his heart (10:31). In almost every instance, the report of having done evil in Yahweh's eyes continues with a qualifying statement that the king "followed the way of Jeroboam and his sin, which he caused Israel to sin." In the regnal formulae, doing הרע is equated with continuing the sins of Jeroboam. The second part of the formula refers to the sins of Jeroboam and the king's continued association with the cult of Jeroboam. This Jeroboam comparative element takes three different forms, although each expresses the same sentiment. The first pattern says, וילך בדרך ירבעם בן נבט ובחטאתו אשר החטיא את ישראל, "And he followed the way of Jeroboam and his sin, which he caused Israel to sin." In each case, there is a slight variation based on the circumstances of the characters. Nadab, son of Jeroboam, follows the way of his father (unnamed), because he is the actual son of Jeroboam.

---

35. Although Elah (1 Kgs. 16:8-14) does not get an evaluation, Zimri wipes him out because of "the sins of Baasha and Elah" (1 Kgs. 16:13).

Omri follows בכל דרך, "in all the ways of Jeroboam," and Ahaziah, son of Ahab and Jezebel, follows the "way of his father and mother," in addition to the way of Jeroboam. The following table clearly demonstrates the similarities in evaluation.

	Followed the way of Jeroboam/his father and his sin, which he caused Israel to sin	Did evil in the eyes of YHWH
Nadab (1 Kgs. 15:26)	וילך בדרך אביו ובחטאתו אשר החטיא את ישראל	ויעש הרע בעיני יהוה
Baasha (1 Kgs. 15:34)	אשר החטיא את ישראל וילך בדרך ירבעם ובחטאתו	ויעש הרע בעיני יהוה
Omri (1 Kgs. 16:25-26)	וילך בכל דרך ירבעם בן נבט ובחטאתו	ויעשה עמרי הרע בעיני יהוה וירע מכל אשר לפניו
Ahaziah (1 Kgs. 22:53)	וילך בדרך אביו ובדרך אמו ובדרך ירבעם בן נבט אשר החטיא את ישראל	ויעש הרע בעיני יהוה

The second pattern is more stereotyped and occurs in the regnal formulae of six of the eight later kings of Israel, Jehoash to Pekah. Instead of "following the way" of Jeroboam, these kings "do not stray from the sins of Jeroboam son of Nabat, which he caused Israel to sin," לא סר מ[כל\על] חטאות ירבעם בן נבט אשר החטיא את ישראל. Most of these kings have very short reigns, and the narrative accounts of their acts do not encompass more than a few verses, not much beyond the regnal formulae.

	Did not turn away from sins of Jeroboam which he caused Israel to sin	Did evil in the eyes of YHWH
Jehoash (2 Kgs. 13:11)	לא סר מכל חטאות יב"נ* אשר החטיא את ישראל בה הלך	ויעשה הרע בעיני יהוה
Jeroboam II (2 Kgs. 14:24)	לא סר מכל חטאות יב"נ אשר החטיא את ישראל	ויעש הרע בעיני יהוה
Zechariah (2 Kgs. 15:9)	לא סר מחטאות יב"נ אשר החטיא את ישראל	ויעש הרע בעיני יהוה כאשר עשו אבתיו
Menahem (2 Kgs. 15:18)	לא סר מעל חטאות יב"נ אשר החטיא את ישראל כל ימיו	ויעש הרע בעיני יהוה
Pekahiah (2 Kgs. 15:24)	לא סר מחטאות יב"נ אשר החטיא את ישראל	ויעש הרע בעיני יהוה
Pekah (2 Kgs. 15:28)	לא סר מן חטאות יב"נ אשר החטיא את ישראל	ויעש הרע בעיני יהוה

יב"נ=ירבעם בן נבט*

Jehoahaz, the king immediately preceding Jehoash, fills a transitional compositional position bridging the two forms of the assessment. Jehoahaz both follows the sin of Jeroboam (although not the דרך) and does not stray from it.

Jehoahaz (2 Kgs. 13:2)

וילך אחר חטאת ירבעם בן נבט אשר החטיא את ישראל   לא סר ממנה   ויעש הרע בעיני יהוה

It is clear in both of these patterns that the focus on doing what is evil is intrinsically connected to being like Jeroboam. The third pattern is reserved for those kings of the house of Omri—Omri, Ahab, and Ahaziah. There is an added element to their regnal formulae. Each of these kings causes Yahweh to anger (*hip̄'il* כעס) because of their added apostasy. The root כעס is also used in several other places when discussing the pending destruction of a dynasty for the sins a king committed, angering Yahweh (house of Jeroboam, 1 Kgs. 15:30; house of Baasha, 1 Kgs. 16:2, 13; house of Ahab, 1 Kgs. 16:33).

In Ahijah's second oracle, Jeroboam is said to "have done worse than all who came before you. You have gone and made for yourself other gods and molten images [מסכות] to anger me [להכעיסני], and me you cast off behind your back." This charge is also made against Baasha and Elah in the report that Zimri has destroyed them: אל כל חטאות בעשא וחטאות אלה בנו אשר חטאו ואשר החטיאו את ישראל להכעיס את יהוה אלהי ישראל בהבליהם, "Because of all the sins of Baasha and the sins of Elah his son which they did and caused Israel to sin, angering Yahweh God of Israel with their idols" (1 Kgs. 16:13). Yet, unlike the accusations against the Omrides, this does not appear in the regnal formula, but instead in the narrator's comments about the oracle of Jehu calling for the destruction of the house of Baasha. Perhaps these statements are reserved for those dynasties that will be destroyed because of their apostasy. כעס is also used in the verdict on the southern kingdom, in the Manasseh narrative referring to Judah's sin: יען אשר עשו את הרע בעיני ויהיו מכעסים אתי, "Because of that which they did that was evil in my eyes and they angered me" (2 Kgs. 21:15). Also, it is interesting to note that כעס in the *hip'il* is thoroughly deuteronomistic. Throughout DtrH, it appears in redactional passages.[36] Returning to the third pattern of regnal formulae, the Omrides add to Jeroboam's apostasy.[37] Omri's sin is that of Jeroboam, with an added comment that he caused Israel to sin against the God of Israel with their idols (בהבליהם). Ahab introduced Baal worship into Israel (1 Kgs. 16:31-33), which Ahaziah continues. Only Jehoram, the last of the Omrides, in 2 Kgs. 3:2 removes Baal worship from Israel, and although he continues the sins of Jeroboam, he does not cause Yahweh to anger. It is interesting to note that despite the presumably praiseworthy act of removing Baal

36. Erik Eynikel, *The Reform of King Josiah and the Composition of the Deuteronomistic History* (Leiden: Brill, 1995), 69.
37. Omri (1 Kgs. 16:25-26), Ahab (1 Kgs. 16:30-33), Ahaziah (1 Kgs. 22:53-54).

worship, Jehoram, in continuing to commit the sins of Jeroboam, still does הרע בעיני יהוה, unlike Jehu, who also continues the sins of Jeroboam but is seen as doing הישר because he carries out the annihilation of the house of Ahab. While it may seem illogical, von Rad suggests that "the judgment passed on the kings is not arrived at on the basis of a balanced reckoning of the number of *pros* and *cons*, by means of an average, as it were, of their achievements and their sins of omission. . . . the Deuteronomist is not concerned with the various good and evil actions, but with the one fundamental decision on which he was convinced judgment and salvation finally depended." [38] The use of כעס in the regnal formula pattern and in the dynastic doom proclamations seems to acknowledge a particularly bad brand of evil kings. These kings are "the worst of the worst." Yet for the Omrides, despite their qualification as being worse than all the kings and also introducing Baal worship into Israel (in addition to the decentralized worship of Jeroboam's cult), the Omrides are not used as the comparative prototype for the bad kings of Israel. This will be discussed further in chapter 6. Jeroboam inhabits the prototype of the evil king because of his Davidic potential. Identifying the use of the Davidic prototype strategy justifies the choice of Jeroboam over Ahab as the prototype of the evil king while also highlighting the evil behaviors of the kings of Israel, namely, decentralized worship. In fact, the only places in which they are comparative are in the evaluation of two Judean kings: Jehoram of Judah, Ahab's son-in-law, and his son Ahaziah of Judah (Ahab's grandson), and in the reign of King Manasseh (to be discussed in chap. 6). Even though they are southern kings, they are associated with the sins of Jeroboam, Ahab, and the kings of Israel. Jehoram followed the ways of the kings of Israel (presumably the cult of Jeroboam, but Jeroboam is

---

38. Rad, "Deuteronomistic Theology," 75–76.

not mentioned explicitly) and was like Ahab (2 Kgs. 8:18). Similarly, Ahaziah follows the ways of the house of Ahab, and does what is displeasing (ויעש הרע), like the house of Ahab (2 Kgs. 8:27-29). In the case of both of these Judean kings, the narrator makes clear that their likeness to Ahab is a consequence of their blood relationship. The comparison to Jeroboam, and the typology of the evil king, is reserved for the kings of Israel.

Did Evil in eyes of YHWH	Omride relationship	Ahab comparative	Followed way of N. kings
Jehoram of Judah (2 Kgs. 8:18)			
ויעש הרע בעיני יהוה	כי בת אחאב היתה לו לאשה	כאשר עשו בית אחאב	וילך בדרך מלכי ישראל
Ahaziah of Judah (2 Kgs. 8:27-29)			
ויעש הרע בעיני יהוה	כי חתן בית אחאב הוא	כבית אחאב	וילך בדרך בית אחאב

The Function of Jeroboam as the anti-David and the Prototype of the Evil King

The prototype strategy is used in the case of Jeroboam not only to evaluate the king but also to denounce his cult and the kingdom of Israel as a whole. This is done through both the pseudo-historical narrative reports and the prophetic oracles. First, the report of the establishment of Jeroboam's shrines (1 Kgs. 12:28-33) reads as a list of deuteronomistically prohibited practices. Then, the proclamation of the man of God from Judah (1 Kings 13) makes a strong statement against the cult. Finally, the prophecy of Ahijah to the wife of Jeroboam makes explicit the consequences for the house of Jeroboam and the kingdom of Israel. Ahijah's oracle, establishing Jeroboam as the anti-David, intrinsically connects the downfall of Israel to the cult of Jeroboam (1 Kgs. 14:16). Reading the fierce reaction of Dtr, it is possible to see that he is not only laboring to promote his program but is also focused on discrediting another tradition. By highlighting Jeroboam's establishment of the shrines at Bethel and Dan, Dtr recognizes a rivalry between the national cults of Israel and Judah.[39] It is clear that Dtr is threatened by Jeroboam's religious "innovations" and writes scathingly against them. Dtr does not seem concerned with the rebuilding of Shechem and establishing Penuel as the royal residence, acceptable within political strategic measures for fortifying kingship; he also does not seem overly troubled by the split of the kingdom; but Dtr is deeply disturbed by changes in cultic affairs.[40] As local worship had previously been the cultic mode for centuries before the deuteronomistic "reform," Dtr fears a return to this standard Israelite tradition, continued support of the status quo, and noncompliance with the deuteronomistic program's innovations. In response, Dtr vilifies Jeroboam and his shrines. As

---

39. Knoppers, *Reign of Jeroboam*, 7. This is particularly true about discrediting the traditional importance of the Bethel shrines. It is no coincidence that Dtr focuses on the dedication at Bethel specifically (rather than Dan or both), because of its historical importance (Mark Leuchter, "Between Politics and Mythology: Josiah's Assault on Bethel in 2 Kings 23:15-20" [paper presented at the 2013 Moskow Symposium, "Theorizing Ritual Violence in the Hebrew Bible," Brown University, May 5, 2013]; I thank Mark Leuchter for sharing the contents of this essay with me in advance of its publication). Elijah, a northern prophet who fights vigorously for the eradication of foreign cults (1 Kgs. 18:22), does not respond negatively to the Bethel cult. He is even told to go there to meet a group of prophets in Bethel before his death (2 Kgs. 2:2-4) (Danelius, "Sins of Jeroboam ben-Nabat, Part I," 95–114; Danelius, "Sins of Jeroboam ben-Nabat, Part II," 96). Similarly, Knoppers contends that "indulging Jeroboam with this attention, the Deuteronomist concedes the antiquity and appeal of the sanctuaries at Bethel and Dan." If they were not popular and well established, Dtr would not have to deal with them (*Reign of Jeroboam*, 40). This demonstrates the prominence of these locations, in particular Bethel. Also, the bizarre interlude of the old prophet of Bethel (1 Kgs. 13:11-32) highlights the illegitimacy of Bethel. This prophet is a liar, tricking the man of God to violate Yahweh's commands (for his own gain), in order to prove whether the man of God is a true prophet (Erik Eynikel, "Prophecy and Fulfillment in the Deuteronomistic History (1 Kgs 13; 2 Kgs 23, 16-18)," in *Pentateuchal and Deuteronomistic Studies: Papers Read at the XIIIth IOSOT Congress, Leuven 1989*, ed. C. Brekelmans and J. Lust [Leuven: Leuven University Press, 1990], 234). There appears to be nothing prophetic about this old prophet; he does not speak with Yahweh, initially deliver an oracle, or lead the people. Instead, he exists to demonstrate the corruption of the northern kingdom and to legitimate the man of God from Judah, as prophet and the truth of his prophecy.

40. Knoppers, *Reign of Jeroboam*, 36.

such, Dtr attempts to make a previously acceptable mode of worship appear unacceptable—by casting local worship as entirely foreign, tantamount to idolatry; using the prototype strategy, the Deuteronomist works hard rhetorically to discourage and prohibit local shrines. Through his history (and his historiographical method), Dtr demonstrates that the cultic innovations of the deuteronomistic program should replace older forms of worship. Furthermore, in comparison with the LXX version of the Jeroboam narrative, it is possible to see the effects of the prototype strategy. The rise and fall of Jeroboam as the potential David and anti-David is a literary strategy only apparent in the MT. The ordering of episodes and changes in LXX illustrate this unique literary perspective. The Jeroboam narrative in LXX contains a significantly different narrative from MT.[41] Jeroboam is not initially presented positively. The Septuagint includes two versions of the story of Jeroboam's rise. The first account is roughly parallel to the MT account. The second account, often called the

41. For more scholarship on the Septuagint addition, see Mordechai Cogan, *1 Kings: A New Translation with Introduction and Commentary*, AB (New York: Doubleday, 2001), 355–56; David Willoughby Gooding, "Jeroboam's Rise to Power," *JBL* 91, no. 4 (1972): 529–33; Robert P. Gordon, "Second Septuagint Account of Jeroboam: History or Midrash?," *VT* 25 (1975): 368–93; John Gray, *1 and 2 Kings: A Commentary*, Old Testament Library, 2nd ed. (Philadelphia: Westminster, 1970), 286–88; James A. Montgomery, *A Critical and Exegetical Commentary on the Books of Kings*, ed. Henry Snyder Gehman, International Critical Commentary (New York: Scribner's, 1951), 251–54; Adrian Schenker, "Jeroboam and the Division of the Kingdom in the Ancient Septuagint: LXX 3 Kingdoms 12.24 a-z, MT 1 Kings 11-12; 14 and the Deuteronomistic History," in *Israel Constructs Its History: Deuteronomistic Historiography in Recent Research*, ed. Albert de Pury, Jean-Daniel Macchi, and Thomas Römer (Sheffield: Sheffield Academic, 2000), 214–57; Marvin A. Sweeney, "A Reassessment of the Masoretic and Septuagint Versions of the Jeroboam Narratives in 1 Kings/3 Kingdoms 11–14," *Journal for the Study of Judaism in the Persian, Hellenistic and Roman Period* 38, no. 2 (2007): 165–95; Zipora Talshir, "Is the Alternate Tradition of the Division of the Kingdom (3 Kgdms 12:24a-z) Non-Deuteronomistic," in *Septuagint, Scrolls and Cognate Writings*, ed. George J. Brooke and Barnabas Lindars (Atlanta: Scholars Press, 1992), 599–621; Talshir, *The Alternative Story of the Division of the Kingdom: 3 Kingdoms 12:24a-z* (Jerusalem: Simor, 1993); Talshir, "Literary Design—A Criterion for Originality? A Case Study: 3 Kgdms 12:24a-z; 1 K 11-14," in *Double Transmission Du Texte Biblique: Études D'histoire Du Texte Offertes En Hommage à Adrian Schenker*, ed. Adrian Schenker, Yohanan Goldman, and Christoph Uehlinger (Göttingen: Vandenhoeck & Ruprecht, 2001), 41–57; T. Michael Law, "How Not to Use 3 Reigns: A Plea to Scholars of the Books of Kings," *VT* 61, no. 2 (2011): 280–97.

addition, supplement, alternative story, or LXX B story, contains a narrative different from that found in MT Kings. The long addition found in the Septuagint follows 3 Kgdms. 12:24. Ahijah's doom oracle, presented at the end of the MT account, appears at the beginning of Jeroboam's story in the LXX addition. The first oracle, making Jeroboam king, follows later in the story and is not made by Ahijah at all, but instead by Shemaiah, a false prophet known from the time of Jeremiah (Jer. 29:24-32).[42] The difference in the ordering of the LXX from the MT version emphasizes the use of the prototype strategy in the MT. Without the inclusion of the two Ahijah oracles and the originally positive and David-like portrayal of Jeroboam, the strategy is not used. As with many LXX–MT differences, there are two approaches to explaining the differences. For those who argue that the LXX version predates the deuteronomistic version and is thus primary, it is possible to read the absence of the prototype strategy as a later deuteronomistic strategy only added into a late manuscript tradition that continues into the MT. But it does not make sense for Dtr to construct an initially positive Jeroboam when the manuscript tradition included a thoroughly negative portrayal. Instead, for many reasons (some discussed in chap. 2 concerning the variation in the narrative of Solomon's adversaries), the LXX tradition is more likely secondary.[43] The LXX tradents ignored the necessity of MT's ordering for the prototype strategy and instead are focused on solving a serious theological problem present in MT. Since Jeroboam turns out to be an evil king who leads Israel to sin and ultimately to its destruction, who was wrong in choosing Jeroboam? Was it Yahweh or Ahijah? And did Yahweh deliberately set up the north for failure by making Jeroboam king? Did Yahweh know (or more

42. Sweeney, "A Reassessment," 170.
43. Law argues that we should not view it as secondary, just different, reflective of a translation of a different Hebrew manuscript ("How Not to Use 3 Reigns").

problematic, not know) that Jeroboam would turn out so bad and doom the North even before its inception? Sweeney suggests that the LXX addition attempts to address this problem of Yahweh/Ahijah's righteousness and good judgment by taking away the agency from Yahweh/Ahijah and instead presents Jeroboam as a self-promoter who raises himself up.[44] In this way, according to Sweeney, the LXX addition is an interpretation or correction of the MT. In the MT, Ahijah's two prophecies highlight the "conversion" of Ahijah. Additionally, true to deuteronomistic theology, the MT emphasizes Yahweh's role in history: the split of the kingdom is the punishment of Solomon. Similarly, Jeroboam is initially conceived of as a second David figure that when unrealized makes the evil Jeroboam as the Davidic antitype even more powerful. Also, the doom oracle against Jeroboam is extended to the people of Israel and Jeroboam's dynasty (parallel and in contrast to the promise of the Davidic dynasty, which even when punished will persist). This is later linked to their destruction in 2 Kings 17. (The close connection between the prophecy and fulfillment is clearly seen through the language and images of the prophecy/destruction report.) Extending the doom to the entire kingdom also sends a clear message to Judah that the same fate could happen to them. With this in mind, it does not make sense for those scholars who argue for a primary LXX, because Dtr would not invent a positive portrait of Jeroboam if the thoroughly negative legacy already existed and was circulating in the LXX *Vorlage*. In this way, the role of Dtr's perspective in shaping the Jeroboam story—its episodes and Jeroboam's actions and character—is apparent when considering the historical plausibility (even the commonsensical motivations) of the narrative. The idea that Jeroboam would disobey the covenantal charge articulated by Ahijah seems illogical, given

---

44. Sweeney, "A Reassessment," 176, 177, 190.

that he "inherits" the throne in the wake of Solomon's apostasy. The consequences of disobedience should have made an impact on Jeroboam, effectively inspiring, or more accurately scaring, him into submission.[45] The absurdity of this occurrence can be interpreted in two different ways: first, from a historical perspective, Jeroboam does not commit what at his time was considered apostasy, and he believed he was faithful to the covenant; yet the Deuteronomist casts his behavior as apostasy. The second perspective is intentionally illogical; perhaps Dtr preserves this story for the sake of making Jeroboam look ridiculous. What kind of person would benefit from another's mistake and repeat the same mistake? Only one who is ineligible to attain such benefit. Dtr may have retained the prophetic investiture of Jeroboam along with its charge of covenantal fidelity to illustrate that Jeroboam should have known better and his inability to attain David-like status was his own fault. It is most likely that Jeroboam's disobedience is a deuteronomistic invention, created to further highlight deuteronomistic theology, demonstrating the punishment for those, especially kings, who violate the covenant. Furthermore, the account of Jeroboam's shrines is presented in two parts. The first is Dtr's narrative account of Jeroboam's decision to build the shrines and the establishment of his own cult in 1 Kgs. 12:25-33. The second is the prophecy by the man of God from Judah in 1 Kgs. 13:1-5. The sin of Jeroboam is his undoing and determines the fate of the kingdom of Israel. Most northern kings are accused of following the sin of Jeroboam. Therefore, it is important to consider what exactly the sin of Jeroboam is. The first way the Deuteronomist indicts Jeroboam is through his violation of the conditions of the promise given to him by Yahweh. Jeroboam does not trust that Yahweh will be with him, even though Ahijah assures him in the oracle that Yahweh will (1 Kgs. 11:38). Through Jeroboam's words

---

45. Van Winkle, "1 Kings XII 25-XIII 34," 110.

in 1 Kgs. 12:26-27, we are given a rare instance in which the reader is privy to the interior monologue of one of the characters.

> And Jeroboam said to himself, "Now the kingdom will return to the house of David. If this people continues to go up to offer sacrifices in the house of Yahweh in Jerusalem then the heart [לב] of this people will return to their lord, to Rehoboam, king of Judah, and they will kill me and return to Rehoboam, king of Judah." (1 Kgs. 12:26-27)

Jeroboam sets up these cultic shrines because he is afraid that the people will return to Judah since Jerusalem is still necessary to their cultic practice. Here, typical of deuteronomistic language, לב (v. 27) designates loyalty. Instead of being concerned that the people direct their לב to Yahweh, Jeroboam is anxious that their לב will return to Rehoboam and their loyalty to the Davidic king. Jeroboam's concern also emphasizes the deuteronomistic position: that the temple in Jerusalem is the only proper site of worship. Jeroboam knows this well and therefore schemes to counteract its political effect on his kingdom. Jeroboam takes agency in securing the kingdom rather than relying on Yahweh's promise.[46] This is the first part of the condemnation of Jeroboam by the Deuteronomist. Jeroboam does not trust Yahweh.[47] For theological reasons, the effect of ordering the first Ahijah oracle before the establishment of the cult is clear; Ahijah's prophecy in 1 Kings 11 should have been sufficient reassurance for Jeroboam. Not only does Ahijah promise Jeroboam he will be king of ten tribes, but he also assures him that he will have a בית נאמן,

---

46. Saul is also condemned for an act of agency; he does not obey Yahweh's command concerning the destruction of Amalek. Yahweh commanded Saul to "go and smite Amalek, and destroy all that belongs to them. And do not spare them. Kill [every] man and woman, from child to infant, from the camel to the donkey" (1 Sam. 15:3). Instead, Saul spares the Amalekite king Agag and the best of the flocks (1 Sam. 15:8-9). It is for this reason, and the agency that Saul takes on in carrying out the will of Yahweh, that the kingdom is torn from him (1 Sam. 15:16-29).

47. It is interesting to contrast this transgression with the praise of Hezekiah, one of the few exceptional kings of DtrH. Hezekiah is praised for his incomparable trust in Yahweh (2 Kgs. 18:5).

a "lasting house" (1 Kgs. 11:38). Despite this, Jeroboam works proactively to ensure the sustainability of the split kingdom.[48] Jeroboam should have been secure in Yahweh's promise. Jeroboam's act also shows that he does not have faith in his followers. According to Stuart Lasine, "Jeroboam's quoted thoughts in verses 26–27 imply that he views his followers as so fickle and violent that they might kill him and return their allegiance to Rehoboam, in spite of the fact that they had so recently killed Rehoboam's *corvée* officer Joram, an act which prompted Rehoboam to rush back to Jerusalem in his chariot to avoid the same fate (12:18)."[49] Through the revelation of his thoughts, in one short verse, Dtr convicts Jeroboam as a paranoid leader—afraid that both Yahweh and Israel will leave him. This is certainly not David-like. Dtr forces the reader to wonder, if Jeroboam does not fully believe in the legitimacy of his kingship, should others? Also, Dtr portrays Israel as politically unfaithful (again, the לב) and will later convict them of being religiously unfaithful; they have recently deserted one king (Rehoboam) and because of their nature, as Jeroboam fears, may just as quickly leave their new king. The evaluation of Jeroboam and Israel in this short statement is thoroughly negative. Although he is vilified for this act, Jeroboam is politically and not religiously motivated to erect the countercults at Bethel and Dan (1 Kgs. 12:26–33). He views it as a necessary act in order to secure his rule and secession from the South. Jeroboam attempts to solidify his control of the northern kingdom by establishing a northern shrine so that the people would not return to a southern (or united) kingdom since it included Jerusalem and Solomon's temple. By erecting new shrines in the North, he works to guarantee the maintenance of divided kingdoms.[50] J. A. Montgomery

48. Van Winkle, "1 Kings XII 25–XIII 34," 110.

49. Stuart Lasine, "Reading Jeroboam's Intentions: Intertextuality, Rhetoric, and History in 1 Kings 12," in *Reading Between Texts*, ed. Danna Nolan Fewell (Louisville: Westminster John Knox, 1992), 143.

says that "Jeroboam's enterprise was purely political indeed cleverly founded on the opposition to Solomon's autocracy and centralization of religion. But he had no religious interest beyond the restoration of the local cults."[51] It is Dtr's evaluation of these sites that gives them their negative thrust. While Jeroboam's reasons for instituting the new cult sites seem somewhat justified on a political level, he is fiercely condemned for it. The temerity of Jeroboam's cultic activity is only shocking according to deuteronomistic proscriptions. His is an act of decentralization, rather than idolatry. Jeroboam's cult corresponds to standards of predeuteronomistic worship. According to Knoppers, "Jeroboam's goal was undoubtedly to reorganize and preserve a cult, not to create a new one *ex nihilo*. Whether the issue is iconography, location, priesthood, or festival, there is good reason to believe that Jeroboam's cultus was essentially conservative, especially when contrasted with the religious innovations of David and Solomon in Jerusalem."[52] Jeroboam's cult may have been a return or a continuation of previously established cults, which had never ceased to function, yet according to the Deuteronomist, Jeroboam's act is as grave as one of idolatry. Despite his decentralized shrines, Jeroboam is primarily convicted of not being like David. Dtr constructs a narrative in which Jeroboam sets himself against Davidic and religious tradition. Dtr works very hard literarily to condemn Jeroboam's shrines. Using a rhetoric of idolatry, Dtr renders the cult shrines idolatrous even though they were likely Yahwistic. While the concept of noncentralized Yahwistic shrines would have been acceptable (even standard) religious practice in Jeroboam's tenth-century Israel, the seventh-century Jerusalemite Deuteronomist is adamant about rendering it unacceptable and transgressive. Von Rad

---

50. *CMHE* 279.
51. Montgomery, *Books of Kings*, 256.
52. Knoppers, *Reign of Jeroboam*, 35.

speaks to this historiographical impulse: "The Deuteronomist makes absolutely no claim to appraise the kings at a given moment in relation to the particular historical situation confronting them."[53] What was contemporaneously permissible has no bearing on the judgment of the king. Dtr's standard of centralization was likely unknown during most of the monarchical period.[54] The narrator's report of Jeroboam's cultic actions, while delivered matter-of-factly, reads like a list of all things prohibited by deuteronomistic theology.

> So the king took counsel and he made two golden calves and said to them, "Enough going up to Jerusalem. Behold, your gods, Israel, who brought you up out of the land of Egypt."[55] (29) And he installed one at Bethel and the other at Dan. (30) This thing became a sin and the people went before the one as far as Dan.[56] (31) And he made a shrine

---

53. Rad, "Deuteronomistic Theology," 75.

54. Ibid., 76.

55. The story of Aaron's golden calf in Exodus 32 may express a northern polemic against Jeroboam's shrines. For more on this, see Richard E. Friedman, *The Bible with Sources Revealed: A New View into the Five Books of Moses* (San Francisco: HarperSanFrancisco, 2003), 173; Gary N. Knoppers, "Aaron's Calf and Jeroboam's Calves," in *Fortunate the Eyes That See: Essays in Honor of David Noel Freedman in Celebration of His Seventieth Birthday*, ed. Astrid B. Beck et al. (Grand Rapids: Eerdmans, 1995), 92–104; William Henry Propp, *Exodus 19–40*, AB (New York: Doubleday, 2006), 547–83.

56. As it stands, the MT does not make sense. LXX (Lucianic) includes וילכו העם לפני האחד עד דן ולפני האחד בית-אל. It is difficult to adjudicate which one is primary. The MT should be considered better on the basis of *lectio difficilior* (Martin Noth, *Könige* [Neukirchen-Vluyn: Neukirchener Verlag des Erziehungsvereins, 1968], 266; Cogan, *1 Kings*, 359). For those scholars who consider the LXX to be the original, the MT omission could be explained by haplography, *homoioteleuton* (Volkmar Fritz, *1 and 2 Kings: A Continental Commentary*, trans. Anselm Hagedorn, Continental Commentaries [Minneapolis: Fortress Press, 2003], 146; Gray, *1 and 2 Kings*, 289), but it is difficult to sufficiently explain how this error may have occurred. The suggestion of *homoioteleuton* is attractive, especially because of the similarity in the words, and the scribe may have jumped from one לפני האחד עד to לפני האחד עד, but that would mean the original would have had Bethel in the middle, lost by haplography, and Dan at the end of the verse, וילכו העם לפני האחד בית אל ולפני האחד עד דן. As the Lucianic is usually a reliable witness, Knoppers is inclined to order according to that manuscript (Knoppers, *Reign of Jeroboam*, 27), but how can we explain that the Bethel clause falls off the end? Haplography could have occurred, but then Bethel would have been lost from the middle of the verse. It is not possible to posit haplography and hold to the Lucianic LXX reading. An alternative is that the MT is the original and the Greek added Bethel as a gloss. This seems to be the best explanation. In order to make sense of the MT verse, the LXX translator added the second, לפני האחד בית אל, in order to clarify the Dan clause or because the shrines at Dan and Bethel were

at the high place and appointed priests from the whole population who were not from the Levites. (32) And Jeroboam established a festival in the eighth month on the fifteenth day of the month, like the festival in Judah. And he ascended the altar, which he made in Bethel, sacrificing to the calves, which he made, and he stationed in Bethel the priests of the high place that he appointed. (33) And he went up to the altar which he made in Bethel on the fifteenth day of the eighth month which he devised himself. And he made a festival for the Israelites and he ascended the altar to make an offering. (1 Kgs. 12:28-33)

In the simple installation of this cult, Jeroboam violates many tenets of deuteronomistic theology. He institutes noncentralized worship and (in Dtr's interpretation) image worship, installs non-Levitical priests, changes the holiday, and creates a system of possible polytheism. While the institution of noncentralized Yahwistic cult sites would have been permissible and common in Jeroboam's time, Dtr makes clear that in his reading of history, Jeroboam's religion is akin to idolatry. The rhetoric of idolatry is accomplished through Jeroboam's words of dedication and in the dual iconography. In verse 28, he says, "Behold your gods [אלהים]." While it is possible to read אלהים both as a singular and plural, the plural form of the verb indicates that Dtr intends it to be read as plural (and I have translated it as such). Dtr heaps on the accusations, including one of polytheism. Had Jeroboam actually uttered these words (not likely), he could have meant אלהים in the singular, suggesting that the calves were representatives of the one God, Yahweh, who had taken them out of Egypt, and Jeroboam was participating in permissible monotheistic, Yahwistic worship. This ambiguity, and the potential innocence of אלהים, may be intentional. Montgomery suggests that the introduction of two calves (rather than one, although the narrative focuses only on

a fixed pair and almost always appear together. Both of these scenarios could be true. Noth also suggests that Dan is mentioned alone since the narrative focuses on the dedication of the calf at Bethel; here is a comment and judgment that in their enthusiasm the people of Israel journeyed as far as Dan in order to install the other calf (Noth, *Könige*, 285; Cogan, *1 Kings*, 359).

the installation of one at Bethel) is to make certain that the calves are seen as polytheistic. "With only one calf there was danger of confusion of the image with YHWH." [57] Similarly, the report leaves the direction of the offerings ambiguous. In verse 33, when Jeroboam ascends the altar to make an offering, does he offer it to Yahweh or to the calves? While Dtr may not go as far as to accuse Jeroboam of worshiping the calves themselves (perhaps this is a reflection of the collective memory that the shrines were permissible, the tradition against which Dtr writes), the ambiguity (there is no indirect object following להקטיר) and the mere suggestion is enough to color the episode and add suspicion to Jeroboam's intentions.[58] While this passage looks like a strict "factual" report, each step Jeroboam takes in establishing his new cult violates another tenet of deuteronomistic religion. The prophecy of the man of God makes the condemnation of the shrines unequivocally clear. While Dtr attempts to represent worship at Jeroboam's cult site as akin to idolatry, he still maintains them in two disparate categories. This is apparent when enumerating the sins of Ahab; the Deuteronomist distinguishes the sins of Jeroboam, which Ahab continues to do, from those that Ahab adds (1 Kgs. 16:30-31): Baal worship to Jeroboam's decentralized worship. This goes back to the way in which Dtr conceives of idolatry: wrong place, wrong symbols, and wrong deities. Jeroboam is only guilty of the first two, while Ahab adds the worship of another deity. Still, for Dtr, the effect of connecting the act of decentralized worship with blatant idolatry puts them in the same category—local worship is wrong. For the most part, Dtr appeals to a pious audience and tries to undermine the acceptance of local worship. These people already

---

57. Montgomery, *Books of Kings*, 255.

58. This tendency toward ambiguity and indeterminacy is described by Sternberg not as confusion or sloppiness, but as an intentional strategy, inserting multiple possible meanings into the interpretation of the text (Meir Sternberg, "Gaps, Ambiguity and the Reading Process," in *The Poetics of Biblical Narrative* [Bloomington: Indiana University Press, 1985], 186–229).

considered idolatry to be sinful, and Dtr tells them that decentralized worship is just as bad. The message is clear—if someone might have thought that worship at any Yahwistic shrine was permissible, through his literary and historiographical technique, Dtr lets his audience know that decentralized worship is just as bad as idolatry, or actually becomes idolatry. Still, Dtr separates these two modes of illegitimate worship and runs independent campaigns against them since the deuteronomistic policy of centralization sets up Jeroboam as the anti-David, the prototype of the evil king. Jeroboam's sin is a literary construction rather than an actual cultic violation. In his important and influential essay, Frank Cross contends that the major theme of the northern kingdom in DtrH is the "sin of Jeroboam" and it is this theme that guides the narrative; I would like to suggest that the sin of setting up the competing cult sites is secondary to the narrative and that the major transgression is a literary one, reflecting the construction of the Davidic prototype. First and foremost, Jeroboam was primed to be "like David," but he is not. The cultic violations are the "how" he was not like David. While Cross also highlights two themes that pit Jeroboam and David against each other (their religious behavior—Jeroboam's establishment of the countercult and David's fidelity), the typology of opposition is primary.[59] The contrast of David and Jeroboam is a literary construction; their behavior is part of that construction. Cross argues that the preexilic Dtr presents two theologies: "One stemming from the old Deuteronomic covenant theology which regarded destruction of dynasty and people as tied necessarily to apostasy, and a second, drawn from the royal ideology in Judah: the eternal promises to David."[60] While the role of the kings underlies this theory and I do not intend to reject his assessment, Cross does not sufficiently

59. *CMHE* 282–84.
60. Ibid., 284.

recognize the literary design of the portrait of the kings and instead focuses on the themes as identifying levels of redaction and the theological concerns of the author/editor through cultic violations rather than literary construction. Framing the use of the prototype in terms of David versus Jeroboam lends greater precision and literary consciousness to our understanding of the Jeroboam narrative. The importance of the oppositional prototype (over the physical cults) is further supported by the absence of mention of the calves and countercult at Dan and Bethel in Ahijah's doom prophecy. How can the cult violation be primary if it is not even mentioned in Jeroboam's judgment and renunciation? It is only the ordering of the narrative, putting the condemnation of the man of God before Ahijah's second prophecy, that directs us to read the sin of the cult as implying that verdict. Furthermore, if it were all about cultic (in)fidelity, we would expect Ahab, who adds to the sins of Jeroboam by introducing Baal worship in Israel, to be excoriated as the evil king (see chap. 6). But he is not. This is also apparent in the use of Jeroboam rather than Ahab as the prototype of the evil king. Given that the Omrides, and in particular Ahab, are seen as the worst of all the kings of Israel, it is surprising that they are not used as the standard for measuring evil kings. The Ahab comparative only exists among those of the house of Omri (including two Judean kings), and the exilic version of the Manasseh account. The regnal evaluation for Ahab cements his place as building on the sins of Jeroboam:

And Ahab son of Omri did more evil in the eyes of Yahweh than all who preceded him [ויעש אחאב בן עמרי הרע בעיני יהוה מכל אשר לפניו]. It was a light thing to him to add to the sins of Jeroboam son of Nabat. He took Jezebel daughter of Eth-Baal, king of the Sidonians, as a wife and he went and served Baal and worshiped him. And he erected an altar to Baal in the house of Baal which he built in Samaria. And Ahab made an Asherah and Ahab continued to do and angered Yahweh, God of Israel, more than all the kings of Israel before him

לעשות להכעיס את יהוה אלהי ישראל מכל מלכי ישראל אשר היו]
[לפניו. (1 Kgs. 16:30-33)

Dtr's assessment that it was not a small thing to increase the sins of Jeroboam is quite right. Since Jeroboam is established as the *Unheilsherrscher* in 1 Kings 13–14, to be worse than the prototype of evil (this comparative is articulated twice in the regnal formula, 1 Kgs. 16:30 and 33) sets up Ahab in a position of surpassing Jeroboam in claiming this title. But Ahab is not taken up as the literary model for the evil king. Instead, the first, founding kings are adopted as the prototypes and points of reference—David for good and Jeroboam for evil. This is not the result of the accident of chronology; the kings who succeed Ahab (more than half of the total number of kings of Israel) are still compared to Jeroboam, using the prototype of the evil king, the anti-David, established in 1 Kings 13–14. It may be possible to attribute this to Jehoram's act of removing the *maṣṣēbat* Baal and not being like his mother and father (2 Kgs. 3:2-3), so that the major innovation of Ahab (bringing Baal worship to Israel) only lasts two generations. But it is more likely that the Jeroboam prototype is an intentional literary tool used by Dtr to construct the entire existence—rise and fall—of the northern kingdom. Jeroboam (and not Ahab) is the prototype of the bad king, constructed in contrast to the Davidic prototype, the exemplum of the good king. In so doing, Dtr creates two models that are polar opposites, the prototype and its antitype. This highlights the use of the prototype strategy. According to Paul Ash, "The Deuteronomist condemns Jeroboam for one primary reason: failure to be like David (1 Kgs. 14:8). Jeroboam's construction of the calves is secondary, a specific act of being unlike David."[61] Jeroboam is the comparative, the prototype and exemplum of the evil king developed in opposition to the Davidic prototype, but

---

61. Ash, "Ideology of the Founder," 19.

he is hardly the worst of Israel's kings. The focus on Jeroboam as the evil king demonstrates that the preexilic Dtr is most concerned with centralization of the cult in his religious program rather than fighting against Baal worship. The use of the prototype strategy in the portrait of Jeroboam illustrates the intentional literary plan of Dtr in crafting the entirety of his history. The kings, the theology, and the major events are all part of that scheme.

5

Josiah: "No One Arose Like Him"

"Josiah appears to be the climactic figure of the DtrH who sees the realization of YHWH's promise to the house of David." So says Marvin Sweeney.[1] Statements such as this have long confused the readers of the account of Josiah's reign. Much ink has been spilled on acclaiming Josiah as the great hero of the Deuteronomistic History, but it is somewhat surprising that the two-chapter account of Josiah's reign (2 Kings 22–23) pays little attention to the person of Josiah, and has more to do with the book finding and the reform report.

The book of Kings chronicles the reigns of each king and the history of the monarchy. The fate of Israel and Judah rises and falls with the cultic behavior of the kings. Throughout, the history builds to the reign of Josiah. A prediction of his future appearance is even articulated in 1 Kgs. 13:2. Despite this, the character of Josiah seems quite minor. This shift of gaze from the king to his actions highlights what is important in this story: the "found" law book

---

1. Marvin A. Sweeney, *King Josiah of Judah: The Lost Messiah of Israel* (Oxford: Oxford University Press, 2001), 26.

and its application, while the use of the Davidic prototype strategy maintains the importance of the figure of Josiah.

The use of the Davidic prototype, through intertextual comparisons with other kings and their cultic actions, sets up Josiah as the ultimate king. This technique is effective even though the account of Josiah's reign spends little time on the king himself. By using the typological conventions, the development of the character is implicit. Dtr is able to focus on the individual reforms while setting up Josiah as surpassing the best of kings, based on the Davidic prototype. The use of the prototype strategy illustrates how the entirety of the history is focused on the coming of Josiah and his reform. He eliminates the sins of both the North and South, ultimately reuniting them, "returning" worship to the temple in Jerusalem. By fulfilling deuteronomic law, doing הישר בעיני יהוה, and walking in the ways of David, according to the Torah of Moses, Josiah is a figure compared to Moses and Joshua, surpassing even David, the model of the prototype of the good king.[2] In Dtr's unparalleled acclaim, Josiah "out-Davids" even David. The figure of Josiah bears a heavy literary burden; he is the second David and the anti-Jeroboam and anti-Solomon, the antithesis of the Davidic antitype.

Historiographical Hero: Book or King?

The narrative of King Josiah begins with the finding of the lost scroll of the law during the eighteenth year of Josiah's reign (2 Kgs. 22:3-11). Upon hearing the book read, Josiah tears his clothes and sends emissaries to inquire of the prophetess Huldah about the meaning of the scroll. Huldah predicts Josiah's peaceful death and the complete destruction of Judah (22:12-14, 15-20).[3] Following

---

2. Ibid., 173.

this, Josiah embarks on a large-scale reform to purge Israel and Judah of all foreign cults. The reform includes the covenant (23:1-3), cultic purge (23:4-20), and culminates with the celebration of the Passover (23:21-23). The account ends with the death of Josiah on the battlefield of Megiddo at the hands of Pharaoh Neco, falsifying Huldah's prophecy.

The account of King Josiah, the incredible book finding and the illustrious reform, is set in the larger history following the disastrous reign of King Manasseh and preceding the ordinary and terse accounts of the final four bad kings of Judah. There is disagreement among scholars as to how to date the Josiah narrative and the reform. While some suggest that the final version of the narrative is almost entirely exilic,[4] Josiah's reform only makes sense in a context in which there was an opportunity to overturn Yahweh's anger.[5] In the wake of the extreme judgment pronounced on Manasseh, as reflected in

3. The prophecy of Huldah will not be addressed in this chapter because it does not play a role in the development of Josiah in the Davidic prototype strategy, although it is a linchpin in the argument for determining the compositional date of the Josiah narrative and DtrH as a whole. It is important to note that the oracle is another example of the extensive use of the prophetic tradition in Kings, an essential part of Dtr's historiographical poetics, and the use of prophecy-fulfillment as a framing strategy. For my treatment of this oracle, see the earlier dissertation version of this volume, Alison L. Joseph, "The Portrait of the Kings and the Historiographical Poetics of the Deuteronomistic Historian" (PhD diss., University of California, Berkeley; Ann Arbor: ProQuest/UMI, 2012), 101–4 (Publication No. AAT 3527138).

4. Philip R. Davies, "Josiah and the Law Book," in *Good Kings and Bad Kings: The Kingdom of Judah in the Seventh Century BCE*, ed. Lester L. Grabbe (New York: T&T Clark, 2005), 75–76; Christof Hardmeier, "King Josiah in the Climax of the Deuteronomic History (2 Kings 22–23) and the Pre-Deuteronomic Document of a Cult Reform at the Place of Residence (23.4-15*)": Criticism of Sources, Reconstruction of Literary Pre-stages and the Theology of History in 2 Kings 22–23*," in Grabbe, *Good Kings and Bad Kings*, 142; Thomas Römer calls 2 Kings 22–23 "the foundation myth" of the Deuteronomistic school (Thomas Römer, *The So-called Deuteronomistic History: A Sociological, Historical, and Literary Introduction* [New York: T&T Clark, 2007], 49–56). In this way, scholars date these chapters in congruence with their overall dating of the entire history.

5. This is in contrast with Monroe's argument that the postmonarchic, deuteronomistic layer of the account is focused on demonstrating that despite his best efforts, even Josiah and his reform could not save Judah from its fate, proving that if even the best of kings is unable to prevent the destruction of Judah, "governance by kings is insufficient" (Lauren A. S. Monroe, *Josiah's Reform and the Dynamics of Defilement: Israelite Rites of Violence and the Making of a Biblical Text* [New York: Oxford University Press, 2011], 71–72, 115).

the current version of text, the reform of Josiah appears futile and ridiculous. If the fate of Judah were already sealed, why would Josiah put into effect such a thorough reform? As such, composition of the majority of the reform account only makes sense in a preexilic context. For that reason, I consider almost the entirety of the Josiah narrative a product of Dtr[1], with the exception of 2 Kgs. 22:15-17, 19b, 20b; 23:10-11, 12b, 24, 26-27.[6] These verses are primarily those that deal with the Babylonian exile and the sins of Manasseh. There will be further discussion of dating the Manasseh account and the corresponding verses in the Josianic reform in the following chapter.

The reform report and its introduction by the book finding is focused on demonstrating that the innovations of the reform are antique and that Josiah is a great reformer, clearly topping any reform previously attempted in Israel and Judah. All previous reforms were unsuccessful or insufficient, and only Josiah has the ability to create real and lasting reform. In this way, Josiah's reform unites the entirety of the history, rectifying all the wrongs of the monarchy. Josiah's reform removes the cultic sites of Ahaz, Manasseh, Solomon, Jeroboam, and the people of Israel, almost all the players primarily responsible for the majority of problems in the cultic lives of Israel

---

6. While these chapters incorporate extensive pre-Dtr sources (designated by many as the *Auffindungsbericht* and *Reformbericht*), and Dtr clearly borrows from 2 Kings 12 and Jehoash's construction narrative, even to the extent of leaving in details superfluous and irrelevant to the Josiah narrative, the sources are so highly rewritten, rhetoricized, and redacted that it is impossible to reconstruct the original source documents. The reform report, while rewritten to mirror the sins of the kings of Israel and Judah and to correspond with the previous reforms of the good kings of Judah, maintains its list-like character, a vestigial characteristic of the original document, as well as features *wāw*-conjunctive perfect constructions, usually seen as a feature of late Biblical Hebrew. Barrick suggests that while it is "compositionally suspicious," it is not enough evidence to date late on the grammar (W. Boyd Barrick, *The King and the Cemeteries: Toward a New Understanding of Josiah's Reform*, VTSup 88 (Leiden: Brill, 2002), 65. See also Monroe, *Josiah's Reform*, 14–17. One of the ways we see the deuteronomistic adaptation is the point-by-point correspondence between each stage of the reform with other parts of the history. Dtr may have reworked a preexisting royal report of the reforms, but he makes it thoroughly his own. The correspondence with deuteronomistic concerns and direct and indirect connections to acts of other kings makes it clear that the final version of this report thoroughly reflects a deuteronomistic hand with a view of the entire DtrH.

and Judah.[7] The focus on the law and reform, and lack of focus on Josiah himself, function as something of a justification of the history as a whole. DtrH chronicles the history of the monarchy through the lens of cultic fidelity, primarily derived from the deuteronomic code. The book finding and Josiah's reading of the law declare the value of the written law. We know of no other king who acclaims the law in this way, using it as the basis for the covenant with Yahweh. The book finding legitimates the entire deuteronomistic project—the writing down of history, the application of the law, and the value of the written law. This corresponds with the view that Josiah's book-finding account focuses attention on establishing the "religion of the book," a movement that has ancient Near Eastern parallels.[8]

The found scroll has long been associated with an early version of Deuteronomy. Since W. M. L. de Wette's identification of the book (1805), scholars have made the connection between the content of the law of Deuteronomy and the concerns of Josiah's reform.[9] This focus underscores the importance of the book for the deuteronomistic covenant and the deuteronomistic project. The lack of focus on the king and increased interest in the book of the law are all part of Dtr's complete narrative plan.

---

7. Sweeney, *King Josiah of Judah*, 44.

8. Jonathan Ben-Dov, "Some Precedents for the Religion of the Book: Josiah's Book and Ancient Revelatory Literature," in *Constructs of Prophecy in the Former and Latter Prophets and Other Texts*, ed. Lester L. Grabbe and Martti Nissinen (Atlanta: Society of Biblical Literature, 2011), 43–64.

9. Wilhelm Martin Leberecht de Wette, *Dissertatio Critico-exegetica Qua Deuteronomium a Prioribus Pentateuchi Libris Diversum, Alius Cuiusdam Recentioris Auctioris Opus Esse Monstratur* (Jena, 1805). Mordechai Cogan and Hayim Tadmor, *2 Kings: A New Translation*, AB 11 (Garden City, NY: Doubleday, 1988), 294. Monroe, referencing Berry, suggests that perhaps the found scroll is a version of the Holiness Code, claiming that there are insufficient grounds to assume that Josiah's book is Deuteronomy. They are in the minority (Monroe, *Josiah's Reform*, 19).

Josiah and the Davidic Prototype

Josiah is certainly viewed through the Davidic prototype, yet it is surprising, given that the history seems to have been leading up to his arrival (especially 1 Kgs. 13:2), that the character of Josiah is literarily flat in comparison with the character development of other kings. Reticence in the presentation of Josiah as a character may be explained by the nature of typology in general. The goal of the use of a type is to establish a pattern that can be repeated. Similar to Robert Alter's discussion of the use of type-scene motifs in biblical narrative, the use of character typology carries with it all the information that an audience knows about a pattern or motif. In this way, the author does not always need to lay out all of the information because it is implicit by using such a type. Alter suggests that an awareness of conventions helps us read. We recognize patterns of repetition, symmetry, and contrast.[10] In his definition, the "type-scene" demonstrates "certain prominent elements of repetitive compositional pattern[s] . . . that are conscious convention[s]."[11] Alter states that "the biblical authors, counting on their audience's familiarity with the features and function of the type-scene, could merely allude to the type-scene or present a transfigured version of it."[12] Similarly, with the typology of characters, when the author activates any given character type, the audience is already clued in to the convention. When a character is plugged in to the prototypes discussed above, the Davidic and anti-Davidic, the reader already knows a lot about a figure. A king like David is faithful to Yahweh, and a king like Jeroboam is not and worships at and supports noncentralized cult sites. Typology is a helpful tool and results in concision of language on the part of the biblical author.

10. *ABN* 47.
11. *ABN* 50.
12. *ABN* 58.

Similar to type-scenes as Alter states, "What is really interesting is not the schema of convention but what is done in each individual application of the schema to give it a sudden tilt of innovation or even to refashion it radically for the imaginative purposes at hand."[13] It is with this in mind that the audience begins to read the character development of King Josiah. He is squarely set within the Davidic typology, but the narrative does not focus on him as a character. The use of a typological convention allows the reader to know about Josiah, to recognize him as the inheritor of the Davidic literary tradition, and to view him as an adherent of Yahweh's law, while simultaneously shifting the focus away from the character of the king and toward the book of the law and the reform.

The way the typology is applied to Josiah is unlike any other instance in the history. Dtr's insistence that Josiah is the paradigm of the good king is overly emphatic. Like the other good kings, he does what is right in Yahweh's eyes. As are two others, he is like David. But he is the only king to comply with the law of the king (Deut. 17:15-20).[14] As a type, he is pitted against and triumphs

---

13. *ABN* 52.

14. While many scholars attribute the deuteronomic law code to the court of Josiah, there is some question about whether Josiah and his court would really have composed this law that widely limits his power and breaks with ancient Near Eastern and Israelite standard attributions of royal power. The law of the king is not always reflected in DtrH. The law seems to convict the king more than permit authority. It contains five prohibitions about what the king should not do, but includes only one positive duty, to read the Torah every day. It is that same Torah that limits his power. The law of the king denies the king's role in the cult. The scholarly view that suggests that Deuteronomy is promulgated by King Josiah is somewhat problematic given that the role of the king is so limited by the law. Would Josiah be responsible for a law that limits his power? Monroe says that it is doubtful that Josiah would implement the laws of Deuteronomy, implementing a law code "with the express purpose of restricting his own authority. . . . While a limited kingship may be Deuteronomy's prerogative, it is unlikely to have been Josiah's" (Monroe, *Josiah's Reform*, 114). Conversely, Sweeney suggests that the conflict between Dtr and the law of the king is not as problematic and the law does not limit the king's power as much as many scholars contend. "The 'Torah of the King' does not restrict royal authority; it merely defines the conditions by which it may be exercised. It does not compromise the judicial role of the king; rather, it testifies to it by requiring the monarch to write and observe a copy of 'this Torah'—that is, the lawcode that defines the legal system administered of the land" (Sweeney, *King Josiah of Judah*, 162).

over Solomon and Jeroboam; he undoes both of their sins with his reform. He does better than any of the previous reforming kings: Asa, Jehoshaphat, and even Hezekiah. And he celebrates the Passover in a way it has never been celebrated by any king. This portrayal justifies the assertion made in chapter 3 that the Davidic prototype is modeled on the character of Josiah rather than the "historical" David we know from Samuel. There is no other king who can measure up to the paradigm of Josiah.

The development of the prototype, as previously discussed, begins with the introductory regnal formula. The reign of Josiah characteristically starts with this formula. Josiah is the best of the

In order to justify this position, we must consider, more generally, the relationship between Deuteronomy and the Deuteronomistic History. This is particularly pressing in the book of Kings, where the kings and the people are presumably held to a deuteronomic standard, although the law presented in Kings is often very different from Deuteronomy. This also goes back to the original question of "Is there a Deuteronomistic History?" The entire concept of a DtrH relies on an assumption that the history is crafted in relation to the themes and laws expressed in Deuteronomy.

Quite obviously, it seems that DtrH is influenced by Deuteronomy, but Dtr is still willing to reinterpret and reject some of deuteronomic law. Dtr seems to implement deuteronomic law, but also changes it. Knoppers suggests that "the Deuteronomist's recourse to the Deuteronomic law in judging the monarchy is selective. The Deuteronomist does not always define what the 'statutes' (חקים), 'testimonies' (עדות), 'judgments' (משפטים), and 'commandments' (מצות) are, but as most commentators have stressed, their primary reference is cultic. By comparison, the Deuteronomic code contains a wide range of legislation affecting social, economic, cultic, and political aspects of Israelite society" (Gary Knoppers, "Rethinking the Relationship Between Deuteronomy and the Deuteronomistic History: The Case of Kings," *CBQ* 63, no. 3 [2001]: 406). Also, Knoppers describes the relationship between DtrH and the deuteronomic code in this way: "If the Deuteronomist is indebted to and informed by the deuteronomic program, he also undermines it. While the deuteronomic writers engage problems in Israelite history by carefully dispersing powers among a variety of institutions, the Deuteronomist champions the exercise of monarchical power as a resolution to Israel's ills" (Knoppers, "The Deuteronomist and the Deuteronomic Law of the King: A Reexamination of a Relationship," *ZAW* 108, no. 3 [1996]: 334). Similarly, Bernard Levinson suggests that Dtr "actually abrogates Deuteronomy, the very normative standard that he purports to implement" (Bernard Levinson, "The Reconceptualization of Kingship in Deuteronomy and the Deuteronomistic History's Transformation of Torah," *VT* 51, no. 4 [2001]: 526). In this way, DtrH is connected to the law in Deuteronomy, but not necessarily constrained by it. He makes choices to use, change, and reject individual elements of the law. This stance can be reflected back on the specific issues concerning the law of the king, suggesting that Dtr and the characters of his history are not strictly beholden to all the laws of deuteronomic code, but it does not resolve the problem of why Josiah (or his court) would have penned such a law.

best kings. He did הישר בעיני יהוה, "what was right in the eyes of Yahweh," and he was like David. Josiah's comparison to David is more robust than the two others who are also compared positively to him (Asa and Hezekiah). Josiah וילך בכל דרך דוד אביו ולא סר ימין ושמאול, "walked in all the way[s] of David his father. And he did not stray to the right or left" (2 Kgs. 22:2). The resemblance with David, while similar to the other kings compared, is constructed in a unique way. Asa merely does what was right כדוד אביו, "like David," while Hezekiah does what is right ככל אשר עשה דוד אביו, "like all that David did." Josiah is the only one to walk in all the ways of David, parallel to and contrasting those bad kings of Israel who walk in the way of the anti-David, Jeroboam. This is a highly rhetorical collocation, functioning as one of the first indicators that Josiah and his reform are set up to oppose Jeroboam and undo his sin.

Furthermore, the concept of following in David's path establishes a strong connection with the laws of Deuteronomy. Josiah is explicitly set up as an adherent to the deuteronomic law. The phrase "to walk in the way(s) of Yahweh" is used throughout Deuteronomy. It is an expression of covenantal loyalty.[15] As previously discussed, this instruction first appears in Kings in David's deathbed instructions to Solomon; David lays out the criteria for being a good king. He tells Solomon: "Keep the mandates of Yahweh your God, following his ways [ללכת בדרכיו],[16] keeping his statutes and commandments, laws and testimonies, as is written in the instruction of Moses [בתורת משה], so that you will be successful in whatever you do and to whatever you turn" (1 Kgs. 2:3). Being like David and following David's way is following the way of Yahweh (as in 1 Kgs. 3:4). By connecting Josiah with David using these words (as opposed to

---

15. Moshe Weinfeld, *Deuteronomy and the Deuteronomic School* (Winona Lake, IN: Eisenbrauns, 1992), 333–34.

16. Here we have the same use of the root הלך with indirect object, דרך. The possession is of Yahweh, rather than a monarchic prototype.

the other Davidic comparisons), Dtr intrinsically links Josiah and his actions with the stipulations of deuteronomic law and following the ways of Yahweh, while simultaneously contrasting Josiah with Jeroboam and those kings who continue Jeroboam's sin. Furthermore, it is said of Josiah that he did not "stray to the right or left." Josiah is the only king to whom this deuteronomic phrase is applied. This expression also appears in the law of the king in Deut. 17:20 as well as Deut. 5:29; 17:11; and 28:14. The connection with this verse in 1 Kings 2 is made further by the reference to following תורת משה. In another evaluative comment toward the end of 2 Kings 23, Dtr remarks that there was no king before Josiah "who turned back to Yahweh with all his heart and all his soul and all his might, as all the instruction of Moses [תורת משה]" (2 Kgs. 23:25). This is the only instance in the account that the found scroll is referred to as תורת משה (elsewhere ספר התורה, ספר הברית). Josiah's fidelity to the law connects him with Moses and Mosaic law.

The king is charged with reading the law (תורה) every day, following the laws and statutes, and not straying to the right or left. Unlike any previous king, Josiah is the first to follow the mandate of reading the Torah (Deut. 17:18-19). While we are not told whether he did it every day, Josiah is the first and only king we are told read the Torah at all. The introduction to Josiah is a companion to this law in Deuteronomy. Josiah, the paradigm of the good king, fulfills the injunctions made to kings. By using the language of the law of the king, Dtr announces in this regnal introduction that Josiah perfectly exhibits kingly behavior. In the regnal evaluation, Josiah is established as one of the few good kings, one who is like David, surpassing those who are also compared to David. He is clearly set in the Davidic prototype, even contrasted with the antitype, Jeroboam. He exceeds all other kings in his strict adherence to the law of the king. It is not just that Josiah is the idealized king of kings since David and the "cult reformer *par excellence*" who puts others to shame, but also there has been no one like him, since Moses and Joshua; Josiah is the first leader to understand deuteronomic law and put it into application.[17] Josiah's adherence to Deut. 17:19 is a nod to this literary position.

Dtr is focused on demonstrating how a king, like Josiah, should follow the law of Yahweh. The example presented here extends to the entirety of the book of Kings. In relaying the history of the monarchy, Dtr evaluates the kings of Israel and Judah primarily according to their fidelity to the law and the covenant. While the other kings are never given a specific outline of how to behave (like the presentation and reading of a book of the law), they are still held to Dtr's standards. In reading the law, Josiah acclaims the importance of the written law code, promoting its dispersion and weight in Israel. The book-finding account has a similar function.

Additionally, the portrayal of Josiah in the Davidic prototype relies heavily on the connection to Solomon. One way this link is made is by reference to the law of the king. Many scholars have suggested that this law was written specifically against Solomon, citing his accumulation of horses and wives;[18] Solomon was well known to have many of both. But it is not likely that this law was composed during the time or shortly following Solomon's reign, as some scholars contend. If the law were written in response to Solomon's reign, it would suggest that 1 Kings 1–11 predates the deuteronomistic school.[19] Also, in Dtr's Solomon narrative (1 Kings 3–10), Solomon's wealth and prosperity are viewed as rewards from Yahweh (1 Kgs. 3:4-15), not as means for criticism.[20] This is further

17. Hardmeier, "King Josiah," 130.
18. Knoppers, "Rethinking the Relationship," 409; Knoppers, "The Deuteronomist and the Law of the King," 331; Marc Zvi Brettler, "The Structure of 1 Kings 1–11," *JSOT*, no. 49 (1991): 91–93.
19. Knoppers, "The Deuteronomist and the Law of the King," 334.
20. Ibid., 338.

evidenced by the fact that even within the censure of Solomon in 1 Kings 11, he is not condemned for having many wives but for having foreign wives who corrupt his religious practices. Despite this, even though the law is not necessarily a comment against Solomon, it certainly calls him to mind, further highlighting the disparity between Solomon, who violates the prohibitions of the law of the king, and Josiah, who is the only king to fulfill them.

Furthermore, the contrast between Josiah and Solomon is also apparent in Josiah's exploits in purging the cults of Judah. In a final act of reform in the southern kingdom, Josiah sets his sights on the altars of Solomon. The narrative first describes the general action Josiah took against the noncentralized and idolatrous cults of Judah, but Dtr also specifically focuses on Josiah's actions against the cult of Solomon (2 Kgs. 23:13). Rather than just being another undertaking in the list of the reform measures, this act has strong literary ramifications. It is not coincidental that it is included as the final feat in Judah. Undoing the sins of Solomon is another important element of correspondence with other parts of the history, contributing to setting Josiah up as the Davidic prototype. As previously discussed (chap. 3), the portrait of Solomon helps contribute to the development of the Davidic prototype (especially 1 Kings 2–3) and its antitype (1 Kings 11). By countering Solomon's sins of 1 Kings 11, Dtr constructs Josiah in the Davidic prototype, opposing Solomon's portrayal of the antitype. In this way, according to Sweeney, "The narrative concerning the reign of Solomon is especially important in the Josianic DtrH because it points to Solomon as the cause of most of the problems that Josiah must resolve."[21] In destroying Solomon's altars, Josiah removes the sin that split the kingdom and essentially restores the Davidic promise of

---

21. Sweeney, *King Josiah of Judah*, 174.

2 Samuel 7. The correspondence between these two acts (erecting and demolishing the altars) is made clear in the word choice. Josiah removes the altars of Solomon, using the same words as the report of their installation.

> And Solomon went after Ashtaroth the god of the Sidonians, and after Milcom, the abomination of the Ammonites. . . . (7) Then Solomon built a high place to Chemosh, the abomination of Moab, on the mountain which is next to Jerusalem and for Molech the abomination of the Ammonites. (1 Kgs. 11:5, 7)

Solomon's apostasy causes the rift in the kingdom according to Dtr. The reform account reports Josiah's action in almost identical words of condemnation of its institution.

> As for the altars that were on the face of Jerusalem from the right of the mount of destruction upon which Solomon king of Israel built to Ashtaroth abomination of the Sidonians, and to Chemosh abomination of Moab, and to Milcom abomination of the Ammonites, the king defiled [them]. (2 Kgs. 23:13)

By destroying Solomon's high places, Josiah removes the cause of the split of the kingdom, theoretically reuniting Israel and Judah.[22] In this way, Josiah restores the kingdom that was promised to David. Because Solomon's apostasy was the cause of the division of kingdoms, he bears the responsibility for the cultic sins of the North as well. The split affords the opportunity for Jeroboam to set up the competing shrines at Dan and Bethel. The sites and Jeroboam himself lead Israel to sin. Upon its demise, Israel is primarily convicted for following the sins of Jeroboam. In this way, Solomon sets the stage for the Israelite kings' transgressions. Solomon's high places initiate censure of Judean kings. Solomon's actions, resulting in the division

---

22. Gary N. Knoppers, *Two Nations under God: The Deuteronomistic History of Solomon and the Dual Monarchies*, vol. 2, *The Reign of Jeroboam, the Fall of Israel, and the Reign of Josiah*, Harvard Semitic Monographs (Atlanta: Scholars Press, 1994), 245.

of the kingdom, influence the future apostasy of both the northern and southern kings.[23] Only Josiah is able to overturn Solomon's sins. The contrast with Solomon is essential to the portrait of Josiah.

The disparity between Solomon and Josiah in their fulfillment (or lack thereof) of the law of the king continues in a second judgment formula at the end of Josiah's reign. (This is not the standard regnal formula—the introduction or death-and-burial formula.) This evaluation also contributes to the contrast between Josiah and Hezekiah. Josiah is praised for his incomparability, וכמהו לא היה לפניו מלך אשר שב אל יהוה בכל לבבו ובכל נפשו ובכל מאדו ככל תורת משה ואחריו לא קם כמהו, "And like him there was no king before him who turned back to Yahweh with all his heart and all his soul and all his might, as all the instruction of Moses. And after him, no one arose like him" (2 Kgs. 23:25). There is a short list of characters who receive praise for their incomparability. They are Moses (Deut. 34:10), Solomon (1 Kgs. 10:23), and Hezekiah (2 Kgs. 18:5). Also Jeroboam and Ahab are negatively incomparable. While some scholars, including Gary Knoppers,[24] recognize this verse as produced by exilic Dtr[2], I identify it as preexilic Dtr[1]. Knoppers suggests that these "incomparability formulae are one means by which an exilic Deuteronomist highlights the exceptional accomplishments of major figures within his history."[25] He argues that only an author who knew the kings following Josiah would be able to make a comparison to them.[26] This is not necessary. It is possible for the author to make a hyperbolic statement proclaiming Josiah's unmatched greatness and not intend it literally, while also not having a crystal-ball's view into the future. An author could

---

23. Sweeney, *King Josiah of Judah*, 94.
24. Gary N. Knoppers, "'There Was None Like Him': Incomparability in the Books of Kings," *CBQ* 54, no. 3 (1992): 411–31; Knoppers, *Reign of Jeroboam*, 218.
25. Knoppers, "There Was None Like Him," 411.
26. Knoppers, *Reign of Jeroboam*, 219.

make this claim at the time of Josiah without knowing the fate of the subsequent kings. Similarly, existence of other statements of incomparability, specifically the one about Hezekiah, can be explained, as Iain Provan suggests, by dating. The incomparability statement about Hezekiah predates the Josianic edition, and was the end of an earlier redaction.[27] The Josianic Dtr could be imitating this earlier author's style and replacing Hezekiah with Josiah as the greatest of kings. Similarly, in 1 Kgs. 14:9, Jeroboam is said to have "done worse than all who came before [him]." This too is a literary/ nonliteral comparison. In the case of Jeroboam's negative incomparability, Knoppers argues that the statement is not anachronistic but highlights Jeroboam's "unparalleled apostasy."[28] The same should be said here for Josiah's unparalleled preeminence.

Part of the cause for debate about the provenance of verse 25 may be the interruption by verses 26 and 27 of the closing formula. These verses, which announce that Josiah's attempts to quell Yahweh's wrath are unsuccessful and that Yahweh will reject the temple, Jerusalem, and Judah are undeniably exilic. Verses 26 and 27 are surrounded by the closing statements of Josiah's reign and were inserted here in an exilic context, by a later redactor (Dtr^2 represented by the underlined font):

And like him there was no king before him who turned back to Yahweh with all his heart and all his soul and all his might, as all the instruction of Moses. And after him, no one arose like him. (26) But Yahweh did not turn from his great wrath which burned against Judah, against all the things by which Manasseh caused him to anger. (27) And Yahweh said, "Also Judah I will remove from my sight as I removed Israel. And I will reject this city, which I have chosen, Jerusalem and the house where I said, 'My name will be there.'" (28)

27. Iain Provan, *Hezekiah and the Books of Kings: A Contribution to the Debate about the Composition of the Deuteronomistic History* (Berlin: de Gruyter, 1988), 121, 153.
28. Knoppers, *Reign of Jeroboam*, 106.

> **And the remainder of the deeds of Josiah and all that he did, are they not written in the book of the annals of the kings of Judah?**

The exilic insertion of verses 26 and 27 into the praise for Josiah, with other exilic insertions, transforms the narrative. Unequivocally, Nelson asserts that "there is a definite change in authors between 25a and 26-27."[29] Even this great king is unable to overturn Yahweh's wrath. The king presented in the Davidic prototype is unable to restore the Davidic promise.

Similarly, the ordering of the conclusion of the Josiah narrative is unusual. Unlike any other king, the summation of Josiah's reign and reference to the annalistic sources (vv. 25 and 28) appears before the report of his death. In creating this unconventional ordering, Dtr attempts to focus on the greatness of Josiah and his reign. For a brief moment, Dtr tries to ignore the historical fate of Josiah, which denies the truth of much of deuteronomistic theology and the expected rewards for fidelity to the law. By setting the death report after the closing formula, Dtr wants to end the account with his statement of incomparability. It is also possible that the closing was written before Josiah's death. So sure of Josiah's fate to live long and die peacefully, Dtr completed his history before Josiah's death, and the death report is only added at the end of the account, as many have suggested as an embarrassed addendum.[30] Ending the Josiah account originally with the closing formula before his death may serve as an argument in favor of a preexilic dating. Otherwise, if the entirety of verses 25–28 were a postexilic addition, why wouldn't it appear following Josiah's death in verses 29 and 30? It would be more conventional for the closing evaluation and reference to the annals to be connected with the DBF.

---

29. Richard D. Nelson, *The Double Redaction of the Deuteronomistic History* (Sheffield: JSOT Press, 1981), 84.
30. Stanley Brice Frost, "The Death of Josiah: A Conspiracy of Silence," *JBL* 87, no. 4 (1968): 371.

It is clear from the definitively exilic insertion and unconventional ordering that something redactionally suspicious occurs in these verses, leaving us, as Baruch Halpern and David Vanderhooft describe, in a "boggy mire of uncertainty."[31] It is likely that we will never definitively resolve the compositional provenance of verses 25 and 28, but it still seems to make the most sense that these verses are preexilic and were part of the Josianic edition. Verses 26 and 27 are awkwardly inserted into the closing verses, and Josiah's death is appended to the closing. Had verses 25-30 been composed or even redacted at one time, they would not seem so clumsily constructed. And while Halpern and Vanderhooft assert that kings who die violently have variation in their DBF,[32] Josiah's burial maintains part of the standard DBF (*qbr* + place), but lacks the variation of the other violent deaths. Also, Josiah's notice is extremely brief, "signaling a significant truncation of the formula."[33] Halpern and Vanderhooft argue that the significant change in DBF after Hezekiah gives support for a Hezekian first edition, and therefore a post-Hezekian redactor is responsible, creating variation in the praise for Josiah and his closing formula. At best, we are left with a difficult situation to determine, but one in which there is a redactional gray area that may not be resolved. Regardless, the incomparability formula sets Josiah in the company of Moses, Solomon, and Hezekiah, and in contrast with Jeroboam. And even if one contends that it is thoroughly exilic (which I do not), this grouping together of figures would predate the statement of incomparability.

Similarly, just as the contrast with Solomon contributes to the portrait of Josiah's reform, so too does a comparison between the reforms of Josiah and Hezekiah promote Josiah over Hezekiah. Dtr

---

31. Baruch Halpern and David S. Vanderhooft, "The Editions of Kings in the 7th–6th Centuries BCE," *HUCA* 62 (1991): 179.
32. Ibid., 184.
33. Ibid., 194, 195.

downplays Hezekiah's reform in order to elevate Josiah's above it. Dtr could not let Hezekiah's comment of incomparability stand without adding a comment about Josiah. While Knoppers argues that, contemporaneously composed, the two comments are not competing (that Hezekiah is incomparable in his trust in Yahweh and Josiah is incomparable in his unparalleled reforms),[34] there is no question that the similarity of expression and vocabulary demands comparison and that the two statements be read together. Dtr's statement of incomparability in 2 Kgs. 23:25 positions Josiah as the most loyal of all kings. This verse corresponds with Deut. 6:5: "Love Yahweh your God with all your heart, all your soul, and all your might." This injunction is thoroughly deuteronomistic. It is repeated verbatim in the praise for Josiah, and Josiah is the only person about whom this is said.

As previously discussed, the directing of one's לב is a profession of covenant loyalty. Not only was all of Josiah's heart (בכל לבבו) with Yahweh, but also all his soul and all his might. (See chap. 3 for more on this covenant loyalty.) Loyalty of heart and soul is required for the success of the Davidic dynasty, as seen in David's charge to Solomon: "If your sons are careful in their way to walk before me faithfully with all their heart and with all their soul [בכל לבבם ובכל נפשם], no one will be cut off from the throne of Israel" (1 Kgs. 2:3). Here, David mentions only heart and soul, but not might. Josiah complies but goes further in his fidelity. Only Josiah (not even David) completely fulfills the injunction of Deut. 6:5.

Through these few verses it is clear to see how Dtr activates the Davidic prototype. The use of key phrases and terms is enough to set up Josiah in the model of David and to elevate him beyond all kings: past, present, and future. This verse is made as an addition to the closing regnal formula, which concludes in verse 28. This further

---

34. Knoppers, "There Was None Like Him," 411–31.

suggests that Josiah is idealized in these chapters as the greatest of all Davidic kings, one who walks in the ways of David. Josiah is also set up in the model of Moses as in 2 Kgs. 22:2 and 23:25. Josiah's actions highlight the shortcomings of other kings, namely, Ahaz, Manasseh, Jeroboam, Solomon—and Hezekiah.[35]

Josiah, a Reformer among Reformers?

Establishing Josiah's superiority over the other kings is done primarily through the details of his reform. Josiah's reform is unparalleled in its extent and correspondence with deuteronomic law. It focuses on deuteronomistic principles—fidelity to the law, disavowing other gods, and first and foremost, centralization of the cult to the temple in Jerusalem. Josiah ensures that other sites, both Yahwistic and idolatrous, will be permanently out of commission. He sets about cleaning up not only Judah but also the defunct kingdom of Israel, removing all aspects of idolatry and all noncentralized shrines, and undoing the sins of previous kings. He hits the cult of Jeroboam hard, fulfilling the prophecy of the man of God from Judah, destroying the altar at Bethel, and burning human bones on it. He defiles and completely destroys the locations and accoutrements of these cults, preempting any resurrections of idolatrous and/or noncentralized cults.

Josiah's reform in 2 Kings 23 is broken into several parts. The first part includes the public reading of the law and reaffirming the covenant between Yahweh and the people (vv. 1-3). Then Josiah cleans up Judah, removing idolatrous practices from the temple and outside Jerusalem (vv. 4-14). He then purges Israel, fulfilling the prophecy of the man of God from Judah (vv. 15-20). Finally, Josiah institutes the celebration of the Passover (vv. 21-23). In each element

---

35. Sweeney, *King Josiah of Judah*, 105.

of Josiah's reform, Dtr both connects to individual laws of the deuteronomic code and sets up Josiah as a foil to the bad kings, systematically undoing the specific sins of the kings of Israel and Judah and superseding the good kings. Josiah improves on all previous efforts of reform, outdoing the other kings. In this way, Josiah is further portrayed through the use of the Davidic prototype, culminating with the celebration of Passover, which depicts him as the counterpart not only of David but also of Moses and Joshua.

Josiah's reform is motivated by deuteronomistic concerns. In order to centralize the cult of Yahweh, Deut. 12:2-6 requires the destruction of local shrines, the burning of 'ăšērîm and maṣṣēbôt. Deuteronomy 6:4-5 and elsewhere demand complete loyalty to and worship of Yahweh alone. Josiah eliminates the worship of Baal and Asherah. The importance of the law, obedience to Yahweh and the law, and the covenant based on law are enumerated in Deut. 26:16-19. These important tenets of the deuteronomistic program, especially centralization of the cult, represent a break with previous Israelite religion. Even the commandment that there is only one God is something of an innovation. While throughout Israelite history only the worship of one God was permitted, Yahweh was the God of gods, essentially admitting the existence of other, albeit lesser, gods (e.g., Exod. 15:11; 18:11; 22:19; 23:13, 24).

Josiah mounts a comprehensive reform that reestablishes the covenant between Yahweh and the people. This raises the observance of the law—Yahweh's commandments, testimonies, and laws (2 Kgs. 23:3)—to the highest priority. In making this covenant, the people take an oath of loyalty, committing themselves with their heart and soul (similar, as above) to keep the covenant as prescribed by the scroll. The language of the covenant account is thoroughly deuteronomistic. Josiah gathers the people, reads the scroll, and facilitates the covenant with Yahweh:

And the king sent and all the elders[36] of Judah and Jerusalem assembled before him. (2) And the king went up to the house of Yahweh and all the men of Judah and all the inhabitants of Jerusalem with him and the priests and the prophets and all the people, from the young to the old, and he read to their ears all the words of the scroll of the covenant [ספר הברית] found in the house of Yahweh. (3) And the king stood by the pillar [cf. 2 Kgs. 11:14] and cut the covenant before Yahweh, to follow Yahweh and to observe his commandments and his testimonies and his laws with all [their] heart and all [their] soul, to establish the words of this covenant prescribed in this scroll. And all the people stood in the covenant. (2 Kgs. 23:1-3)

According to the deuteronomistic expression of covenant loyalty articulated here, the people should follow the laws with all their heart and all their soul, corresponding to Deuteronomy 6 and elsewhere. The narrator explicitly states that this covenant is a direct response to the finding of the scroll: "To establish the words of this covenant prescribed in this scroll" (v. 3). The terms and language of the covenant contribute to the identification of the scroll with Deuteronomy.

There is only one other place in Kings where we see a similar covenant. Following Jehoiada's successful coup, overthrowing the queen Athaliah in 2 Kings 11, the priest Jehoiada renews the covenant with Yahweh and starts a small reform against Baal.

Then Jehoiada made a covenant between Yahweh and the king and the people to be a nation to Yahweh and between the king and the people. Then all the people of the land came to the house of Baal and they tore down its altars and its statues they broke into pieces. And they killed Matan, the priest of Baal, before the altars and the priest set guards over the house of Yahweh. (2 Kgs. 11:17-18)

---

36. Elders are important in Deuteronomy. This may be an indicator that it belongs to Dtr; cf. 1 Sam. 8:4: elders ask Samuel to appoint a king (Erik Eynikel, *The Reform of King Josiah and the Composition of the Deuteronomistic History* [Leiden: Brill, 1995], 162–63).

Jehoiada's covenant is the first covenant of this sort in the history of the monarchy.[37] While Josiah's covenant is established in a similar way, there is a difference in the content of the covenants. Jehoiada's covenant is not specific, while Josiah's corresponds to the law in the scroll. While Jehoiada's covenant and reforms precede Josiah's, they appear as inferior. The covenant is not specific, and the reform is limited to removing the temple of Baal in Jerusalem and killing the priest of Baal. It does not deal with centralization. While praiseworthy, the purge of Baal is either incomplete or short-lived. Josiah also attacks the cult of Baal in Judah. Jehoiada, a priest and not a king, puts these measures into effect, but he is neither praised nor evaluated by the historian. Instead, Josiah takes on similar but greater measures and is given the highest praise. In this way, the narrative is set up to present the acts of Josiah as eclipsing and surpassing even the positive acts of earlier figures in the history. This also highlights the importance of the scroll of the law. Josiah's covenant is based on the written word. Joshua in Josh. 8:30-35 also celebrates a covenant renewal, connecting the portraits of Josiah and Joshua.[38] Just as Josiah's covenant is presented as better than Jehoiada's, throughout the history of the monarchy, when a figure mounts a reform, Dtr makes sure that Josiah's measures supersede those of the others.

Following the covenant, Josiah's first acts of reform are to remove the idolatrous cults of Baal and Asherah from Judah.[39] His acts closely

---

37. Cogan and Tadmor, *2 Kings*, 132.

38. Richard D. Nelson, "Josiah in the Book of Joshua," *JBL* 100, no. 4 (1981): 532.

39. For more on the role of Asherah in Israelite worship, see Judith M. Hadley, *The Cult of Asherah in Ancient Israel and Judah: Evidence for a Hebrew Goddess* (Cambridge: Cambridge University Press, 2000); Hadley, "Yahweh and 'His Asherah': Archaeological and Textual Evidence for the Cult of the Goddess," in *Ein Gott Allein?: JHWH-Verehrung Und Biblischer Monotheismus Im Kontext Der Israelitischen Und Altorientalischen Religionsgeschichte*, ed. Walter Dietrich and Martin A. Klopfenstein OBO 139 (Fribourg: Universitätsverlag, 1994), 235–68; Ziony Zevit, *The Religions of Ancient Israel: A Synthesis of Parallactic Approaches* (New York: Continuum,

correspond with the injunction in Deut. 12:3. The worship of Baal, 'ăšērîm, and the setting up of maṣṣēbôt are widespread in Israel and Judah. The cult of Asherah is brought into Israel by Ahab (1 Kgs. 16:33) and is mentioned again as persisting in the reign of Jehoahaz (2 Kgs. 13:6). Even though in Israel, Jehoram (2 Kgs. 3:2) and Jehu (2 Kgs. 10:18-28) both try to wipe out the worship of Baal, it is reestablished by Ahab. In Judah, there was also a tradition of reform against the maṣṣēbôt and 'ăšērîm. Asa removed the idols, cut down Asherah, and burned them in the Kidron Valley (1 Kgs. 15:12). Similarly, Jehoiada kills the priest of Baal and destroys the altar and images and the temple of Baal (2 Kgs. 11:17-20). Hezekiah also demolishes the maṣṣēbôt and cuts down the Asherah (although we do not have a report that they were rebuilt after Asa's and Jehoiada's reforms, 2 Kgs. 19:4). But Manasseh makes an Asherah like Ahab and builds the altar for Baal and the host of heaven (2 Kgs. 21:3).[40] Josiah then removes the Asherah from the temple and, like Asa, burns it in the Kidron Valley (2 Kgs. 23:6). He also destroys the maṣṣēbôt and cuts down the 'ăšērîm (2 Kgs. 23:14). Josiah completely eliminates Baal worship from Judah. He destroys Manasseh's altars (2 Kgs. 23:12). He removes all the implements of Baal, Asherah, and the host of heaven (2 Kgs. 23:4). And he does away with the idolatrous priests who sacrificed to Baal and the host of heaven (2 Kgs. 23:5).

Josiah seeks not only to remove the idolatrous cults but also to undo the acts of the kings of Judah (v. 5). His position of reversing and surpassing all kings is cemented with these actions. The destruction of the cults is complete. He burns the vessels, carrying the ashes far away. He removes the priests, ensuring that worship cannot

---

2003); Mark Smith, *The Early History of God: Yahweh and the Other Deities in Ancient Israel* (Grand Rapids: Eerdmans, 2002).

40. Baal worship in the South begins with Manasseh. Solomon does not worship Baal. There is no mention of כלים of Baal elsewhere in DtrH. Eynikel suggests this indicates that this chapter has its own redactor, but identifies it as Dtr[1] (Eynikel, *Reform of King Josiah*, 198, 199).

resume, even in secret. He removes the Asherah that Manasseh erected in the temple (v. 7). He also thoroughly eliminates any remnant of Asherah, burning it, crushing it to dust, and dispersing the dust (v. 6).

Josiah's attacks on the foreign cults of Judah are as follows:

> Then the king commanded Hilkiah the high priest, the deputy priests and the doorkeepers to remove from the palace of Yahweh all the vessels made for Baal, Asherah, and all the host of heaven. And he burned them outside Jerusalem, on the terraces of the Kidron, and carried their ashes to Bethel. (5) Then he removed the idolatrous priests who the kings of Judah had set up to offer[41] sacrifices at the high places in the cities of Judah and around Jerusalem, the ones offering to Baal, to the sun, the moon, and the constellations and all the host of heaven. (6) He removed the Asherah from the house of Yahweh, from [to] outside Jerusalem, to the Wadi Kidron, and he burned it in Wadi Kidron and crushed [it] to dust, and threw the dust on the grave of the common people. (2 Kgs. 23:4-6)

The language of destruction is repeated throughout this chapter and in other places in the history—the burning (שרף), crushing (דקק), and throwing (שלך). Josiah does this to Asherah and to the altar at Bethel (v. 15). Deuteronomy 12:3 calls for the destruction of the 'ăšērîm and the maṣṣēbôt. The same language of that injunction is used here, creating an intrinsic intertextual relationship between the law and Josiah's fulfillment of it. These acts follow the prescription of Deut. 12:3: "And you shall tear down your altars and break apart their maṣṣēbôt and their 'ăšērîm, you shall burn with fire and hew down the statues of their gods and you will remove their name from this place." Similarly, Moses does the same thing to the golden calf in Deut. 9:21: את העגל לקחתי ואשרף אתו באש ואכת אתו טחון היטב עד אשר דק לעפר ואשלך את עפרו, "I took the calf and I *burned* it with fire and I *crushed* it, grinding it thoroughly until it was *crushed* into dust

---

41. Reading plural with LXX, ויקטרו for ויקטר in MT.

and I *threw* the dust [into the wadi]." These actions are thoroughly deuteronomistic.[42]

After tackling the idolatrous sites of Judah, Josiah destroys the altars of Solomon in Jerusalem and the altar of Jeroboam in Bethel. The attack on the local cult sites of Israel and Judah, especially the golden calf of Jeroboam in Bethel, demonstrates the importance of centralization and the importance of the deuteronomistic program in action. Despite all of the theologically motivated connections, the entire reform can be seen through a literary lens, literarily opposing Josiah to the earlier kings of Israel and Judah. Josiah systematically removes the cult of Jeroboam, further eliminating the cultic separation between north and south, completing the reunification of the Davidic kingdom: "And also the altar which is in Bethel, the high place which Jeroboam son of Nabat who caused Israel to sin made, even that altar and the high place, he tore down and he burned the high place, he crushed it to dust and he burned Asherah" (2 Kgs. 23:15).

---

42. A further indication of the uniquely deuteronomistic character of the vocabulary is clear in a comparison of the golden calf episodes in Deuteronomy 9 and Exodus 32. In Exodus 32, when destroying the golden calf, the text expresses similar actions but utilizes a somewhat different vocabulary and syntax: ויקח את העגל אשר עשו וישרף באש ויטחן עד אשר דק ויזר על פני המים וישק את בני ישראל, "And he took the calf which they made and he burned it with fire and he ground it to powder and he scattered it in water and made the children of Israel drink [it]" (Exod. 32:20). Instead of שׁלך, Exodus uses זרה. Instead of a verb of דקק, Exodus uses טחן with a nominal form of דק. In deuteronomistic terms, by destroying the altars of Baal and Asherah, Josiah acts like none other than the great Moses.   Monroe argues that the acts of burning, beating, scattering, casting of dust, and defiling are common in Priestly texts (Leviticus and Numbers), not Deuteronomy and deuteronomistic texts, and are representative of priestly purification rituals (Monroe, *Josiah's Reform*, 24). This does not take into account the differences we see in the report of the golden calf event in Exodus 32 and Deuteronomy 9, and the unique correspondences between Deuteronomy 9; 12; and 2 Kings 23.   As a side note, in verse 12 Josiah destroys the altars on the roof, of the upper chamber of Ahaz and the altars of Manasseh in the courtyard of the temple. Here Josiah "tore down and threw their dust into the Wadi Kidron," נתץ המלך וירצם משם והשליך את עפרם אל נחל קדרון. There is no crushing into dust, but the dust is thrown. There is no burning, just tearing. The sequence and vocabulary are different here and may be an indicator that this verse derives from a later hand who imprecisely attempted to imitate the expressions of Dtr[1].

Parallel to the dedication of Jeroboam's calves in 1 Kings 12, Josiah's reform focuses on Bethel (rather than also on Dan). With the destruction of the northern cult, the entire kingdom (north and south) comes under the religious auspices of the Jerusalem temple. This is a curious act. The northern kingdom had been destroyed one hundred years previously and had fallen under foreign dominion, but Josiah takes it upon himself to clean up Israel's cult in addition to Judah's (2 Kgs. 23:4-14). Was he really concerned that those who remained in Israel continued in the sins of Jeroboam? Was he anxious about the foreign people installed in Samaria who even after being taught how to properly worship Yahweh continued to also worship at the high places and their own gods (2 Kgs. 17:26-41)? Would the king of Judah really have had the jurisdiction to go into a foreign kingdom and clean up its religious sites?[43] The prospect of this may be possible politically because of the breakdown of power of the Assyrian Empire, but this is beside the point.[44] Similarly, Barrick states that there is no historical claim to Josiah's purge of the "Samaria" territory of the defunct northern kingdom.[45] Consideration of the actual likelihood and lack of pragmatic necessity in this act highlights its literary value. Similar to destroying Solomon's high places, in demolishing the shrine at Bethel and the high places throughout the North, Josiah reunites Israel and Judah, restoring the Davidic promise.[46] Taken in connection with the complex construction of the

---

43. Knoppers, *Reign of Jeroboam*, 213.

44. This cultic reach, while politically plausible, is likely an artifact of Dtr. The archaeological evidence does not support the historicity of Josiah's reform. For more, see Lisbeth Fried, "The High Places (Bāmôt) and the Reforms of Hezekiah and Josiah: An Archaeological Investigation," *JAOS* 122, no. 3 (2002): 437–65; Christoph Uehlinger, "Was There a Cult Reform Under King Josiah? The Case for a Well-Grounded Minimum," in Grabbe, *Good Kings and Bad Kings*, 279–316.

45. Barrick, *The King and the Cemeteries*, 36.

46. Frost, "Death of Josiah," 370.

Davidic prototype, Josiah's act is even more significant—Dtr's portrait of Josiah is the embodiment of David and the anti-Jeroboam.

The Josiah-Jeroboam opposition is further emphasized in the overturning of the sins of Jeroboam as the fulfillment of the prophecies made against him, highlighting the importance of the prophecy-fulfillment schema as an essential element of Dtr's historiographical poetics. After tearing down the altar at Bethel, Josiah fulfills the word of the man of God from Judah spoken at the dedication of the same altar. He also legitimates the proclamation of the old prophet of Bethel as well.

> When Josiah turned and saw the graves that were on the hill, he sent and took the bones from the graves and he burned [them] on the altar and he defiled it according to the word of Yahweh foretold by the man of God, who has foretold these things. (17) And he said, "What is that grave marker that I see?" And the men of the city said to him, "The grave of a man of God who came from Judah. He foretold these things which you did upon the altar [at] Bethel." (18) And he said, "Leave him, let no man disturb his bones." And they left his bones and the bones of the prophet, who came from Samaria.[47] (19) And also [נגב] all the shrines of the high places which are in the cities of Samaria, which the kings of Israel had made to anger [Yahweh], Josiah tore down and he did to them just as he had done in Bethel. (20) And he sacrificed all the priests of the high places, who were there on the altars, and he burned the human bones on them. Then he returned to Jerusalem. (2 Kgs. 23:16-20)

This report is the fulfillment of the prophecy of the man of God. As prophesied in 1 Kings 13, Josiah does indeed burn human bones on the altar at Bethel, permanently defiling it. Josiah's actions in verses 15 and 16 directly correspond to the words of the man of God, creating a clear example of the prophecy-fulfillment schema that structures DtrH. Just as the man of God predicts in 1 Kgs. 13:2, such is done: "And he called out against the altar by the word of Yahweh. And he

---

47. In 1 Kings 13, the old prophet came from Bethel, not Samaria.

said: 'O Altar, Altar, thus says Yahweh, "Behold, a son will be born to the house of David, Josiah by name, and he will sacrifice upon you the priests of the high places, the ones making offerings upon you, and human bones will be burned upon you."'" In case the connection was lost on the reader, the direct discourse between King Josiah and the townspeople makes the association even clearer. Josiah asks for identification of the graves on the hill. In response, the men tell Josiah that it is the grave of the man of God "who foretold these things which you did upon the altar at Bethel."

As the old prophet from Bethel (here, Samaria) predicted, Josiah does not disturb the bones of the man of God. The old prophet was shrewd to throw his lot in with the man of God. In sparing the bones of the man of God, the bones of the old prophet are left in peace. The fulfillment of the old prophet's prediction further confirms the value of the prophecy of the man of God. It is clear that these verses were composed in conjunction with the events and composition of 1 Kings 13.

Further correspondence with the prophecy of the man of God continues in verses 19 and 20. The prophecy of the man of God is extended to apply to the whole of Israel. Josiah tears down the high places of the North and sacrifices the priests of those high places, burning their bones on the altars. He not only counteracts the sins of Jeroboam (v. 15) but also overturns the continued sins of those kings of Israel who follow the sins of Jeroboam (v. 19). In his role as the Davidic prototype and the opposition to the antitype, Josiah undoes the sins of the bad kings, renewing the Davidic promise, eliminating the noncentralized shrines and removing the illegitimate priests.

Contrasting Josiah with the evil acts of Solomon and Jeroboam is not the only way Dtr uses Josiah's acts of reform to further elevate him over the other kings as well as successfully setting Josiah up as the Davidic prototype. In addition to the statement of incomparability that pits Josiah against Hezekiah, they are further compared in their acts of reform. In the reform report, between the very specific descriptions of the destruction of the altars of Solomon (v. 13) and those of Jeroboam (v. 15), a general and vague verse appears: "And he broke the *maṣṣēbôt* and cut down the *'ăšērîm* and filled their places with human bones" (v. 14). The verse does not specify whether this act against the *maṣṣēbôt* and *'ăšērîm* refers to the North or to the South or to both. Josiah has already removed the Asherah from the temple (v. 6) and torn down the houses of the *qĕdēšîm*, which (only in this context) have some connection to the cult of Asherah (v. 7). In both Israel and Judah, worship of Baal and Asherah is prevalent.

The lack of specific location in this act of removing the *maṣṣēbôt* and *'ăšērîm* may be intended to indicate that it was included to call to mind (and denigrate) the reform of King Hezekiah, the only other reformer who receives unqualified praise. Hezekiah, like Josiah, is said to be like David, doing what is right in Yahweh's eyes, ככל אשר עשה דוד אביו, "like all that David his father did" (2 Kgs. 18:3). While Hezekiah's reform is significant, it is only recounted by Dtr in one verse in the regnal formula at the beginning of his reign: "It was he [הוא] who removed the high places and he broke the *maṣṣēbôt* and cut down the Asherah and smashed the bronze serpent that Moses made, for until those days Israel was sacrificing to it (all verbs perfects) and it was called[48] Nehustan" (2 Kgs. 18:4). Through the syntax, it is clear that the report of reform is part of the judgment formula rather than an account of Hezekiah's actions in narrative time, similar to that of Josiah's reform report. All of the verbs, until the end of the verse, are perfect forms. This demonstrates simultaneous action, even an aside, rather than the normal narrative syntax of *wāw*-conversive verbs, which actively move along the plot. Instead of an account that

---

48. Literally, "he called it." This is the only *wāw*-conversive form in the verse.

includes "real-time" action, reporting Hezekiah's deeds, the reform is part of the judgment evaluation.

The verse focuses on Hezekiah, illustrated by the fronting of the subject and the inclusion of the unnecessary third-person masculine singular pronoun. This terse account detracts from the significance and importance of Hezekiah's acts. Hezekiah attacks the high places, reinforcing the doctrine of centralization. He removes the cultic objects of syncretism, the Asherah and *maṣṣēbôt*, and he removes the icon erected by the great Moses. Presumably, it stood for half a millennium before anyone deigned to remove it. Most certainly the worship of the Nehustan did not begin at the time of Hezekiah. We have no reason to assume that Hezekiah's efforts toward reform were not genuine and attempted to be effective, but the outcome is short-lived and literarily overshadowed. Within one generation, Hezekiah's own son Manasseh rebuilds the high places and the Asherah (2 Kgs. 21:3). Manasseh undermines Hezekiah's cult reform. Minimizing Hezekiah's reform report is an intentional strategy by Dtr to lessen Hezekiah's reform.[49] (This short report is in stark contrast with the extensive account of Hezekiah's reform in 2 Chronicles 29–31.)

The necessity for Josiah to repeat the same actions undercuts the effect of Hezekiah's reform and demonstrates that Josiah was an even greater reformer and king than Hezekiah, who must have been well known as a reformer.[50] Josiah's act of removing (again) the Asherah

---

49. Nelson, "Josiah in the Book of Joshua," 536.

50. Reading between the lines, it is clear that Dtr has a problem with giving Hezekiah's reform its due. Yet, if, as it seems in Dtr's mind, reporting on a significant reform like Hezekiah's detracts from the greatness and uniqueness of Josiah's reform, why does the Josianic Dtr even include it? Hezekiah's reign is filled with many other events that the reform could have been left out. But this is not Dtr's modus operandi; this does not reflect his historiographical poetics. Dtr includes the reform of Hezekiah because it must have been well known and could have been included in his source material. Some scholars, including Provan, view the reign of Hezekiah, his reform, and the statement of his incomparability (2 Kgs. 18:5) as the climax of a first edition of the history written during or shortly after the reign of Hezekiah (Provan, *Hezekiah*). Provan views the *bāmôt* theme as a pervasive and framing theme throughout the book, which culminates in the reign of Hezekiah and his destruction of the high places. Hezekiah removes the sin of

and the *maṣṣēbôt* in 2 Kings 23:14 is expressed by using the same verbs as the Hezekiah account: ‏ושבר את המצבות ויכרת את האשרים‏ ‏וימלא את מקומם עצמות אדם‏, "And he broke the *maṣṣēbôt* and cut down the *'ăšērîm* and filled their places with human bones." This compares with the Hezekiah account in 2 Kgs. 18:4: ‏ושבר את‏ ‏המצבות וכרת את האשרה‏, "And he broke the *maṣṣēbôt* and cut down the Asherah [sg.]." The word choice makes clear that Josiah is literally repeating the same actions.[51] The necessity of this deems Hezekiah's reform unsuccessful.

Another literary indication that Dtr found Hezekiah's reform insufficient is the focus on Ahaz's altars in 2 Kgs. 23:12: "As for the altars which were on the roof, the upper chamber of Ahaz, which the kings of Judah had made, and the altars which Manasseh made in the two courtyards of the house of Yahweh, the king tore down. And he hastily[52] tore down and threw their dust into the Wadi Kidron." While the comment about Manasseh's altars may have been added by Dtr[2], the beginning of the verse may be preexilic. It is somewhat surprising that Dtr specifically mentions Ahaz and his sins here. The only other kings named in the reform report are Solomon, Jeroboam, and Manasseh, the prototypical kings whose cultic transgressions have long-term effects on the history of Israel and Judah. Ahaz is never previously included in this category. (Ahaz seems worse than most of the bad kings, but literarily is never afforded prototype status.) Instead, Ahaz's altars are mentioned as a backhanded jab at Hezekiah's reform. Ahaz's reign immediately precedes Hezekiah's; the altars stood at the time of Hezekiah's reform, but he leaves them standing. The message conveyed from this is: "Good thing Josiah

Jeroboam, namely, the high places, but not explicitly Dan and Bethel. Literarily, Josiah must both do and outdo the righteous acts of Hezekiah and his reform. Hezekiah removes the high places; Josiah needs to burn Bethel, fulfilling the prophecy of the man of God.

51. This is also similar vocabulary to the injunction in Deut. 12:3.

52. ‏וירצם משם‏ for ‏וירץ משם‏. Loss of ‏מ‏ from haplography (Cogan and Tadmor, *2 Kings*, 289).

arrived to clean up the wrongdoing of the kings of Judah, even the reformers." The destruction of the Bethel altar further cements Josiah's position. Only Josiah, the greatest of all the kings, has the ability to return Israel to the "son of Jesse." All other reforms, literarily, pale in comparison.

A final intertextual association that illustrates how Josiah's reform and Josiah himself supersede all other kings is the removal of the *qĕdēšîm* ("cult prostitutes"). The *qĕdēšîm* have been the target of reforms by earlier Judean kings, even ones praised for their rightness. The *qĕdēšîm* are mentioned four times in DtrH. *Qĕdēšîm* and cult prostitution seems to be a southern problem and is not listed among the sins of the North. Josiah's destruction of the houses of the *qĕdēšîm* demonstrates, as Erik Eynikel suggests, a "continuity and tension with the previous texts."[53] The first reference to the *qĕdēšîm* is in the reign of Rehoboam (1 Kgs. 14:24). Judah is said to do evil in the eyes of Yahweh, building high places throughout the land. At that time there were also "*qĕdēšîm* in the land." The prohibition against *qĕdēšîm* appears in Deuteronomy 23:18: "None of the daughters of Israel shall be a *qĕdēšāh*; none of the sons of Israel shall be a *qādēš*."

Asa is the first of three kings who attempts to remove the *qĕdēšîm*. He appears to be the first cult reformer of the southern kingdom and is the first of the kings to be given a positive evaluation (see chap. 3). He gets rid of the *qĕdēšîm*, removes the idols, and deposes his mother from the position of queen mother because she worships Asherah (1 Kgs. 15:12). Even though Asa removes the *qĕdēšîm* from the land, they persist, and Asa's son Jehoshaphat also strikes against them, as it says in 1 Kgs. 22:47, "The remnant of the *qĕdēšîm* who remained from the days of Asa his father, he exterminated from the land." Clearly, Asa's reform was incomplete in eradicating the existence of

---

53. Eynikel, *Reform of King Josiah*, 331.

the *qĕdēšîm* from the land.[54] There seem to be *qĕdēšîm* in existence long past the time of Asa. And while Jehoshaphat is credited with removing the remnant, something continues against which Josiah strikes.

Josiah's reform destroys the houses of the *qĕdēšîm*: "He tore down the houses of the *qĕdēšîm* who were in the house of Yahweh, where women weave coverings for Asherah" (2 Kgs. 23:7). Dtr is unwilling to let stand a reform by other kings (even those who receive praise) that Josiah does not also undertake. At every stage of his reign, Josiah must supersede and eclipse the other kings. Does Josiah really attack the practice of *qĕdēšîm* or just destroy the location? It is unclear what it means that Josiah tore down the houses of the *qĕdēšîm*. There is no specific mention that he removed the *qĕdēšîm* themselves, as do Asa and Jehoshaphat. Perhaps this belies the fact that there were no *qĕdēšîm* left in the land at the time of Josiah. Instead of fabricating Josiah's removal of them, Dtr includes the comment about removing the houses rather than the *qĕdēšîm* themselves. An alternative explanation that may give Josiah more credit is that he attacks the site of the *qĕdēšîm* so they cannot return to this practice under a future king. Unlike Asa and Jehoshaphat, who presumably leave the buildings still standing, Josiah does not merely strike against those in the position of *qĕdēšîm*. This concept, attacking the "institutional foundation" of the sins of the kings of Israel and Judah, is a strategy used throughout the reform report, demonstrating the unforgiving, thorough, and definitive nature of Josiah's actions.[55] Josiah outdoes any previous attempt at reform, making his bigger, stronger, longer-lasting, and farther-reaching. This is another indication of how

54. Phyllis A. Bird, "The End of the Male Cult Prostitute: A Literary-Historical and Sociological Analysis of Hebrew Qādēš-qĕdēšîm," in *Congress Volume*, ed. International Organization for the Study of the Old Testament, VTSup 66 (Leiden: Brill, 1997), 61.
55. Knoppers, *Reign of Jeroboam*, 183.

thoroughly Dtr is involved in rewriting the list of the reform report. Each element of the reform corresponds to something else in the history, presenting Josiah as either repairing and/or surpassing the actions of earlier kings.[56]

Through the purge of his reform, Josiah is compared to the few good kings, and his acts supersede those of the others. He outdoes each reform, and his commitment to the deuteronomistic law code is unparalleled. He singularly puts the law of Deuteronomy (the found book of the law) into application, as can be seen through the direct connections between the law and Josiah's acts. This is demonstrated through the common, deuteronomistic vocabulary, focusing on centralization of the cult and removing syncretistic elements from worship. Josiah is like no other king, even David, the prototype of all kings.

With the final act of reform, the celebration of the Passover festival, Josiah is likened not only to David but also to Moses and Joshua. This celebration further focuses on centralization. Having destroyed all of the cult sites of Israel and Judah, Josiah mandates the celebration of Passover, presumably in accordance with Deut. 16:2, 5-6, which requires centralization to the temple in Jerusalem. The report of the Passover is as follows:

> And the king commanded all the people, saying: "Celebrate a Passover to Yahweh your God, as prescribed in this scroll of the covenant [ספר הברית]." For a Passover like this has not been celebrated since the days of the judges who judged in Israel and all the days of the kings of Israel and the kings of Judah. Only in the eighteenth year of the reign of Josiah was such a Passover of Yahweh celebrated in Jerusalem. (2 Kgs. 23:21-23)

---

56. This renders dubious the arguments by Lauren Monroe that Josiah's reform report derived from the hand of the holiness priests (Monroe, *Josiah's Reform*).

There are two important elements in these verses. The first is that this is the only act of reform explicitly linked to the finding of the scroll, and the second highlights the singular quality of Josiah's reform. The connection with the scroll may indicate that the celebration of Passover, which is separated from the book-finding account by the twenty verses describing the covenant and the reform, may have been part of the original book-finding-source account. Also, in this way, it serves as something of a conclusion for the reform, bringing the narrative back to focus on the scroll of the law. This envelope structure, with the book-finding narrative as its opening and the Passover as its conclusion, implicitly contributes to the sense that the entirety of the reform (as expressed in the intervening verses) is enacted because of the book of the law. Invoking this belief is intentional; Dtr wants to make sure that the law code is seen as primary and as the impetus and justification for the reform. The scroll is called ספר הברית similar to 23:2 (the only other instance in the two chapters where the scroll is referred to in this way), describing the reading of the scroll followed by the affirmation of the covenant. The Passover continues this narrative.

The second element is the uniqueness of this celebration to the eighteenth year of Josiah. During all the days of the kings of Israel and Judah, about four hundred years, no king has instituted a festival like the one Josiah proclaims. Without expressing it explicitly, Josiah is set up as an incomparable king (see discussion above). The last Passover celebrated in this way hearkens back to the time of the judges, that mythical time before there was a king in Israel. The statement telescopes the history beyond the period of David and Solomon, to the time of charismatic leadership. Josiah is featured as a Moses-like leader.[57] While throughout the history, the depiction of

---

57. Sweeney, *King Josiah of Judah*, 105.

the divided monarchies is primarily negative, the united monarchy was seen as a golden age; the comment about the quality of the celebration of the festival raises Josiah above David and Solomon, the kings of the united kingdom. Dtr further emphasizes the importance of Josiah's Passover since throughout DtrH no Passover has been mentioned since Joshua 5. (This is in contrast to the Chronicler, who includes a Passover during the reform of Hezekiah; see 2 Chronicles 30.)[58] The connection to Joshua is not only in the celebration of the Passover but also in the way Joshua in the book of Joshua is constructed as a Josiah-like figure, further highlighting the dynastic king akin to the charismatic leaders of Joshua and Moses.[59]

We must ask, what does it literally mean that there had been no Passover celebrated like this since the period of the judges? We have no record of any Passover celebrations (similar or different) during the entirety of the monarchy. Was it truly not celebrated or just not recorded? How was the Passover of Josiah celebrated differently from any other Passover (presumably, although not reported, they did occur)? Is this a nod to centralization? That this is the first time the Passover sacrifices have only been offered in Jerusalem? Is this a reflection of Deuteronomy 16, where the two separate festivals of Passover and Unleavened Bread, as expressed in the Tetrateuch (Exodus 23; Leviticus 23; Numbers 28), are conflated into one holiday for the first time? None of the answers to these questions is made explicit.

---

58. Nelson, "Josiah in the Book of Joshua," 536.
59. Ibid., 531–40. In contrast, Monroe, in separating what she views as the priestly and deuteronomistic strata of the reform report, suggests that Josiah is depicted in the model of Joshua, "the great ḥērem warrior" (Monroe, Josiah's Reform, 10, 56–58). And while she acknowledges an overall schema to DtrH that begins with Joshua's violent purge of the cities of Canaan and ends with Josiah's reform, considering the relationship between Joshua and Josiah in this way (Joshua as the model for Josiah, rather than the reverse) does not acknowledge the intentional use of the Davidic prototype strategy that exists throughout the presentation of the kings.

Finally, the last verse brings up some important questions; it was only in the eighteenth year of Josiah's reign that the Passover was celebrated in this way. Josiah reigned for a total of thirty years. While many scholars have questioned what happened in the first eighteen years of Josiah's reign, I ask, What happened in the final thirteen years of his reign? We do not know anything about them, until his death on the battlefield of Megiddo. Perhaps they were not noteworthy. It is not uncommon for Dtr to regularly focus on the events of specific years in the reigns of his kings and gloss over the rest, but why was the Passover not celebrated after the eighteenth year? Or more precisely, why is Dtr explicit in stating that the Passover was not celebrated after the eighteenth year? Is this an indication that Josiah's reform never caught on? Was the Passover celebrated after this year, but not in this way: as elaborately? Centralized? These unanswered questions highlight the literary, rather than historical, value of the report of the Passover celebration. The account lacks the details of reality. Instead, we are left with a picture of a festival that is described as being unique in the history of the monarchy, another nod to setting up Josiah as the incomparable king. This is further supported by the report in Chronicles of Hezekiah's great Passover celebration. Even if the Passover had been celebrated during the monarchy, Josiah is still depicted as an incomparable reformer and champion of deuteronomic law.

The use of the Davidic prototype strategy in the Josiah narrative allows Dtr to present his ultimate king, the reformer who out-reforms others, the only king to read the Torah, the king who surpasses even the literary construct in which he is molded, while focusing on the importance of the deuteronomistic law code (the found scroll), the implementation of centralization, and the purge of syncretistic cultic elements. The prototype strategy grants Dtr the ability to activate the typology with a few concise clues, and Josiah is immediately situated among and evaluated against the kings of Israel and Judah. As readers, we know exactly what to expect of a king who is like David (deuteronomistically adherent) and not like Jeroboam. This strategy frees up the historian to use the narrative of Josiah and his great reign to focus on his programmatic purposes. The events of the reform that put deuteronomistic law into application remain the main character of the narrative.

The Davidic prototype is a literary strategy that Dtr uses throughout the history. It not only evaluates the individual kings, the good ones (like David) and the bad ones (like the anti-David, Jeroboam), but it also provides an overall framework in which to portray and view the literary figures of the individual kings. The kings cast in the model of the prototype signify much more than themselves as individuals; they are the means for constructing the history in general. Israel falls because of the acts of Jeroboam, and Josiah attempts to rescue Judah from the same fate. Each king, of both Israel and Judah, is evaluated in the same way, and the portrait of Dtr's important kings is constructed similarly, allowing for easy and clear comparisons and contrasts. Using this strategy, the explicit comments of incomparability are almost unnecessary. The use of the model makes incomparability within comparison clear, while also recognizing that the essential nature of something being incomparable is that it is indeed compared, and found unique, to other things.

The prototype strategy also allows Dtr to connect the climax of the history, the coming of Josiah and his reform, to the early monarchy and even the beginning of DtrH in the period of the conquest. The arrival of Josiah and his role in putting into effect the tenets of deuteronomistic theology is anticipated from almost the very beginning of the history of the monarchy. And while the man of God's reference to the future coming of Josiah during Jeroboam's dedication of his cult shrines is, of course, not historical and not contemporaneous to Jeroboam's reign, it creates a literary situation in which the entirety of the history is constructed around Josiah and his fulfillment of the Davidic prototype.

It is important to recognize that while the literary prototype of the good king is based on the portrait of David, it is truly based on the figure of Josiah himself. The literary David constructed in the Davidic prototype strategy is reflective of the portrait of Josiah. David is bolstered as the model for the best of kings, better than he appears in his own story in Samuel, and only Josiah can achieve his likeness, and even surpass David, loving Yahweh with all his heart, soul, and might, while David only loves Yahweh with his heart. Similarly, Josiah as a model for the prototype is also used in the portrait of Joshua. As Richard Nelson argues, Joshua is "pictured by Dtr as a royal figure . . . a sort of proto-king sketched out along the lines of the ideal deuteronomic monarch."[60] Like Josiah, Joshua (as discussed above) makes a covenant and mediates on the book of the law (Josh. 1:8) similar to the requirement in the law of the king. Joshua's succession of Moses and his installation are similar to that of a monarch, rather than the charismatic leadership of Moses, and he is the only other deuteronomistic figure to celebrate the Passover, According to Nelson:

> Although the kings of Judah were ostensibly judged by the example of David, the perfect king . . . actually David's piety was not the decisive criterion. Josiah's was. Even the kings who met the level of David's faithfulness only received partial approval, . . . unless by practicing cult centralization they met Josiah's standards as well. . . . The David who was the prototype of the perfect king was not really the David whom the historian met in his sources, but, as in the case of Joshua, an image of Josiah projected back into history.[61]

60. Nelson, "Josiah in the Book of Joshua," 534.
61. Ibid., 540.

In this way, it is seen that the Davidic prototype, which governs the historiographical poetics of the preexilic DtrH, is complete in its use but is not based on a model of David after all. Instead, it is modeled on the only figure who fully achieves that paradigm, Josiah. The prototype strategy is fully integrated into the construction of the history and the portrait of Dtr's kings, both good and bad.

The preceding chapters focused on the development of the prototype strategy in the portraits of David, (Solomon,) Jeroboam, and Josiah. The prototype strategy is a crucial literary technique used by Dtr[1], essential to his overall historiographical poetics, in creating the portrait of each king and constructing the history of the monarchy as a whole, in order to promote the deuteronomistic agenda focused on fidelity to the covenant and centralization. The account of Josiah functions as something of a break not only in the compositional history (the end of the preexilic Josianic edition) and the climax of the literary strategy to which the entire history builds but also in my treatment of the kings and the overall argument of this book. The following chapter will deal with the account of King Manasseh as a counterexample, demonstrating the afterlife of Dtr[1]'s historiographical poetics in a secondary, exilic context, and demonstrating the ways in which the prototype strategy was modified during the exile. Chapter 6 represents a shift in my argument, concluding that Manasseh is indeed portrayed by using the prototype strategy, but that the model used in depicting him is not the anti-David, Jeroboam, but Ahab, reflecting exilic concerns of Baal worship rather than syncretistic, noncentralized worship.

6

Manasseh, "Who Did More Evil than All . . . Who Were Before Him": A Counterexample

This chapter, in its treatment of the portrait of King Manasseh, will deal primarily with the exilic perspectives addressed in the text, contrasting them with the preexilic historiographical style. Through this analysis, it will be possible to see that the historiographical poetics in the Manasseh account are somewhat different, but it is not entirely disparate. The specific thematic concerns may be altered, but much of the methodological process is similar. In this way, it is possible to see that both Dtr^1 and Dtr^2 were part of the same scribal school with a similar method and poetics, but the historical circumstances of the exile require that the method and content be recalibrated.[1] This

---

1. On the deuteronomistic scribal school, see Moshe Weinfeld, *Deuteronomy and the Deuteronomic School* (Winona Lake, IN: Eisenbrauns, 1992); Weinfeld, "The Emergence of the Deuteronomic Movement: The Historical Antecedents," in *Das Deuteronomium: Enstehung, Gestalt, Und Botschaft*, ed. Norbert Lohfink (Leuven: University Press, 1985), 76–98; Raymond Person, *The Deuteronomic School: History, Social Setting, and Literature* (Leiden: Brill, 2002); Ernst Axel Knauf, "Does 'Deuteronomistic Historiography' (DtrH) Exist?," in *Israel Constructs*

is most prominent in the use of the prototype strategy, according to which Manasseh is still constructed using a prototype, but one modeled on Ahab, not the anti-David, Jeroboam, as is seen in the preexilic accounts of other bad kings. I look at the portrait of Manasseh as a counterexample to the portraits of the other kings. It is for this reason that I address the Manasseh narrative out of order, following the treatment of Josiah, who chronologically and narratively succeeds Manasseh.

The Problem of the Manasseh Account

The account of Manasseh, found in 2 Kgs. 21:1-18, has long been a topic of discussion and disagreement among scholars. This passage, with its explicit declaration of the impending fall of Jerusalem and Judah and its naming of Manasseh as the responsible cause, has been seen as an integral part in the shaping of the Deuteronomistic History, as well as a major key to identifying redactional theories.[2] The Manasseh account, with its irreversible-doom proclamation, transforms the meaning and function of the entire history, disavowing the eternity of the Davidic promise and calling into question the conditional or unconditional character of that promise. This passage, among others, led Martin Noth to describe the history as a pessimistic one, in which exile and punishment were inevitable.[3]

Its History: Deuteronomistic Historiography in Recent Research, ed. Albert de Pury, Jean-Daniel Macchi, and Thomas Römer (Sheffield: Sheffield Academic, 2000), 388–97; Norbert Lohfink, "Was There a Deuteronomistic Movement?," in *Those Elusive Deuteronomists: The Phenomenon of Pan-Deuteronomism*, ed. Linda Schearing and Steven L. McKenzie, JSOTSup 268 (Sheffield: Sheffield Academic, 1999), 36–66; Richard E. Friedman, "The Deuteronomistic School," in *Fortunate the Eyes That See: Essays in Honor of David Noel Freedman in Celebration of His Seventieth Birthday*, ed. Astrid B. Beck et al. (Grand Rapids: Eerdmans, 1995), 70–80.

2. Ben Zvi describes the account as "one of the most important test cases for a comprehensive theory about the redactional history of the Book of Kings" (Ehud Ben Zvi, "The Account of the Reign of Manasseh in II Reg 21:1-18 and the Redactional History of the Book of Kings," *ZAW* 103, no. 3 [1991]: 355).

3. Martin Noth, *The Deuteronomistic History* (Sheffield: JSOT Press, 1981), 101, 123–27.

Because the perspective of certain doom seems to contradict much of the history, with its unconditional, eternal promise, many have seen the oracle against Judah as a later addition to the original Josianic history.[4]

Throughout, I have primarily maintained the double redaction theory expounded by Frank Moore Cross, positing that the majority of the history was composed during the time of Josiah and later updated by an exilic editor. These exilic additions are usually composed of short comments, often just a verse or two, sprinkled throughout the history. In contrast, the narrative of King Manasseh in 2 Kings 21 includes a significant insertion of exilic material that changes the meaning and function of the account of Manasseh's reign, as well as influences the way we read the entirety of the history, leading us to ask: Is the history primarily positive or negative? The Cross theory accounts for both these perspectives; the exilic version of the history is largely pessimistic, while the preexilic version is hopeful. Because of this late passage, the final version has a very different focus and thrust from its preexilic precursor. Placing the blame on Manasseh marks a significant shift in theological perspective, allowing for the destruction of Judah and the end of the Davidic dynasty. As such, Cross unequivocally states that "the attribution of Judah's demise to the unforgivable sins of Manasseh is tacked on and not integral to the original structure of the history."[5]

The effect of the new perspective created in this updated account also has ramifications for the way we view the function and

---

4. Especially *CMHE* 278–85; Mark A. O'Brien, *The Deuteronomistic History Hypothesis: A Reassessment*, OBO 92 (Fribourg: Vandenhoeck & Ruprecht, 1989), 227–34; Jeremy Schipper, "Hezekiah, Manasseh, and Dynastic or Transgenerational Punishment," in *Soundings in Kings: Perspectives and Methods in Contemporary Scholarship*, ed. Mark Leuchter and Klaus-Peter Adam (Minneapolis: Fortress Press, 2010), 81–105; Marvin A. Sweeney, *King Josiah of Judah: The Lost Messiah of Israel* (Oxford: Oxford University Press, 2001), 52; Richard D. Nelson, *The Double Redaction of the Deuteronomistic History* (Sheffield: JSOT Press, 1981), 65–69.

5. *CMHE* 286.

intentions of the reform of Josiah in 2 Kings 23. In the context of the present text, Josiah's reform (following the ill-fated reign of Manasseh) appears futile and even ridiculous. Judah's fate has already been sealed in 2 Kgs. 21:10-15 because of the deeds of Manasseh; even the great King Josiah is unable to overturn this outcome. If it were the case that the fate of Judah had already been decided before Josiah's reign, why would Dtr even include his portrait of Josiah as the hero of the history? The irreversible verdict pronounced on Manasseh undermines the greatness of Josiah and his ability to change the fate of Judah.

In places, the redactional layers in 2 Kings 21 are easily discernible, while in others it is more difficult and perhaps even impossible to separate the redactions. And while we will never definitively know which verses are from the original Dtr[1] and which from the exilic Dtr[2], my consideration of their literary and historiographical function can help us to identify the layers. I would first like to offer what I feel confident identifying as Dtr[1]. Verses 1, 2a, 3a, and 17-18 are all preexilic. These verses roughly correspond to our typical Dtr[1] regnal formula. I also feel secure attributing 3b, 6c, and 7b-15 to Dtr[2]. Verse 5 is also probably exilic. The host of heaven is mentioned five times in DtrH.[6] Nelson identifies all of these as secondary.[7] Beyond the oracle in verses 10-15, much of the rest of the account is also probably exilic. The blame on Manasseh extends beyond these verses. We see it also in verses 3, 6, and 9. Therefore, if blame of Manasseh is exilic, these verses need to be reconsidered.[8] I will discuss these choices further below. For its heuristic value, I present the following as my best guess at the original, preexilic account of the reign of Manasseh in 2 Kings 21:

---

6. Deut. 4:19; 2 Kgs. 17:16; 21:3, 5; 23:4, 5; also in Jer. 8:2; 19:13; Zeph. 1:5.
7. Nelson, *Double Redaction*, 65.
8. Sweeney, *King Josiah of Judah*, 54.

Manasseh was twelve years old when he became king. And he reigned fifty-five years in Jerusalem. And his mother's name was Hephzibah. (2a) He did what was evil in the eyes of Yahweh. (3a) He rebuilt the high places that Hezekiah his father had destroyed. (4) And he built altars in the house of Yahweh of which Yahweh said, "In Jerusalem I will set my name." . . . (16) The innocent blood Manasseh spilled was very great until it filled Jerusalem from end to end, apart from his sin which he caused Judah to sin [החטיא], doing evil in the eyes of Yahweh. (17) The rest of the deeds of Manasseh and all that he did and the sin he committed, are they not written in the book of the chronicles of the kings of Judah? (18) And Manasseh slept with his fathers and was buried in the garden of his house, in the garden of Uzzah; and Amon his son became king in his place.

The exilic rewrite of the narrative also affects the ways we consider the historiographical process, especially in the use of the prototype strategy, but also in the thin reference to prophetic oracles. The differences in theological perspective of the exilic editor manifest themselves in an update of the Manasseh account in which the basic elements of the historiographical poetics are utilized, but not necessarily as fully or with the same substantive content. Previously, I have assessed Dtr[1]'s historiographical poetics and focused on the portrait of a few select kings Dtr highlights for their role in influencing the history of the monarchy: namely, David, Solomon, Jeroboam, and building up to the coming of Josiah and his reform. These kings fill unique roles in the history, embodying the Davidic prototype and its antitype. Dtr[1] affords these select kings fuller portraits than other kings. Given that Manasseh is blamed for the destruction of Judah and the Babylonian exile, the reader expects an extraordinary literary presentation of the king who plays such an extraordinary role, but does not find it. Instead, Klaas Smelik describes the account as "dull" and "lacking" in narrative.[9] This is the first clue that the process of composition in this account is different from that of other kings. Instead, Manasseh is initially presented as an ordinary bad king. We do not know much more about him than many of the inconsequential kings; he does not speak or act directly. Stuart Lasine describes him as a "faceless portrait . . . set against a blank background." He has no emotions or backstory like other essential kings.[10] Similarly, Richard Nelson describes even the "arch-villain Manasseh" as a "cardboard" character.[11] Also, Francesca Stavrakopoulou says, "Given the fact that Manasseh plays what is arguably the most crucial role within Kings in causing the destruction of Judah and the exile of her people, this brief and flimsy characterization is surprising, presenting Manasseh as little more than a man of straw."[12] The inconsistency of the literary style and the lack of literary intention displayed in the style of the blaming of Manasseh further highlights its late addition to the narrative. It was not part of the greater literary plan of Dtr^1. Instead, Dtr^2 creates a composite figure who performs the most sinful actions of the bad kings. The account of Manasseh's reign operates as a "textual magnet," attracting every sin that a king ever committed into the list of Manasseh's sins.[13] Those sins are so severe that they create a caricature of a villain, not real, but a fictional scapegoat.[14] Like Josiah, the best of kings, who surpasses the good deeds of the few good kings, Manasseh exceeds the bad kings in wickedness, doing all the sins of the bad kings and more, making him the one "who did [more] evil than all . . . who were before him" (2 Kgs. 21:11).[15]

9. Klaas A. D. Smelik, "The Portrayal of King Manasseh: A Literary Analysis of II Kings XXI and II Chronicles XXIII," in *Converting the Past: Studies in Ancient Israelite and Moabite Historiography*, Oudtestamentische studiën (Leiden: Brill, 1992), 132.

10. Stuart Lasine, "Manasseh as Villain and Scapegoat," in *New Literary Criticism and the Hebrew Bible* (Sheffield: JSOT Press, 1993), 164.

11. Nelson, *Double Redaction*, 126.

12. Francesca Stavrakopoulou, *King Manasseh and Child Sacrifice: Biblical Distortions of Historical Realities* (Berlin: de Gruyter, 2004), 22.

13. Many thanks to Mark Smith for this phrase (in conversation, December 12, 2011). Also, Marc Zvi Brettler, *The Creation of History in Ancient Israel* (New York: Routledge, 1995), 133; Smelik, "Portrayal of King Manasseh," 133–34.

14. Lasine, "Manasseh as Villain and Scapegoat," 163.

Furthermore, the account of Manasseh's long reign is very sparse. Manasseh becomes king after the death of his father Hezekiah. He reinstitutes the cultic sites and symbols that Hezekiah destroyed and then inaugurates and/or restores a host of other cultic practices, including the worship of Baal, Asherah, and the host of heaven, and a variety of divination practices. He also embarks on building projects to support those practices. The list of Manasseh's transgressions is followed by a pronouncement of the impending doom of Judah. Manasseh's reign ends with the stereotypical notice that he slept with his fathers and that his son succeeded him. Nothing actually happens during the account of Manasseh's reign, even with the extensive exilic updating. There are no events to be rechronologized or juxtaposed. Manasseh does not speak or interact with prophets, foreign nations, or even the people. The account basically consists of the regnal formula, the list of sins, the doom oracle against Judah, and the closing death and burial formula (DBF). The lack of events is one of the things that makes the original portrait of Manasseh's reign like that of the other ordinary bad kings. (It may have only included 5-6 verses.) In those accounts, the ordinary bad kings ascend to the throne, are evaluated as having done what is evil in Yahweh's eyes, commit some sins, and then die and are buried. The remainder of the things that presumably must have happened during their reigns is relegated to the annals of the kings (as in the accounts of Joash of Israel, 2 Kgs. 13:10-13; Jotham, 2 Kgs. 15:32-38). Yet the parallels are not perfect because, unlike these kings, Manasseh reigns for an unprecedented length of time. The account of Manasseh began as one of an ordinary bad king with the regnal formula that he did evil in the eyes of Yahweh, like other bad kings. Only the additions of Dtr[2] make Manasseh extraordinary as a bad king.[16]

---

15. Smelik, "Portrayal of King Manasseh," 139-40.

Also, the doom oracle delivered against Judah in 2 Kings 21 does not have the same prophetic thrust as other oracles. The oracle begins with the introduction that "Yahweh spoke by the hand of his servants the prophets." Unlike the prophetic texts of Dtr[1], these are generic, nameless, collective prophets. Such anonymous prophets are uncommon in DtrH, and their appearance may indicate a late addition to the text.[17] Also, the message of the prophets lacks warning. The first communication to Judah is a proclamation of doom. The difference in this oracle leads us to believe that it is in the style of Dtr[1], but derives from Dtr[2] for several reasons. First, the term עבדי הנביאים is usually exilic.[18] Second, unlike Dtr[1], there is no prophet here. There is a nod to the use of prophecies, but it is somewhat weak.[19] The oracle is announced as Yahweh's words, which he said through his prophets. These generic, plural prophets do not seem to exist. Was there actually a warning? The oracle is cast in the prophetic pattern of Dtr[1], but it is not quite the same. Jonathan Rosenbaum describes this as a "quasi-prophetic" statement.[20] Similarly, Cross emphasizes that "no prophecies concerning Manasseh's great sin, and the inevitable rejection it entailed, are to [be] found in the earlier part of the Deuteronomistic history. Not one."[21]

---

16. Previously, unless otherwise indicated, Dtr referred to the preexilic Dtr[1]. In this chapter, unless specified, Dtr will still refer to the preexilic redactor or both the exilic and preexilic Deuteronomistic Historians.

17. Ehud Ben Zvi, "'The Prophets'—References to Generic Prophets and Their Role in the Construction of the Image of the 'Prophets of Old' within the Postmonarchic Readerships of the Book of Kings," *ZAW* 116, no. 4 (2004): 391n8.

18. William M. Schniedewind, "History and Interpretation: The Religion of Ahab and Manasseh in the Book of Kings," *CBQ* 55, no. 4 (1993): 350. It appears in 2 Kgs. 17:13, 23; 21:10; 24:2; Jer 7:25; 44:4; Amos 3:7; Zech. 1:6.

19. *CMHE* 286.

20. Jonathan Rosenbaum, "Hezekiah's Reform and the Deuteronomistic Tradition," *HTR* 72 (1979): 25.

21. *CMHE* 286.

This is also in contrast to the oracle against Israel in 2 Kings 17, where we have the mention of similar generic prophets and seers, but there is a real prophetic warning: "And Yahweh warned Israel and Judah by the hand of all prophets[22] and every seer, saying: 'Turn back from your evil ways and observe my commandments and statutes, in accord with all the Torah which I commanded your fathers, and which I sent to you by the hand of my servants the prophets'" (v. 13). Israel has an opportunity to change its ways. In contrast, there is no warning in 2 Kgs. 21:10. This is one example of how Dtr[2] mirrors the historiographical poetics of Dtr[1], but changes the content. Dtr[2] knows that a doom proclamation such as this would usually be announced through a prophetic oracle, and while he does not possess such a prophetic source, he makes light allusion to such a revelation.

Second Kings 21 is clearly composite, but it is difficult to know whether there is a use of independent sources. Scholars, including those who posit single, double, or triple redaction theories, identify multiple redactional layers in this narrative. Even those scholars, primarily the Cross school, who see a comprehensive, primary, preexilic history, do not suggest that the entirety of the narrative is preexilic. Still, the extent to which the exilic editor was at work is contested.[23] There is some consensus that at the least 2 Kgs. 21:11-15

22. Corrected on the basis of Qumran, נביאי for נביאו.

23. Early on Driver, Kuenen, and Wellhausen all identified vv. 10-15 as intrusive (Mordechai Cogan and Hayim Tadmor, *2 Kings: A New Translation*, AB 11 [Garden City, NY: Doubleday, 1988], 270). There is a lack of agreement on the extent of that intrusion and further additions. Some of the major positions include the following: Frank Cross points to vv. 7-9 and 10-15 in the exilic redaction (*CMHE* 285–86). In their commentary, Cogan and Tadmor agree with 10-15, but they attribute vv. 7-9 to Dtr[1] (*2 Kings*, 270). John Gray ascribes vv. 8-15 to a late deuteronomistic addition (Gray, *1 and 2 Kings: A Commentary*, 2nd ed. Old Testament Library [Philadelphia: Westminster, 1970], 644–45). Similarly, Richard Friedman also identifies vv. 8-15 as exilic (Friedman, *The Exile and Biblical Narrative: The Formation of the Deuteronomistic and Priestly Works* [Chico, CA: Scholars Press, 1981], 11). Erik Eynikel identifies vv. 4, 6, 7b-16 as part of the exilic redaction (Eynikel, "The Portrait of Manasseh and the Deuteronomistic History," in *Deuteronomy and Deuteronomic Literature* [Leuven: Peeters, 1997], 241). Richard Nelson includes vv. 3-7 in addition to 8-15, but suggests that these verses also incorporate several predeuteronomistic annalistic notices (4a, 6a, and perhaps 7a) "floating somewhere in

is exilic. Unlike other passages where Dtr^2's additions are minimal and appear as comments or corrections pinned to Dtr^1's text, Dtr^2 completely rewrites and expands the Manasseh account.

On the axis of composition, we most clearly see the differences and similarities in the work of Dtr^1 and Dtr^2. In this account, there is an attempt to use some of Dtr^1's historiographical methods, but they are either misapplied or Dtr^2's agenda is different so that he uses the same method as means to a different end. (This is similar to the Chronicler, who in writing history has a different ideological focus from Dtr and therefore a different story that he wants to tell.)

The Prototype Strategy—Ahab as Model

In the preexilic history, Dtr establishes Jeroboam as the evil king par excellence, the anti-David, and the prototype of the evil king. This prototype is then used as a comparative for the evil kings of Israel. In establishing Manasseh as the most evil king of Judah, the one on whom the destruction is blamed, Dtr^2 uses the prototype strategy in two ways. First, he establishes Manasseh as an evil king, on par with those of northern Israel. Then, in order to express his theological concerns (the problem of idolatry and foreign worship), he constructs Manasseh in the model of Ahab rather than Jeroboam, the anti-David and prototype of the evil king in the preexilic edition. These two strategic moves are not entirely independent. In his own account (as discussed in chap. 4), Ahab is established as the worst of the northern kings, even surpassing Jeroboam, although he is not taken up by Dtr^1 as the prototype of the evil king.

---

between" the exilic composition (Nelson, *Double Redaction*, 43, 65–67). It is interesting to note that even those who do not subscribe to the double redaction model see multiple hands at work in these verses. For example, Ehud Ben Zvi similarly breaks up the sections and identifies vv. 4, 7b, 8-9 (DtrN) and 10-14 (DtrP) as secondary additions to DtrH(G) (Ben Zvi, "The Reign of Manasseh," 365, 370, 373). A major difference is that the Göttingen school views all of these three redactions as exilic.

Most notably in the exilic version of this passage, we see a shift in the prototype strategy used, but Dtr[2] still utilizes the historiographical poetics of Dtr[1] and employs a prototype strategy. In the preexilic edition, the prototype has been based on that of David. The evil king is constructed as an anti-David. Jeroboam is the comparative prototype for the evil king throughout, especially in the evaluations of the northern kings. In 2 Kings 21, exilic Manasseh is constructed in the model of Ahab as prototype. (The preexilic version of the narrative reveals traces of the Jeroboam comparison.) We can attribute this modification to the different concerns of the exilic writer. The use of Ahab as prototype is apparent in several places, both explicitly and implicitly. Affinity between the Ahab and Manasseh accounts exists on stylistic, lexical, and theological levels.[24]

The prototype strategy is established similarly to the preexilic portraits of the kings in the regnal formulae as Manasseh is initially evaluated like all the other kings.[25] The regnal evaluation begins as usual that he did הרע בעיני יהוה. This judgment evaluation sets the tone for the rest of the narrative. Manasseh is thoroughly portrayed as an evil king. Beginning with this instance, רע, as both noun and verb, functions as a *Leitwort* in this passage.[26]

Manasseh was twelve years old when he became king. And he reigned fifty-five years in Jerusalem. And his mother's name was Hephzibah. He did what was evil in the eyes of Yahweh, <u>like the transgressions of the nations whom Yahweh dispossessed before the children of Israel.</u> **He rebuilt[27] the high places that Hezekiah his father had destroyed.** (2 Kgs. 21:1-3a)

---

24. Schniedewind, "History and Interpretation," 649.
25. Stavrakopoulou suggests that Manasseh's regnal formula is somewhat different from other Judean kings, including only the name of his mother, but not her patronym or place of origin. She argues that this has potential significance, but is unremarkable for my arguments using the regnal formulae in setting up the judgment of the king and his role in the prototype strategy (Stavrakopoulou, *King Manasseh and Child Sacrifice*, 26).
26. Dtr[1] is represented by the bold, text while Dtr[2] is designated by underline.
27. Literally, "returned and built."

Here, Dtr² makes a slight addition to the preexilic judgment formula. Manasseh "did what was evil in the eyes of Yahweh, like the transgressions [תועבת] of the nations whom Yahweh dispossessed [הוריש] before the children of Israel." Usually, at this point of the regnal formula, the king is compared with his father or the ancestral prototype. Instead, Manasseh is compared with the dispossessed nations. This accusation directly connects Manasseh's sin with that of Israel in the oracle against the North in 2 Kgs. 17:8. There Israel is punished because the people "followed the statutes of the nations [חקות הגוים], whom Yahweh dispossessed [הוריש] before the children of Israel and the kings of Israel, which they practiced." In the context of Israel, the sin of the nations was noncentralized worship at the high places and following the sin of Jeroboam, as well as the building and worshiping of *maṣṣēbôt* and *'ăšērîm* (2 Kgs. 17:9-11). As previously discussed, these practices in the preexilic context were primarily syncretistic rather than idolatrous and were considered "traditional" in standard Israelite religion.[28]

Throughout DtrH, Dtr¹ uses a rhetoric of othering, depicting noncentralized and syncretistic Yahwistic practice as idolatry. While Dtr¹ is concerned with and fiercely condemns the worship of other gods, his primary focus on cultic infractions is noncentralized worship. The *maṣṣēbôt* and *'ăšērîm* were worshiped at these high places with or alongside Yahweh, but not necessarily as a deity or as a replacement for Yahweh. In general, cultic malpractice is evaluated in three distinct ways: wrong place, wrong symbols, and wrong deity. For the most part, the preexilic redactor is concerned with place and symbols. The specific language of comparison to the sins of the nations, identifying them as those whom Yahweh dispossessed [הוריש], lends itself to link Manasseh's sin with that of

28. Schniedewind, "History and Interpretation," 650.

Israel—uncentralized and syncretistic worship. This is an expansion on the explicit comment that Manasseh rebuilds the high places destroyed by his father (v. 3), aligning Manasseh with the kings of Israel who continued to worship at the high places and followed the sin of Jeroboam. Similarly, this connection with the blame placed on Manasseh is made in verse 11, which clearly collocates the vague "what Manasseh king of Judah did" with "these transgressions," again, תעבות. The תעבות הגוים are practices prohibited in Deut. 18:9, where Yahweh warns that upon entering the land, the people should not learn to do the תועבת הגוים, which include passing children through fire and a list of divination practices, similar to those in 2 Kgs. 21:6. Manasseh does these things. This insertion into the standard regnal formula sets the stage for Dtr[2]'s portrait of Manasseh. He is like the nations, and he is like the destroyed kingdom of Israel; because of this, Judah will be punished. The rhetoric of preexilic Dtr is quite effective. An exilic editor would have read the preexilic edition of the history convinced of the fact that the uncentralized, syncretistic cult was indeed idolatry.

The casting of Manasseh as a northern king begins in the preexilic account, providing fertile grounds for an exilic editor to blame him for the destruction of Judah.[29] Manasseh's first evil act belongs to the original, preexilic account. Manasseh "rebuilt the high places that Hezekiah his father had destroyed" (2 Kgs. 21:3). As discussed in the last chapter, Hezekiah's reform, and the praise he receives for his righteousness, is focused on removing these noncentralized and syncretistic sites, with their foreign symbols, *maṣṣēbôt* and *'ăšērîm*. Hezekiah does not fight a battle against the worship of other gods. In verses 2-3a, Manasseh is established as similar to the Israelite

---

29. Francesca Stavrakopoulou, "The Blackballing of Manasseh," in *Good Kings and Bad Kings: The Kingdom of Judah in the Seventh Century BCE*, ed. Lester L. Grabbe (London: T&T Clark, 2005), 283.

kings who build and worship at the high places and follow the sins of Jeroboam. Manasseh not only continues these practices but also returns to them (וירשב), rebuilding the sites that Hezekiah destroys, restoring the practices of the kingdom of Israel in Judah. Manasseh is likened to the arch-villain of Israel and of the preexilic history, Jeroboam. Both Jeroboam and Solomon build condemned altars.[30]

It is interesting to note that even Manasseh's name contributes to this connection with Jeroboam. He is the only biblical king to share his name with a northern tribal territory. Francesca Stavrakopoulou suggests that Manasseh's northern name makes him a Judean version of an evil northern king, contending that this may be one of the things that attracts Dtr[2] to blaming Manasseh. This casting makes him a fitting candidate to shoulder the responsibility of the fall of Judah.[31] Blaming a quasi-northerner also removes some of the responsibility from Judah, because the punishment is for the king's, rather than Judah's, sins. Stavrakopoulou argues that Manasseh's northern name, rather than a historical reputation of extreme evil as others claim, could be the reason he is vilified. Graeme Auld describes this act of Dtr as portraying Manasseh as a "southern scoundrel dressed in northern colours."[32]

Dtr[2] in choosing Manasseh for his arch-villain is not bothered by defying a general theological perspective: Manasseh has the longest reign of any king of Israel or Judah. He rules for fifty-five years in peace. For Dtr, length of reign and prosperity are a reward for fidelity (as in 1 Kgs. 3:14).[33] Historically, Manasseh may have been

30. Smelik, "Portrayal of King Manasseh," 143.
31. Stavrakopoulou, "Blackballing of Manasseh," 253.
32. A. Graeme Auld, *Kings Without Privilege: David and Moses in the Story of the Bible's Kings* (Edinburgh: T&T Clark, 1994), 85.
33. The Chronicler offers an exegetical solution to the problem of the long reign by including a picture of a repentant Manasseh. Smelik also suggests that the blame of Manasseh for the punishment of Judah is a resolution to the theological problem of his long reign and peaceful death. We would expect Manasseh's fate to be bad, but the historical reality does not support

one of Judah's most successful monarchs. Beginning his reign in the late seventh century BCE, he recovered from the Assyrian siege in 701 BCE. During his long reign, the kingdom flourished.[34] This historical inconsistency, among others, prompts the debates about the dating of the narrative, acting as a clue that Dtr^2's portrait of Manasseh is a secondary retelling of his account. The accusation that the destruction of Judah, Jerusalem, and the temple is blamed on Manasseh highlights him as the worst of all the kings, but his reign is long and nonviolent. A single author would not have allowed both these details to stand. As such, Dtr^2 uses the prototype strategy in the model of Ahab and establishing Manasseh as a northern-like king to justify blaming Manasseh. As such, Dtr^2 portrays Manasseh as Stavrakopoulou describes, as the "ultimate idolater," worse than the worst of Israel and Judah's kings.[35]

After Manasseh is introduced as a northern-like king, using elements of the anti-David (Jeroboam) prototype, the exilic editor connects him to and recasts him in a prototype based on Ahab. The choice of Ahab as the model for Manasseh is an easy one for Dtr^2, as Ahab is presented as an evil king who goes beyond the sins of Jeroboam. Most of the evil kings are satisfied to continue Jeroboam's sin, but Ahab adds to it. The text makes this clear:

> And as if it had been a light thing to follow the sins of Jeroboam son of Nabat, he took as wife Jezebel daughter of King Ethbaal of the Phoenicians, and he went and served Baal and worshiped him. He erected an altar to Baal in the temple of Baal which he built in Samaria. Ahab also made an Asherah. Ahab did more to anger Yahweh, God of Israel, than all the kings of Israel who preceded him. (1 Kgs. 16:31-32)

---

that. Instead, because Manasseh is not personally punished, punishment is meted out on Judah (Smelik, "Portrayal of King Manasseh," 154, 161.)

34. Stavrakopoulou, "Blackballing of Manasseh," 248.

35. Stavrakopoulou, *King Manasseh and Child Sacrifice*, 28.

Ahab not only participates in the uncentralized worship supported by Jeroboam but also goes further to introduce foreign women and foreign cults into the kingdom. It is not surprising that Ahab's reign is filled with fighting between Israel and Judah and with foreign kings, and that he dies on the battlefield in a "random" act that is such a stroke of luck that the coincidence can only be attributed to Yahweh's will.[36]

The choice of Ahab as model, with his reputation of instituting Baal worship/idolatry in Israel (versus Jeroboam and his uncentralized cult), makes it clear that the author of the Manasseh account emphasizes different tenets of deuteronomistic theology from the author/redactor of the earlier kings' accounts. This exilic author is concerned with idol worship, not just uncentralized and syncretistic worship, meting out punishment (even for a king with a long and peaceful reign) regardless of whether it violates the eternal Davidic promise and the eternal covenant between Israel and Yahweh, and transgressions against Yahweh are connected to specific violations of deuteronomic law. According to Stavrakopoulou, "The list of Manasseh's cult crimes is carefully crafted, for each of his transgressions is specifically prohibited in the Deuteronomic codes."[37]

First, in the initial list of Manasseh's sins, after rebuilding the altars Hezekiah destroyed, Dtr[2] adds that Manasseh "erected altars [מזבחת] to Baal and he made an Asherah like those which Ahab, king of Israel, made. He worshiped all the host of heaven and served them" (2 Kgs. 21:3). Here, the worship of Asherah is connected to the worship of Baal, unlike the worship of Asherah as connected to the

---

36. Ahab's death is a particularly poignant censure by the Deuteronomist. Although he tried to protect himself in battle, both by having Jehoshaphat of Judah disguise himself as the king of Israel and by wearing protective armor, "a man drew his bow at random and he hit the king of Israel between the plates of the armor" (1 Kgs. 22:34). According to the Deuteronomist's theological and literary sensibilities, this is anything but random. Ahab's death is an act of divine retribution.

37. Stavrakopoulou, *King Manasseh and Child Sacrifice*, 29.

worship of Yahweh in the preexilic accounts. Similarly, Ahab also erected an altar to Baal and made an Asherah (1 Kgs. 16:32-33). The narrator explicitly likens Manasseh and his sin to Ahab. In fact, the clause הקים מזבח is rare. It only appears in these two instances. Both Manasseh and Ahab erect altars to Baal. The infrequent use of this clause links the two verses.[38] But this connection is one Manasseh exceeds. Ahab made an altar (מזבח), while Manasseh constructs more than one (מזבחת). Similarly, Ahab is the only other person who עשה an Asherah. There are other instances of constructing 'ăšērîm, for example, 1 Kgs. 15:13 (Maacah עשתה) and 14:23 (Judah בנה). While the 'ăšērîm were a real problem in Judah and not unique to Manasseh's sin, here the building of 'ăšērîm generates a comparison with an Israelite king. The connection to Ahab is intentional. This act is also one in which Manasseh proves more evil than Ahab; while Ahab builds an altar to Baal, Manasseh builds multiple altars; while Ahab makes an Asherah, Manasseh makes one and installs it in the temple (v. 7).[39]

Manasseh's transgressions continue and are intertextually connected with the whole of Israel's past, from the exodus to Hezekiah's reign. The list of Manasseh's sins contains the offenses of all the kings of Israel and Judah. These sins mark a distinct change in the theological focus, dealing with the worship of Baal, the host of heaven, and other idolatrous practices. But they are also a return to the תעבות הגוים enumerated in Deut. 18:9. The list of Manasseh's transgressions includes the following:

> And he erected altars to Baal and he made an Asherah like those which Ahab, king of Israel, made. He worshiped all the host of heaven and served them. **(4) And he built altars in the house of Yahweh of**

38. P. S. F. van Keulen, *Manasseh through the Eyes of the Deuteronomists: The Manasseh Account (2 Kings 21:1-18) and the Final Chapters of the Deuteronomistic History* (Leiden: Brill, 1996), 95.

39. Stavrakopoulou, "Blackballing of Manasseh," 251.

which Yahweh said, "In Jerusalem I will set my name."[40] (5) And he built altars to all the host of heaven in the two courtyards of the house of Yahweh. (6) And he passed his son through the fire and conjured and sought omens and made a ghost and a spirit and greatly increased doing what is evil in the eyes of Yahweh to cause [him] to anger. (7) Then he put the statue of Asherah that he made in the house about which Yahweh said to David and Solomon his son, "In this house and in Jerusalem which I have chosen from all the tribes of Israel, I will set my name forever. (2 Kgs. 21:3b-7)

These verses are primarily an addition of exilic Dtr². They illustrate an exilic concern with Baal worship.[41] In attributing Baal worship to Manasseh, we see a shift in the focus of the deuteronomistic program, from the battle against noncentralized and syncretistic worship (wrong place and symbols), including ʾăšērîm and maṣṣēbôt, to full-on idolatry in the worship of Baal and the host of heaven (wrong deities). The description of Asherah in verse 7 is also somewhat different from what we have seen from the preexilic writer; Manasseh makes a פסל of Asherah. This is the only instance of a פסל האשרה. Because this expression is unique, Mark Smith suggests that we do not necessarily know that this is a statue of the goddess Asherah, as many have argued. It is possible that it "may have been a more elaborate form of the asherah in the royal cult of Jerusalem." Smith makes clear that what we do know is that there is "no question" that the author considered this object to be idolatrous.[42] The coupling of Asherah

---

40. This verse seems to be repetitious or a doublet with v. 7. It is unlikely that both derive from the same hand. More likely, v. 4 was part of Dtr¹'s account and Dtr² expands on it in v. 7, connecting it with the oracle against Judah. The building of these "new" altars, as opposed to rebuilding the altars Hezekiah tore down (v. 3), further connects Manasseh with Jeroboam and Solomon, who also build new altars, a strategy of preexilic Dtr¹.

41. The preexilic concerns about cultic purity are focused on centralization and worship of Yahweh alone. And while Dtr¹ scorns all idol worship, as in Deut. 4:15-19, for the most part, he is not focused on fighting Baal worship, but more concerned with cultic rigorism. Even though in Jerusalem the priest Jehoiada acts against Baal worship, killing one of Baal's priests (2 Kgs. 11:18), until the reign of Manasseh, Baal worship is primarily a northern problem, introduced by Ahab and his wife Jezebel.

worship with Baal and the host of heaven is a change from the ʾăšērîm that likely were part of standard Israelite worship during the monarchy that Dtr[1] casts as idolatrous. The verses I attribute to Dtr[2] show a new deuteronomistic focus on the sin of Baal worship and other modes of idolatry, namely, the worship of the host of heaven, demonstrating a shift from concern about place and symbols to that of the wrong deity.

Following the construction of the altars to Baal and making an Asherah like Ahab, Manasseh "worshiped [וישתחו] all the host of heaven and served [ויעבד] them." Manasseh is the only king accused of worshiping the host of heaven; previously only the people of Israel have participated in this practice (2 Kgs. 17:16).[43] These sins are similar to those found in Deut. 17:2-3. Deuteronomy 17:2 presents something of a definition of what it means to do הרע בעיני יהוה and violate the covenant. One who does evil in Yahweh's eyes "follows and serves [ויעבד] other gods and worships [וישתחו] them, whether the sun or the moon or all the host of heaven, which I have forbidden."[44] Similarly, in Deut. 4:19, these heavenly bodies are established as modes of worship that are particularly foreign. Yahweh reminds the people, "And when you lift your eyes heavenward and you see the sun and moon and stars, all the host of heaven, do not be led astray and worship [והשתחוית] them and serve them [ועבדתם], which Yahweh your God allotted them to all the nations [העמים] under heaven." The host of heaven is not an acceptable part of Israelite worship, and the use of the same verbs of these two prohibitions in 2 Kgs. 21:3 highlights the foreignness and

---

42. Mark Smith, *The Early History of God: Yahweh and the Other Deities in Ancient Israel* (Grand Rapids: Eerdmans, 2002), 128.

43. Stavrakopoulou, *King Manasseh and Child Sacrifice*, 28–29.

44. It is interesting to note that the objects of worship in 2 Kgs. 21:3 only include the host of heaven, while the parallel verse in Josiah's reform includes the sun, moon, host of heaven, and the constellations (2 Kgs. 23:5). The list in 2 Kgs. 23:4, that the priests removed the vessels used for Baal, Asherah, and host of heaven is more similar to what we see in 2 Kgs. 21:3.

forbiddenness of Manasseh's sin. Despite these prohibitions present in the deuteronomic law code, these transgressions were not a focal point of Dtr[1]'s theological program.

These verses, particularly 6 and 7, create a long list of Manasseh's sins. The sins of passing sons through fire and divination practices are somewhat limited in Kings. Both of these acts are linked in several parallel texts, including the oracle against Israel (2 Kings 17) and Josiah's reform (2 Kings 23). While verses 6 and 7b find parallels in 2 Kgs. 17:17; 23:6, 24, it is unclear in which direction these correspondences go. Many have discussed the parallels between the Manasseh and Josiah accounts and that the evil Manasseh in the preexilic account has been constructed as a foil for the hero Josiah. This leads us to ask, Are the sins of verses 6 and 7 included by Dtr[1] in the Manasseh account in order for Josiah to remove, or are they added to the Manasseh account by Dtr[2] and then, for symmetry's sake, also added by necessity (in an exilic update) to 2 Kings 23 for Josiah to counter? Smelik offers an interesting and compelling observation that Manasseh is created as the negative counterpart to Josiah, but "to designate Josiah as the positive counterpart of Manasseh . . . would not do justice to the overall importance of this king." Instead, Josiah is the positive counterpart of Jeroboam.[45] This is consistent with my theory of Josiah and Jeroboam's roles in the prototype strategy. Additionally, while the sins of passing his son through fire and divination practices have other correspondences within Kings, it is difficult to reason why they are included here. Are they part of the original list of ordinary bad king Manasseh's sins, or are they included here by Dtr[2], gleaned from the accounts of other bad kings to highlight Manasseh as an extraordinarily evil king, attributing to him every sin that was ever committed by a king?

---

45. Smelik, "Portrayal of King Manasseh," 160.

Evaluating the literary function of these verses and their contribution in shaping the Manasseh account, they are most likely exilic. Dtr^2 collects the sins of all the kings of Israel and Judah and in constructing Manasseh as the most evil king attributes all of them to Manasseh himself. Ahaz is the only other king to pass his son through fire (√עבר *hip'il*). It is interesting to notice that even though Ahaz also commits this unique transgression, he does not play an important role in the overall history. He is not referenced in 2 Kings 21 directly. Also, in his own account, Ahaz plays something of a minor role. (This is in contrast to the portrayal of Ahaz in Chronicles, where he is depicted as the worst king of Judah, taking the place of Manasseh in that history.) Ahaz did what was evil in the eyes of Yahweh, and although he was a southern king, he followed the ways of the kings of Israel. He "passed his son through fire" and made sacrifices at all the shrines and to things in nature (2 Kgs. 16:1–4). This is the only specific mention of his sins. The rest are reasonably generic. Nonspecific accusations of sins are not characteristic of the kings whom Dtr^1 highlights as the paradigmatic good and evil kings. Ahaz, while he does not come to play an important role, is also characterized as something of a northern king, said to follow those kings. Ahaz builds an altar in the temple, styled after the one he sees in the court of Tiglath Pileser III. Ahaz's actions are not necessarily indicative of participating in foreign worship, but they follow the comment that Ahaz did what was evil. Without this, we might have read his building of the altar neutrally or as cult reform, but we do not. Also, connecting him with the kings of Israel reminds us of another northern king who built his own altar and was severely condemned: Jeroboam.[46] And while it is not fully understood what

---

46. Peter R. Ackroyd, "The Biblical Interpretation of the Reigns of Ahaz and Hezekiah," in *In the Shelter of Elyon*, ed. David J. A. Clines and Philip R. Davies (Sheffield: JSOT Press, 1984), 254–55.

is meant, Ahaz is also mentioned in Josiah's tearing down of altars (2 Kgs. 23:12). Dtr² seems to incorporate some elements from the reign of Ahaz to further vilify Manasseh and connect him with the bad kings of Israel.

In addition to the enumeration of his sins, Manasseh is said to have done "what is evil in the eyes of Yahweh to cause [Yahweh] to anger" (2 Kgs. 21:6). This transgression, to cause Yahweh to anger, the *hip'il* of כעס, is a variation on one pattern of the standard Israelite regnal formula (see chap. 4). Before Manasseh, this collocation is primarily used for the Omrides. In the regnal formulae, only Omri (1 Kgs. 16:26), Ahab (1 Kgs. 16:33), and Ahaziah (1 Kgs. 22:54) are said to cause Yahweh to anger. This accusation is missing from the rest of the bad kings. The use here in the Manasseh narrative contributes to the analogy between Manasseh and Ahab. He is evil like Ahab. In Dtr²'s reconstruction of the Manasseh narrative, this comment, that Manasseh caused Yahweh to anger, serves as the close to the introductory regnal formula. Following the accusation that Manasseh did what was evil in the eyes of Yahweh and the list of his sins, Dtr² repeats that Manasseh "greatly increased" doing what was evil in Yahweh's eyes, to cause him to anger, emulating the regnal formulae of the Omrides.

Also, in addition to the use of *hip'il* כעס in the regnal formulae of the Omrides, it is also used in several other places when discussing the destruction of the dynasties of kings who angered Yahweh (house of Jeroboam, 1 Kgs. 15:30; house of Baasha, 1 Kgs. 16:2, 13; house of Ahab, 1 Kgs. 16:33). The use of this verb does three things. First, it sets up Manasseh as like Ahab and the Omrides. Second, Manasseh is the only Judean king accused of provoking Yahweh to anger (הכעס). All the others are northern. In this way, Manasseh is further set up as the Judean counterpart of the bad Israelite kings.[47] Third, Dtr uses it to describe the acts of those kings whose punishment is the destruction of their dynasty. Here, because of Manasseh's sins and his causing Yahweh to anger, the house of David will be removed from the throne, and not only his personal house but also the entire kingdom of Judah will be punished.

The verb הכעס when used by Dtr[1] (in the above-mentioned places) always has Yahweh or a suffix referring to Yahweh as its object. The exilic editor uses this same expression, but the object (namely, Yahweh) is implicit. Nelson astutely suggests that "only the exilic editor also uses a kind of shorthand phrase which leaves the object of the verb understood. . . . It seems that the cliché has become so familiar that only half of it communicated the whole."[48] Alternatively, this could be an example of Dtr[2] trying to replicate (somewhat inexactly) the prose of Dtr[1].

The shift in prototype strategy from Jeroboam to Ahab, emphasizing the change in theological concern (idolatry versus noncentralized worship), is clearly seen in the words of the doom proclamation.

"And I will not continue to cause the foot of Israel to wander from the land that I gave to their fathers, if they will carefully observe all that I commanded them [ככל אשר צויתים] and all the Torah that my servant Moses commanded them."[49] (9) But they did not listen[50] and

---

47. Keulen, *Manasseh*, 102.
48. Nelson, *Double Redaction*, 68.
49. Throughout Dtr[1], obedience to Yahweh's laws and commandments, statutes and testimonies is primary, but in the oracle against Judah, it is almost entirely absent, even though the specific sins have direct correlations to deuteronomic law. The only mention of the law is in a retrospective comment. In v. 8, first, we see an abbreviated reference to the law; ככל צויתים stands in for the more characteristic enumeration of laws, commandments, statutes, and testimonies common to Dtr[1]. Second, the rejection of Judah in 2 Kings 21, despite this verse, is not explicitly connected to the violation of the law, just that they did not listen. There is no specific indication of to what or how they did not listen. This was the perfect setup for admonition for not following the law. We would expect that they are told to follow the law, but instead they did not listen.
50. A contrast can be seen in the similar setup of accusation in the oracle against Israel. The differences highlight that the exilic oracle in 2 Kings 21 is less concerned with the violation of the covenant per se, and more with the actual practice of idolatry. 2 Kgs. 21:9 and 17:14

Manasseh caused them to err [וַיַּתְעֵם] doing the evil[51] of the nations whom Yahweh destroyed from before the children of Israel.

(10) And Yahweh spoke by the hand of his servants the prophets, saying: (11) "Because of what Manasseh king of Judah did, these transgressions [הַתֹּעֵבוֹת], he did [more] evil than all that the Amorites who were before him did and also caused Judah to sin [וַיַּחֲטִא] with his idols. (2 Kgs. 21:8-11)

In verse 9, the originality of Manasseh's sins is seen in the verb choice. Here, Manasseh's act of causing Judah to err is expressed differently from the sin of Jeroboam, which he caused Israel to sin (הֶחֱטִא), the quintessential sin of the kings of Israel presented in the anti-David prototype. In 2 Kings 21:9, the *hipʿil* of תעה is used. This is the only use of the form of this verb in DtrH. It also appears in Jer. 23:13, 32. This is possibly an indicator of its exilic usage. It is interesting to note that the *hipʿil* of חטא, which is one of the primary sins of Jeroboam, is not used in this verse as it is in 2 Kgs. 21:11 and 16. (There its use automatically activates a comparison to Jeroboam.[52]) This may be an unintentional slipup of Dtr[2] in copying the style of Dtr[1]. (For

---

begin similarly, but the way they continue is significant. 2 Kgs. 21:9 says, וְלֹא שָׁמֵעוּ וַיַּתְעֵם מְנַשֶּׁה לַעֲשׂוֹת אֶת הָרַע מִן הַגּוֹיִם אֲשֶׁר הִשְׁמִיד יְהוָה מִפְּנֵי בְּנֵי יִשְׂרָאֵל, "But they did not listen and Manasseh caused them to err doing the evil of the nations who Yahweh destroyed from before the children of Israel." Conversely, 2 Kgs. 17:14-15 demonstrates to what and how they did not listen, employing the characteristic covenant language of Dtr[1]: וְלֹא שָׁמְעוּ וַיַּקְשׁוּ אֶת עָרְפָּם כְּעֹרֶף אֲבוֹתָם אֲשֶׁר לֹא הֶאֱמִינוּ בַּיהוָה אֱלֹהֵיהֶם. וַיִּמְאֲסוּ אֶת חֻקָּיו וְאֶת בְּרִיתוֹ אֲשֶׁר כָּרַת אֶת אֲבוֹתָם וְאֵת עֵדְוֹתָיו אֲשֶׁר הֵעִיד בָּם, "But they did not listen and were stiff-necked like their fathers who did not trust in Yahweh their God. And they rejected his statutes and his covenant, which he made with their fathers, and his warnings, which he gave them." The two verses begin with לֹא שָׁמְעוּ, but 2 Kings 21 does not make explicit to what they do not listen, while 2 Kings 17 makes it clear that it is the warning to keep the covenant. In turn, they rejected it. The slight variation in these two accusations against Israel and Judah is another illustration of the difference in the theological foci of Dtr[1] and Dtr[2].

51. This is the only place in Kings where הָרַע is used in this way. Everywhere else it is the evil in Yahweh's eyes. The phrase of practicing like the nations more frequently uses תּוֹעֲבוֹת, as in v. 2, cf. 1 Kgs. 14:24; 2 Kgs. 16:3, or less commonly חֻקּוֹת הַגּוֹיִם, cf. 2 Kgs. 17:8. This is a similar sentiment to the evaluation made in v. 2 that Manasseh "did what was evil in the eyes of Yahweh like the transgressions of the nations." Yet, in that verse remains the common הָרַע בְּעֵינֵי יְהוָה.

52. Smelik, "Portrayal of King Manasseh," 140.

example, Dtr^2 attempts to use a *hip'il* form of a sinning verb, but uses the wrong one.)

On the other hand, and perhaps more likely, the difference in the verb used in verse 9 may be intentional rather than inexact modeling. The use of תעה√, meaning "to lead astray," recalls the image of the king pasturing his people. Manasseh's leadership is contrary to how the shepherd is supposed to act.[53] The conjuring of this image makes the sin of Manasseh even more poignant. The king, who is the shepherd of his people, is supposed to care and look out for them, steering them away from danger. Instead, Manasseh guides them toward evil. Also, this act, causing Judah to err in doing the evil of the nations (הרע מן הגוים), connects this verse to the accusation in verse 2, that the evil Manasseh did was like the תעבות הגוים. This sentiment continues further in verse 11. There the verse uses the more common החטא. While verse 9 addresses the new ideas of Dtr^2, it is clearly modeled after Dtr^1's regnal formulae and the use of Jeroboam as the anti-Davidic prototype, further connecting Manasseh to the evil kings of Israel.

The Ahab association continues implicitly in verse 11. Here, Manasseh is specifically blamed for doing "more evil than the Amorites." Ahab is said to have been like the Amorites: "And he acted very abominably, going after the idols [גלולים] like all [ככל] that the Amorites did, whom Yahweh dispossessed [הוריש] before the children of Israel" (1 Kgs. 21:26). There, the Amorites are set up as the evil standard against which Ahab is measured. Ahab sinned like the Amorites. Manasseh, however, does more evil than the Amorites (הרע מכל אשר עשו האמרי) and Ahab.[54] Like Ahab, the sin Manasseh causes Judah to do is the worship of idols (גלולים). The term for foreign idols, גלולים, appears only six times in Kings, five of which

---

53. Keulen, *Manasseh*, 117.
54. Stavrakopoulou, "Blackballing of Manasseh," 252.

concern the sins of Ahab and Manasseh.[55] (The sixth is in the oracle against Israel, 2 Kgs. 17:12.) The use of this specific word further connects Manasseh and Ahab.

The most explicit connection to Ahab, his sin and fate, as well as linking Manasseh and Judah with Israel, is made in verses 12 and 13. This is the true doom oracle:

> Therefore, thus said Yahweh God of Israel: "Behold I am bringing evil on Jerusalem and Judah, all who hear [of] it, his two ears will ring. (13) I will stretch the measuring line of Samaria over Jerusalem and with the plummet of the house of Ahab and I will wipe [out] Jerusalem as one wipes clean the bowl, wiped out and turned over on its face."

We see here, in Yahweh's proclamation against Manasseh and Judah, continuity with other similar announcements. Yahweh will "bring evil on Jerusalem and Judah" (הנני מביא רעה). This phrase is also used in the oracles against the house of Jeroboam (1 Kgs. 14:10) and the house of Ahab (1 Kgs. 2:21). Additionally, it appears in the exilic version of Huldah's oracle (2 Kgs. 22:20). Here, Dtr^2 uses the same phraseology of the oracles against northern kings Jeroboam and Ahab and their houses to announce the fate of Judah and Jerusalem. Unlike those oracles, this reused phrase was previously applied to kings and their punishments; in contrast, Manasseh does not receive any individual penalty. This punishment is reserved for Jerusalem and Judah alone. It is interesting to note here that while it is frequent that the fate of the nation depends on the behavior of the king, this is the only instance in which the king does evil, bringing punishment on the people, but is not punished himself. This may also be another indicator that the blame is a secondary addition. In the preexilic version, there was no individual punishment of Manasseh to which this national punishment can be attached. The preexilic Manasseh

---

55. 1 Kgs. 15:12; 21; 26; 2 Kgs. 17:12; 21:11, 21; 23:24 (Schniedewind, "History and Interpretation," 352).

was not so bad as to warrant a remarkable punishment, or any punishment at all.

In these verses, Dtr² begins to connect the collective fate of Judah with that of Israel. This continues with the reference to the "measuring line of Samaria," explicitly linking the sin with the subsequent punishment of the northern kingdom. In 2 Kings 17, Dtr¹ makes clear that the sin of Israel is one of decentralization and syncretism. (Verses 12 and 16 mention sins of idolatry, but these verses are likely exilic.) Israel is also convicted for having rejected the Davidic king and separating from Judah in the first place and for not keeping the covenant (vv. 15, 21-22). The initial charge against Israel is as follows:

> And they followed the statutes of the nations [חקות הגוים], whom Yahweh dispossessed before the children of Israel, and of the kings of Israel which they practiced. (9) And the children of Israel ascribed things that were not so upon Yahweh, their God, and they built for themselves high places in all their cities from the watchtower to the fortified city. (10) And they installed *maṣṣēbôt* and *ʾăšērîm* on every high hill and under every leafy tree. (11) And they made offerings there, at all the high places like the nations, which Yahweh exiled from before them; and they did evil things, causing Yahweh to anger [הכעס]. (2 Kgs. 17:8-11)

The primary charge against Israel is their worship at the high places, which includes the worship of *maṣṣēbôt* and *ʾăšērîm*. With his short reference to the "measuring line of Samaria" in 2 Kgs. 21:13, Dtr² conjures the entirety of the oracle against (and fate of) Israel. They were censured for these many sins and exiled as punishment.

The reference to the fate of the North is to the kingdom as a whole and not to the house of Jeroboam, which was thoroughly destroyed (1 Kgs. 15:27-30), even though in much of DtrH the great sin of Israel is following the sin of Jeroboam. In contrast, the plummet of the house of Ahab refers specifically to the fate of the Omrides, rather than the collective of Israel. This further contributes to the use of Ahab, rather than Jeroboam, as the comparative prototype. P. S. F. van Keulen declares that verse 13 "renders Ahab the perfect counterpart to Manasseh." Ahab bears partial responsibility for the fall of Samaria, while Manasseh bears complete responsibility for Jerusalem.[56] Until Manasseh, Ahab is the most evil king and his house is cut off from Israel.[57] Yet even Ahab, who is an evil king *sans pareil*, is able to repent. He mourns after the oracle and is able to postpone the destruction. Yahweh says: "Because he has humbled himself before me, I will not bring the disaster in his lifetime; I will bring the disaster upon his house in his son's time" (1 Kgs. 21:29). Manasseh, in Dtr^2's narrative, is not given this opportunity (in contrast, Manasseh in Chronicles repents like Ahab in Kings, postponing the impending doom) even though historically the punishment is delayed fifty-plus years.

It is interesting that Dtr^2 does not reuse the oracle against Israel in 2 Kgs. 17:7-23, but makes reference to the fall of Israel with metaphoric connections to the measuring line of Samaria and the plummet of the house of Ahab. Allusion to the oracle against Israel is also present in the link between Manasseh's sin and the transgressions of the dispossessed nations, as discussed above. A third reference to the oracle is present in verse 15. Yahweh says that Judah "did what was evil in my eyes and they angered me from the day which their fathers

---

56. Keulen, *Manasseh*, 131.

57. Elijah pronounces an oracle on Ahab: "Because you have committed yourself to doing what is evil in the sight of Yahweh, I am ready to bring evil upon you. I will make a clean sweep of you, I will cut off from Israel every male belonging to Ahab, bond and free. And I will make your house like the house of Jeroboam son of Nebat and like the house of Baasha son of Ahijah, because of the provocation you have caused by leading Israel to sin [אל הכעס אשר הכעסת ותחטא את ישראל]" (1 Kgs. 21:20-22). The reason for this annihilation is given explicitly: "Indeed, there never was anyone like Ahab, who committed himself to doing what was evil in Yahweh's eyes, at the instigation of his wife Jezebel. And he acted very abominably going after the idols like all that the Amorites, whom Yahweh dispossessed before the children of Israel, did" (1 Kgs. 21:25-26).

went out from Egypt until this day." The mention of Egypt connects this statement with the beginning of the oracle in 2 Kgs. 17:7: "And it was because the children of Israel sinned against Yahweh their God, who brought them up from the land of Egypt from under the hand of Pharaoh, king of Egypt, and they feared other gods." While Dtr^2 does not reuse 2 Kings 17, his allusions make clear connections between the fates of Israel and Judah.

Why Manasseh?

The majority of this chapter has focused on how and why Dtr^2 utilizes the preexilic historian's historiographical poetics, most specifically the prototype strategy. The exilic historian imitates the style of Dtr^1 by choosing one figure, Manasseh, to highlight as a paradigmatic and didactic exemplar to convey his theological beliefs. Dtr^1 portrays David as the paradigm of the good king, comparing other kings to the Davidic standard and emphasizing a few kings, namely Jeroboam and Josiah, as depicted in his model. This illustrates the importance of obedience (and the consequences of disobedience) to the deuteronomic law, including stipulations for centralized and nonsyncretistic worship. Similarly, Dtr^2 chooses the figure of Manasseh to convey the exilic historian's message against idolatry, especially Baal worship and the practices of the nations, and the severe consequences of disobedience. As is characteristic of Dtr's composition, the exilic historian attributes theological meaning to historico-political events. It is the reason for the vilification of Manasseh. The destruction of Jerusalem and Judah and the Babylonian exile are the historical reality of Dtr^2. While the idea of exile and destruction strikes a major blow to preexilic deuteronomistic theology, which promotes the eternity of the Davidic dynasty, the temple and Jerusalem as Yahweh's chosen place, and a connection to the land, in an exilic context, the deuteronomistic theologians look for reasons to explain the calamity of the destruction.[58] Maintaining the strict system of sin and punishment of deuteronomistic theology, Dtr[2] finds a reasonable outlet for this explanation. Judah has sinned, and they will therefore be punished. Also, throughout Kings the fate of the nation has depended on the acts of the kings. Israel is punished for committing the sin of Jeroboam, while in this account Judah is punished for the sin of Manasseh. The attribution of theological causes to this historico-political event is quite clear. The doom oracle (2 Kgs. 21:8-15) explains how the Babylonians will come to rule over Judah and deport them. It is all a consequence of Manasseh's sin and Yahweh's working in history (v. 14). The Davidic monarchy has come to an end. Yahweh has turned the king, the land, and the people over to their enemies. In order to convey his specific, exilic theological concerns, Dtr[2] depicts Manasseh in the model of Ahab,

58. The doom proclamation in 2 Kgs. 21:12-15, although consistent with the deuteronomistic idea of reward and punishment, especially for the sin of idolatry and violation of the divine covenant, does not reflect the concept of an eternal covenant. Following the connections between Judah and Israel, the pronouncement continues: "I will abandon the remnant of my inheritance and hand them over to their enemies and they will be as plunder and booty to all their enemies. Because of that which they did that was evil in my eyes and they angered me from the day which their fathers went out from Egypt until this day" (2 Kgs. 21:14-15). God will destroy and forsake even the remnant of Israel, namely, Judah. There is no sense of pending restoration once punishment is meted out. There is no promise for a return or the continuity of the people after the destruction and exile in this oracle. In fact, the only reference to a remnant, found in v. 14, is one in which the remnant will be forsaken. Here שארית is linked to its earlier connotation of Judah as the only remaining tribe after the destruction of Israel. At the same time, "the remnant" is used differently—even the remnant will be destroyed. This is unlike 2 Kings 19, when Hezekiah asks what to do in the face of the approaching Assyrian army. He is reassured that "the survivors [פליטת] of the house of Judah who remain [הנשארה] will take root downward and bear fruit upward. For a remnant [שארית] will go out of Jerusalem, and survivors [ופליטה] from Mount Zion" (2 Kgs. 19:30-31). In this context, the remnant is those who survive the onslaught, consistent with the deuteronomistic theology of an eternal covenant. Similarly, in the oracle against Israel in 2 Kgs. 17:18: ויתאנף יהוה מאד בישראל ויסרם מעל פניו לא נשאר רק שבט יהודה לבדו, "Yahweh was very angry with Israel and removed them from his presence. Only the tribe of Judah remained alone." Even in the face of extreme punishment and impending destruction, in the preexilic text Judah will always be a remnant, a survivor. In 2 Kgs. 21:14, Dtr[2] uses the language of the remnant to continue to refer to Judah, as in the preexilic edition, but the remnant will no longer remain.

rather than the anti-David, Jeroboam. While I have established this in the preceding pages, we must still ask, Why is Manasseh chosen for this infamous purpose, especially since the blame is not original to his account? In Chronicles (2 Chronicles 28), Ahaz is depicted as the most evil king. Why Manasseh in Kings?

Stavrakopoulou convincingly argues that the historian is first attracted to a southern king with a northern name, allowing the historian to both equate Manasseh with Israel and Israel's sins, and to alleviate some of the blame on Judah.[59] Another reason may be Manasseh's role as an innovator of transgression. In verse 16, Manasseh is said to spill innocent blood: "And furthermore, the innocent blood Manasseh spilled was very great until it filled Jerusalem from end to end, apart from his sin which he caused Judah to sin [החטא], doing evil in the eyes of Yahweh [לעשות הרע בעיני יהוה]." It is possible to see Manasseh's spilling of innocent blood as a "transgression-innovation." No other king is accused of this. The presence of this innovation may be one of the reasons Dtr^2 is captivated by the ordinary portrait of Manasseh and chooses him as arch-villain. In keeping with Dtr's style, the evil kings Dtr^1 highlights, namely, Jeroboam and Ahab, each have their own "transgression-innovations." Jeroboam establishes his countercult at Dan and Bethel, while Ahab, "thinking it light" to merely follow the sins of Jeroboam, adds Baal worship to Israelite practice. In contrast, the ordinary bad kings do not commit "original" sins. They follow the sins of (primarily) Jeroboam and (some) Ahab. But Manasseh contributes a new sin: the spilling of innocent blood. Dtr^2 may have picked up on this sin and expanded the narrative because of it.

---

59. Stavrakopoulou, *King Manasseh and Child Sacrifice*, 63–67; Stavrakopoulou, "Blackballing of Manasseh," 253.

While some scholars see this sin as a later addition,[60] it is quite out of place in the exilic version of the narrative. Manasseh is evaluated as doing what is evil in Yahweh's eyes. His sins are enumerated in the first verses (vv. 2-7) of the account; they are then followed by the oracle against Judah. The sin of spilling innocent blood is not mentioned until after the verdict of Judah and just before the concluding formula of the regnal account. The strange placement of this accusation points to the verse being separated from its original context in the list of sins in the preexilic account. Verse 16 seems to continue the list of the sins from the beginning of the chapter, and the oracle is inserted in the middle of the list. Also, this verse appears more closely related to the preexilic use of Jeroboam as the prototype of the evil king, using the sinning verb *hip'il* החטא. In the preexilic version, this verse functions as the close of the regnal formula and connects Manasseh's sins with those of Jeroboam.[61] Just as Jeroboam caused Israel to sin (החטא), an important element of the prototype strategy of Dtr[1], so too does Manasseh. In the close of this verse, Manasseh is like Jeroboam (not Ahab). Causing Judah to sin has as its consequence the destruction of Judah, but the causation is not made here as in verse 11. This is because verse 16 was composed by Dtr[1], who, while viewing Manasseh as an evil king, does not blame him for the exile. In turn, Dtr[2] picks up on this phrase in verse 16 and reuses it in verse 11, expanding and qualifying how Manasseh caused Judah to sin (with his idols).

Following Manasseh's reign, this sin becomes part of the repertoire of Judah's transgressions. The term דם נקי is often used in prophetic

---

60. Volkmar Fritz, *1 and 2 Kings*, trans. Anselm Hagedorn, Continental Commentaries (Minneapolis: Fortress Press, 2003), 392; Eynikel, "Portrait of Manasseh," 241.

61. This is in contrast with the exilic account, which breaks the regnal formula in order to expand the narrative. The RF of the exilic account closes in the end of v. 6 with the inclusion of הרבה לעשות הרע בעיני יהוה להכעיס, Manasseh "greatly increased doing what is evil in the eyes of Yahweh to cause [him] to anger."

lists of Judah's sins (see Isa. 59:7; Jer. 7:6; 19:4; 22:3; 22:17; 26:15).
It is related to a prohibition in Deut. 19:10: לא ישפך דם נקי מקרב
ארצך, "Don't spill innocent blood within your land." The term is
also used twice more during the reign of Jehoiakim in the report
of the exile, referring to Manasseh and the reminder that he is to
blame for the destruction of Judah: וגם דם הנקי אשר שפך וימלא
את ירושלם דם נקי ולא אבה יהוה לסלח, "And also because of the
innocent blood that he shed. For he filled Jerusalem with innocent
blood, and Yahweh would not forgive" (2 Kgs. 24:4). Also, the
verse begins with וגם, which functions as a redactional juncture,
connecting two redactional levels of the text, showing the seams of
redaction.[62]

While it is possible since this is a sin that we have never seen
before that it may be the invention of Dtr[2], attempting to further
vilify Manasseh as the most evil king, it is more likely that the
sin of spilling innocent blood in verse 16 belongs to the preexilic
account, since it does not play an important role in the narrative, even
though it is unique to Manasseh. One would expect that if the author
who included this transgression were the same one who vilified
Manasseh, it would play a more prominent role in the narrative. If the
preexilic Deuteronomist had initially planned to posit Manasseh as
the figure to "outdo" both Jeroboam and Ahab, surely he would have
highlighted this sin as one that makes Manasseh unique among the

---

62. This crime is not mentioned elsewhere in Kings, which Dtr assimilates from another place.
This verse resumes the list of sins of Manasseh that started the chapter, possibly continuing v.
3a or 4. If this verse were taken from the annals (indicated by the perfect verbs), we can also
see how Dtr[1] integrates it into his text. This is not done smoothly. The verse begins with וגם,
which functions as a redactional juncture, connecting two levels of redaction (Nelson, *Double
Redaction*, 83). The verse continues: לבד מחטאתו אשר החטא את יהודה לעשות הרע בעיני
יהוה, "Apart from his sin which he caused Judah to sin doing evil in the eyes of Yahweh." The
use of לבד here shows a somewhat clumsy redaction. Sweeney describes this as interrupting
the verse. In DtrH, לבד frequently appears in lists or categorizations and is used to introduce
distinct items. Here לבד interrupts the "normal presentation of activities on the part of the
kings in DtrH" (Sweeney, *King Josiah of Judah*, 59).

evil kings and befitting the blame of the destruction of Judah, instead of leaving it to follow the verdict of Judah. At the same time, one would also expect that if this sin in a preexilic version were the cause of exile, it would have been highlighted with the sins of Jeroboam (decentralization and causing the people to sin) and that of Ahab (idolatry), which have already been punished with the destruction of the northern kingdom and Ahab's house, respectively.

Throughout the Manasseh account, we see a shift in the theological focus of the exilic version. The blame of Manasseh is built on several ideological premises. First, the theological denigration of the North throughout the book of Kings has been adopted from the work of Dtr^1. Almost every northern king is portrayed negatively. Also, the fall of the northern kingdom is used for polemical reasons—the northern kings and people behave like foreign nations and despise Yahweh's laws and prophetic warnings. Judah has become like Israel.[63] Manasseh is like an Israelite king. Dtr^2 absorbs this into his narrative. Second, Manasseh does more evil than the nations. He is not the first to participate in foreign cult practices, but the text emphasizes specifically that Manasseh's idolatry leads to exile.[64] Third, a theological premise, or more of a theological omission, is the lack of focus on fidelity to the law. Manasseh's sins are not articulated as his violation of the law (although the underlying assumption is that they are), but that he sins in his cultic practice. The mention of the commandments and the Torah of Moses in verse 8 are phrases included to stand in for the whole of the law, but we do not see the more explicit language of covenant fidelity, common to Dtr^1, articulated.

In 2 Kgs. 21:1-18, Dtr^2 activates the prototype strategy, both positively and negatively, but in a unique way. The use of the verbs

---

63. Stavrakopoulou, "Blackballing of Manasseh," 251.
64. Ibid., 250.

החטא and הכעס connect Manasseh with the worst of Israelite kings, rendering a harsh evaluation. הכעס aligns him with Jeroboam, Baasha, Omri, Ahab, and Azariah, the kings of the destroyed dynasties, while החטא connects him to Jeroboam, Baasha, and Ahab. Manasseh is linked with both Jeroboam and Ahab, but the Ahab parallel is more prominent.[65] He is also contrasted with the best of kings: Hezekiah who tears down the high places in verse 3, David and Solomon, the founders of the centralized temple in verse 7,[66] and in the exilic account of his reign, Josiah. Throughout the Manasseh account, there are many intertextual references in which Manasseh is compared and contrasted with earlier kings. No other king has been portrayed as wicked as Manasseh, even though many of his sins were committed by other Judean kings. None did as many.[67] The historian uses a statement of incomparability in 2 Kgs. 21:11, as Dtr[1] does in his portraits of Solomon, Hezekiah, Josiah, and Jeroboam, demonstrating how Manasseh surpasses the previously incomparable evil king, Ahab (1 Kgs. 16:32).[68]

The use of Ahab as the prototype for the portrait of Manasseh is readily apparent in the narrative, but it is not a straight casting of Manasseh in the model of Ahab. As with the portrait of Josiah, the hero of the preexilic history, Manasseh supersedes all prototypical models. Josiah is better than all of the kings who preceded him, including the illustrious David. At each stage of his reform, his actions supersede those of the other good kings. Likewise, Manasseh surpasses Ahab in the extent of his evil. While Ahab builds one altar to Baal, Manasseh builds more than one (v. 3). While Ahab is evil like the Amorites, Manasseh is more evil than the Amorites (v. 11). Even

---

65. Keulen, *Manasseh*, 147.
66. Ibid., 145.
67. Ibid., 144.
68. See, Gary N. Knoppers, "'There Was None Like Him': Incomparability in the Books of Kings," *CBQ* 54, no. 3 (1992): 411–31.

Ahab has the potential to repent and push off the destruction of his house, but Manasseh has no opportunity to repent. He is not even given prophetic warning. Manasseh commits many sins, all the sins that have been committed by the kings of Israel and Judah—undoing reform, decentralized and syncretistic worship at the high places and of Asherah, worshiping Baal and the host of heaven, passing his sons through fire, a host of divination practices—in addition to a completely unique sin of spilling innocent blood. Smelik argues that Manasseh's reign "constitutes the nadir of the history of kingship in Israel." He is the most evil of all kings.[69] In this way, Dtr^2 creates a portrait of a king who is "worthy" of shouldering the blame of the fall of Judah, the destruction of the temple, the exile of the people, and an overhaul of deuteronomistic theology, reconsidering the eternal promises to the people and the Davidic line.

Analysis of the Manasseh account illustrates a difference in the foci of the historiographical poetics of the exilic Deuteronomist. It is through the exilic account of Manasseh's reign that we see a shift in the Deuteronomist's historiographical poetics. We are unable to view Dtr^2's role in selection, but his compositional poetics are clear. He creates a prophetic-like oracle to pronounce doom on Judah, imitating Dtr^1's use of the prophetic tradition. More significantly, Dtr^2's narrative demonstrates a theological shift, which moves away from the preexilic focus on decentralization and obedience to the law and centers on fighting Baal worship and other forms of idolatry and foreign worship. This change is most clearly seen in the replacement of Jeroboam as the prototype of the evil king. The Manasseh account functions as a counterexample for Dtr's historiographical poetics, particularly in respect to the prototype strategy. The account reflects the priorities of the axis of composition, including the promotion of the deuteronomistic program, the attribution of theological causes to

69. Smelik, "Portrayal of King Manasseh," 148–49.

historico-political events, and the prototype strategy, but reflects a different theological perspective, focused on the eradication of Baal and other foreign worship and explaining the historical reality of the destruction of Jerusalem and Judah and the end of the Davidic monarchy. In this way, Dtr^2 vilifies Manasseh as the worst of all kings by using Ahab as the model for the prototype strategy.

7

Conclusion: "There Shall Be a King over Us"

Throughout the Deuteronomistic History the issue of kingship is a prominent theme, dealt with in comparison to other forms of leadership. The book of Joshua presents Joshua as a protomonarch. Parts of Judges are redacted to express an opinion that the charismatic leadership of the judges is not sufficient to govern Israel, as they sin when there is no king over them. Similarly, 1 Samuel 8 expresses the people's desire and demand for a king. Yahweh's and Samuel's responses are a hesitant acquiescence. By the time the reader reaches the book of Kings, one is already mired in the dilemma of deciding whether kingship is good or bad for Israel. The book of Kings, narrating the history of the monarchy over approximately four centuries, from the reign of Solomon until the Babylonian exile, presents a synchronized chronicle of the reigns of each of the kings of Israel and Judah. Due to their presentation by Dtr, some of the kings are more memorable than others. Those kings who feature more prominently are presented using Dtr's prototype strategy, in relation to the literary portrait of David.

The Effects of the Davidic Prototype Strategy

King David of legend is many things. He is a womanizer, military hero, Shakespearean-like character, mythic warrior. This leads many to assume he must be historical because no people would invent such a flawed character as a national hero.[1] In all of these depictions, it is clear that one thing he is not is cultic hero. However, he becomes one in the imagination of Dtr. David's reputation is enough to inspire Dtr to adopt the mythic David of legend for his own purposes. Beginning with the deuteronomistic addition to Samuel in 2 Samuel 7, continuing into the establishment of David's successor, Solomon, and the first king of the North, Jeroboam, and through the regnal evaluations of the various kings of Israel and Judah, Dtr transforms the character of David, so well known from Samuel (or Samuel's sources), into a figure who is programmatically useful to him in his goal of writing a theologically based, cultically focused history. The David seen in Kings is transformed. He is Yahweh's servant, one who follows the commandments, statutes, laws, and ordinances (esp. 1 Kgs. 9:4-5). He is loyal to Yahweh through the covenant. And he would, of course, only support one centralized shrine in Jerusalem.

This "new" literary David becomes the paradigm of the cultically adherent king, one who serves as the model for all subsequent kings on how to behave. It is through this portrayal that the portrait of the kings is established. Kings are either like or unlike David. They are crafted in a way such that in the accounts of each reign Dtr's evaluation of them reflects back onto the portrait of David. Was such and such a king like David? Was his heart fully with Yahweh as

---

1. Robert Pinsky, *The Life of David* (New York: Schocken, 2005), 4.

David's heart was? Did he do what was right in Yahweh's eyes, as David did?

The recasting of David is an intentional technique used by the preexilic Deuteronomist. Dtr uses this reconstructed portrait of David to demonstrate what it takes to be the ideal king. In the first eleven chapters of Kings, notably the account of the reign of Solomon, Dtr lays out the characteristics and criteria of the Davidic prototype. Simultaneously, while presenting the terms of the Davidic prototype strategy, Dtr applies this prototype to his portrayal of Solomon. He subsequently constructs Jeroboam and Josiah in a similar style. Through each of these narratives, the criteria for what it means "to be like David" is further developed and expanded. A king like David directs his whole heart to Yahweh and "does what is right in the eyes of Yahweh." Most kings, even two of these paradigmatic kings—Solomon and Jeroboam—are unable to achieve the Davidic standard.

The portrait of the covenantally adherent David is primarily created through the investiture of Solomon and the stereotypical regnal evaluations of the kings of Israel and Judah. Most kings are said to do "what is evil in the eyes of Yahweh," while only eight of the more than forty monarchs of Israel and Judah are said to "do what is right in the eyes of Yahweh." Of those, only three are said to be like David—Asa, Hezekiah, and Josiah. As I have discussed, the inclusion of Asa in this praiseworthy group is confounding. He seems no better, and perhaps, even less good, than others who do what is right but are not said to be like David. While Hezekiah is also said to be like David, the account of his reign and the extent of his reform are downplayed by the preexilic Dtr. Only Josiah appears to truly be like David, or perhaps even greater than David. Only Josiah entirely commits his heart, soul, and might to Yahweh, as in the prescription of Deut. 6:5. Not even David himself fulfills this law.

The emphasis on covenant fidelity is a focus on the importance of deuteronomic law. The elevation of Josiah, and even the denigration of Hezekiah, contribute to the likelihood of a Josianic edition of Dtr. The application of the Davidic prototype strategy to the important kings of the monarchic period demonstrates Dtr's theological focus on centralization of the cult and the embodiment of the faithful king in the person of Josiah, the true fulfillment of the Davidic prototype.

The account of the reign of Solomon, both in his investiture and his punishment, outline the criteria for being a good king like David, as applied to the aforementioned kings. In his deathbed instructions to Solomon, David explicitly lays out how Solomon (and all future kings) ought to behave. They should follow Yahweh's ways, keeping his statutes and commandments, laws and warnings, and walk faithfully before Yahweh with all their heart and soul (1 Kgs. 2:3-4). In his own lifetime, Solomon is unable to follow these instructions. His heart is not fully with Yahweh; instead, he loves foreign women and establishes the foreign cultic practices of his wives. He builds the temple but does not restrict worship to it exclusively. And he did not observe what Yahweh had commanded. To make his censure of Solomon clear, Dtr constructs a narrative in which Yahweh sends three adversaries against Solomon to punish him. More severely, Solomon is condemned by losing the majority of the Davidic kingdom. As punishment, ten tribes will join together under a competing king, Jeroboam, and Solomon's son Rehoboam will be left with a diminished kingdom. In both the proclamation of punishment for Solomon and in the description of Jeroboam as the recipient of Solomon's ill fortune, Dtr makes clear the reasons Solomon is censured so harshly: his heart turned away from Yahweh, he was not like David, and he was not faithful to the covenant (1 Kgs. 11:10-11). These "divine" statements further establish the terms of the Davidic prototype strategy.

The narrative of the reign of Jeroboam further develops the Davidic prototype, as begun in the Solomon narrative. Jeroboam is depicted as an oppositional portrait to the Davidic prototype, the anti-David. In the beginning of his reign, Jeroboam is set up as the fulfillment of the Davidic prototype. He is the vehicle for the punishment of Solomon, invested with words of instruction (1 Kgs. 11:38), mirroring those of David in 1 Kgs. 2:3-4, and contrasting the rebuke of Solomon in 1 Kgs. 11:9-11. Jeroboam is commissioned by Yahweh's prophet, like David, in the motif of "prophets as kingmakers"; he is a usurper king; the previous king (Solomon) seeks to kill him. These similarities coupled with the linguistic commonalities create an undeniable comparison between Jeroboam and David. Jeroboam has every opportunity to be like David, to do what is right in Yahweh's eyes, and to direct his heart to Yahweh, but he does not. Instead, he was not "like my servant David, who observed my commandments and who followed me with all his heart, doing only what was right in my eyes. . . . [He did] worse than all who came before" him (1 Kgs. 14:8-9).

In betraying his Davidic potential, Jeroboam establishes a competing prototype, an antitype. He is the anti-David, the northern king who does not keep the covenant and causes his people to sin against Yahweh. As the literary antitype, just as David is the model of the Judean good kings, Jeroboam is the model for the Israelite bad kings. They do not keep the covenant, they worship at the uncentralized shrines established by Jeroboam, and they follow the ways of Jeroboam rather than the ways of Yahweh (הלך בדרך), as prescribed to Solomon by David (1 Kgs. 2:3). Through the regnal evaluations, each of the bad kings of Israel is compared to Jeroboam. The establishment of the Davidic antitype in the person of Jeroboam not only sets up a comparative for the bad kings but also creates a figure against whom Josiah, established as the paradigm of the Davidic prototype, can literarily challenge and counter.

Josiah, as *the* Davidic figure, is the only king fully able to right the wrongs of Jeroboam, not only destroying his uncentralized shrines and finally getting the people to stop worshiping at the *bāmôt*, but also "reuniting" the kingdom, returning it to its ideal, unified state of the Davidic period. The use of the prototype strategy makes the realization of this opposition more integrated and essential to the nature of composition. The competition between Josiah and Jeroboam as the prototype and antitype is more specific than reading only the competing themes of Jeroboam's sin and David's faithfulness, as Cross does.[2]

The mention of Josiah in the Jeroboam narrative highlights their literary bond. The man of God prophesies the future coming of Josiah and the reform measures he will take against Jeroboam's shrines (1 Kgs. 13). Josiah is set up as hero, while Jeroboam is the villain. The use of Jeroboam as the Davidic antitype and the model for the evil kings, even if he is not the most evil of the kings, emphasizes an important deuteronomistic theological focus: centralization of the cult to Jerusalem. Jeroboam's establishment of the countercults at Bethel and Dan is recast by Dtr[1] as the epitome of evil, akin to idolatry. Much of the rhetoric used to portray Jeroboam's shrines in this way is wrapped up in the application of the prototype strategy. As the anti-David, Jeroboam's acts, while they may have been acceptable, and even standard, in Jeroboam's ninth-century context, are seen as violating Dtr's covenant theology. Jeroboam does not follow Yahweh and his laws, statutes, commandments, and testimonies when erecting and dedicating the shrines. Similarly, by contrasting Jeroboam with Josiah, the impetus of Josiah's reform—the

---

2. *CMHE* 282.

book finding and concern with not conforming to the laws of Deuteronomy—emphasizes the acts of reform, purging Judah (and Israel) of forms and symbols of foreign worship, and destroying the uncentralized shrines throughout Judah and Israel. This results in a reification of the covenant with Yahweh. The issue with Jeroboam and the focus of Josiah's reform is not about foreign worship, but the integration of foreign symbols into Yahwistic worship. Using Jeroboam as the failed Davidic prototype and subsequently as the Davidic antitype stresses centralization as the major concern of the author/redactor.

Similarly, in his own account in 2 Kings 22–23, Josiah is depicted as the embodiment of the Davidic prototype. Josiah is the only king to completely fulfill the criteria set up in the Solomon narrative and the regnal evaluations. Josiah is not only like David but also "walked in all the way[s] of David his father. And he did not stray to the right or left" (2 Kgs. 22:2). He does what is right in Yahweh's eyes. Not only is his heart with Yahweh, but so are his soul and might as in Deut. 6:5 (2 Kgs. 23:25). Josiah is said to walk in the way of David (2 Kgs. 22:2), in contrast to all those bad kings who walked in the way(s) of Jeroboam. He is adherent to deuteronomic law, purging the land of foreign cult practices and restoring the covenant. In so doing, he undoes the sins of Solomon and Jeroboam, destroying their uncentralized shrines and restoring the people under one Davidic king.

Many of these accomplishments are literarily established through the use of the prototype strategy. In employing the literary conventions of the Davidic prototype strategy, Dtr is able to establish Josiah as the best of kings, even before he embarks on his reform. Josiah is set up as a king of incomparability, compared to, and surpassing, other incomparable figures, including Moses, Solomon, Jeroboam, and Hezekiah. The use of the conventions of the prototype strategy also allows the historian to focus on the importance of the law code and its role in the deuteronomistic program, without spending much space fleshing out the character of Josiah. His portrayal is tied to the prototype as a recognizable example for Dtr's audience. They know what to expect when the parameters of the prototype are activated. A king like David is covenantally loyal, does what is right in Yahweh's eyes, and his heart is with Yahweh. The description of Josiah depicts him as exceeding the expectations of the good Davidic king.

The presentation of Josiah as the personification of the Davidic prototype is not just in the narrative of Josiah's reign (2 Kings 22–23) but in the entirety of the preexilic history. While throughout the history the kings of Israel and Judah are compared to David, it is clear that the portrait of David is based on one of Josiah. The use of the Davidic prototype strategy illustrates a thorough narrative plan in which Dtr intentionally casts his kings in the prototype and its antitype. When considering the prototype strategy as one of the defining features of the preexilic Deuteronomist's historiographical poetics, it is difficult to accept opinions like Lauren Monroe's in which she says, "Josiah appears to be modeled on David only as an afterthought, part and parcel of the rhetorical process of replacing Hezekiah with Josiah as the hero of the Kings history."[3] Instead, the prototype strategy is an intentional strategy, which creates an integrated literary whole of the narrative, with Josiah and his reform at the center. The connection between the portraits of David and Josiah are integrally linked. Josiah's actions are intertextually connected with the acts of the other kings; he corrects the sins of the evil kings and improves on the reforms of the reformers.

---

3. Lauren A. S. Monroe, *Josiah's Reform and the Dynamics of Defilement: Israelite Rites of Violence and the Making of a Biblical Text* (New York: Oxford University Press, 2011), 126.

The Prototype Strategy and Deuteronomistic Poetics

The value of highlighting the prototype strategy is twofold. First, we see an intentional plan that is used throughout the Josianic edition of the history. The kings who are most interesting to Dtr[1] are constructed using the same prototype. This allows us both to compare them and to know what to expect with each subsequent king. The prototype strategy links the characters as types and antitypes, demonstrating the overall intentional literary plan and highlighting the kind of story that Dtr wants to tell. As Hayden White describes, Dtr has emplotted his characters into a specific narrative story. The commonalities between these kings also highlight what issues are most central to the historian, namely, centralization and the eradication of synchronized cults.

Second, the use of the prototype strategy can help us distinguish redactional levels. The Davidic prototype strategy is used in the portraits of Solomon, Jeroboam, and Josiah, but not in the portrait of Hezekiah. And it is certainly not used in the portrait of Manasseh, considered the most evil king, on whom the destruction of Judah and Jerusalem is blamed. The overall literary plan leads up to Josiah; it does not stop with Hezekiah, and the account of Manasseh seems out of place. The portraits of those kings reflected in the Davidic prototype, namely Solomon, Jeroboam, and Josiah, are all the product of a single author. This is a historian linked to the court of Josiah. The lack of prototype representation in the narrative of Hezekiah, even though he was an exemplary king and the historical memory of him seen between the lines of Kings is likely more complementary than how he is depicted by Dtr, illustrates that the history we have is not Hezekian. The primary first edition is focused on Josiah.

Moreover, the prototype strategy allows us to date this level of redaction. The focus on cultic rigorism and centralization is embodied in the vilification of Jeroboam and his cult. The author's primary theological battle is not with Baal worship and other forms of idolatry, as these are concerns for a later time. If they had been, we might have expected Ahab as the model for the evil king. Also, Josiah is featured throughout DtrH as the hero of the history, the figure to whom the entire narrative seems to build. The Davidic prototype, based on the portrait of Josiah as the ultimate example of the Davidic king, leads the reader to acknowledge the Josianic and preexilic perspective of the narrative.

The portrait of Manasseh in 2 Kings 21 further justifies these contentions. Manasseh is constructed using a prototype strategy, but it is not one based on the figure of David and the anti-David, Jeroboam. Instead, Manasseh is modeled after Ahab. The use of Ahab as the prototype highlights a transition in the theological and cultic concerns of Dtr. His issue is now focused on Baal and other idolatrous forms of worship. While Jeroboam, a bad but not the worst king, is used as the model for the evil kings of Israel (even after the reign of Ahab), illustrating the focus on decentralization, Ahab is truly the worst of kings but is only compared to other Omride kings and Manasseh. This shift, from Jeroboam to Ahab as model, shows a difference in the author's concern. The clearest way to account for the difference in focus is through a change in context. The Manasseh narrative, as preserved in the final version of Kings, is exilic. The exilic Dtr^2 adopts the prototype strategy of Dtr^1 but uses Ahab rather than the anti-David as model.

The prototype strategy is only one of the seven elements of the historiographical poetics that I outline. This historiographical poetics functions on two axes, one of selection and one of composition. Both of these axes work together in the overall literary plan of Dtr and in the portrayal of his kings. On the axis of selection, Dtr collects his sources and chooses what to include and omit, and how to present the sources and the events of history. He has a specific set of priorities, which guides his process of selection and his method for adopting and adapting his sources, using each to conform to his overall narrative goals. In choosing his texts, Dtr maintains a scholarly commitment to his sources, including source documents, even when they may contradict and undermine his narrative goals, rather than excising them from the historical record. He also demonstrates loyalty to the prophetic tradition, both substantially, by including predeuteronomistic prophetic texts in his narrative, and structurally, by using prophecy and its fulfillment as a primary framing strategy to illustrate how Yahweh works in history. Not only does Dtr use the semicomprehensive northern document completed by the time of Hezekiah, but he also searches out, includes, and/or composes prophetic texts that extend in time and space beyond this early document. Dtr further incorporates prophetic oracles from southern prophets regarding the kingdom of Judah until the reign of Josiah, demonstrating the role of prophetic messages and prophecy-fulfillment as selectional, organizational, and interpretative tools.

After these selectional choices have been made, Dtr orders the various texts and the episodes contained therein by rechronologizing them and juxtaposing scenes in order to craft the narrative to most effectively convey his goals. We see these priorities at play in the application and construction of the prototype strategy. For example, Dtr uses the tradition of a positive Jeroboam, likely inherited from his source documents as an opportunity to present Jeroboam with Davidic potential and then ultimately as a failed David and Davidic antitype. Similarly, prophetic texts further highlight the criteria for being like David (e.g., Ahijah in 1 Kings 11), what happens when a king is not like David (Ahijah, again, in 1 Kings 14), and how a figure portrayed in the Davidic prototype (Josiah) is the only one able to counteract the Davidic antitype (Jeroboam), through the prophecy of the man of God from Judah in 1 Kings 13.

On the axis of composition, Dtr employs the prototype strategy to promote the Deuteronomistic program, centered on centralization of the cult, covenant theology, and the Davidic promise. His primary goal in writing Kings is to interpret the history of the monarchy in light of deuteronomistic theology, using that perspective to explain the events of history, and to craft a comprehensive narrative that functions didactically, instructing the kings and the people of Judah how to behave through illustrating the consequences of disobedience. The bad kings and the entire kingdom of Israel serve as examples for Judah and the Judean kings to demonstrate the potential fate that awaits them if they do not follow the deuteronomistic covenant. The Davidic prototype and portraits of the kings provide the measure for kings, good and bad, highlighting the important tenets of deuteronomistic theology.

Also seen in the construction of the prototypical king is the attribution of historico-political events to theological causation, so that everything that happens is a result of Yahweh working in history and is reflective of human fidelity to the deuteronomistic covenant. Individuals, kingdoms, and nations are punished when they violate the tenets of deuteronomistic theology. These transgressions and the resulting consequences are made clear. This is most obvious in the depiction of Jeroboam as the next David. While the rejection of Rehoboam in 1 Kings 12 is given as the historico-political reason for the divisions of the kingdoms, Jeroboam is anointed as king and given the instructions to be David-like by Ahijah in 1 Kings 11 as the punishment for Solomon's apostasy.

These key compositional techniques contribute to the development of the prototype strategy. Dtr focuses on the royal portrait as a literary vehicle to convey his theological program. Dtr

236

can categorize the kings into two groups: those who do what is right and those who do what is evil in the eyes of Yahweh, highlighting a few specific kings to make clear what behavior is to be tolerated and praised in his kings. While the history of the monarchy spans half a millennium, only those kings who contribute to Dtr's metanarrative are constructed using this prototype. It is in the portrait of the kings Dtr highlights that we can most clearly see his poetics and the expression of his theological concerns.

Bibliography

Ackroyd, Peter R. "The Biblical Interpretation of the Reigns of Ahaz and Hezekiah." In *In the Shelter of Elyon*, edited by David J. A. Clines and Philip R. Davies, 247–59. Sheffield: JSOT Press, 1984.

Adam, Klaus-Peter. "Warfare and Treaty Formulas in the Background of Kings." In *Soundings in Kings: Perspectives and Methods in Contemporary Scholarship*, edited by Mark Leuchter and Klaus-Peter Adam, 35–68. Minneapolis: Fortress Press, 2010.

Alter, Robert. *The Art of Biblical Narrative*. New York: Basic Books, 1981.

———. *The Art of Biblical Poetry*. New York: Basic Books, 1985.

———. "Imagining History in the Bible." In *History and—: Histories within the Human Sciences*, edited by Ralph Cohen and Michael S. Roth, 53–72. Charlottesville: University Press of Virginia, 1995.

Amit, Yairah. "The Dual Causality Principle and Its Effects on Biblical Literature." *VT* 37, no. 4 (1987): 385–400.

———. *History and Ideology: An Introduction to Historiography in the Hebrew Bible*. Sheffield: Sheffield Academic, 1999.

Ash, Paul S. "Jeroboam I and the Deuteronomistic Historian's Ideology of the Founder." *CBQ* 60 (1998): 16–24.

Auld, A. Graeme. *Kings without Privilege: David and Moses in the Story of the Bible's Kings*. Edinburgh: T&T Clark, 1994.

Barrick, W. Boyd. *The King and the Cemeteries: Toward a New Understanding of Josiah's Reform*. VTSup. Leiden: Brill, 2002.

———. "On the Removal of the High-Places in 1–2 Kings." *Biblica* 55, no. 2 (1974): 257–59.

Bird, Phyllis A. "The End of the Male Cult Prostitute: A Literary-Historical and Sociological Analysis of Hebrew *Qādēš-Qĕdēšîm*." In *Congress Volume*, edited by International Organization for the Study of the Old Testament, 37–80. VTSup 66. Leiden: Brill, 1997.

Ben Zvi, Ehud. "The Account of the Reign of Manasseh in II Reg 21:1-18 and the Redactional History of the Book of Kings." *ZAW* 103, no. 3 (1991): 355–74.

———. "History and Prophetic Texts." In *History and Interpretation*, 106–20. Sheffield: JSOT Press, 1993.

———. "Prophetic Memories in the Deuteronomistic Historical and the Prophetic Collections of Books." In *Israelite Prophecy and the Deuteronomistic History: Portrait, Reality and the Formation of a History*, edited by Mignon Jacobs and Raymond Person, 75–102. Atlanta: Society of Biblical Literature, 2013.

———. "Prophets and Prophecy in the Compositional and Redactional Notes in I–II Kings." *ZAW* 105, no. 3 (1994): 331–51.

———. "'The Prophets'—References to Generic Prophets and Their Role in the Construction of the Image of the 'Prophets of Old' within the Postmonarchic Readerships of the Book of Kings." *ZAW* 116, no. 4 (2004): 555–67.

Brettler, Marc Zvi. *The Creation of History in Ancient Israel*. New York: Routledge, 1995.

———. "The Structure of 1 Kings 1–11." *JSOT* 16, no. 49 (1991): 87–97.

Campbell, Antony F. *Of Prophets and Kings: A Late Ninth Century Document (1 Samuel 1–2 Kings 10)*. Catholic Biblical Quarterly Monograph Series 17. Washington, DC: Catholic Biblical Association of America, 1986.

Cogan, Mordechai. *1 Kings: A New Translation with Introduction and Commentary*. AB. New York: Doubleday, 2001.

Cogan, Mordechai, and Hayim Tadmor. *2 Kings: A New Translation*. AB 11. Garden City, NY: Doubleday, 1988.

Cohn, Robert L. "Literary Technique in the Jeroboam Narrative." *ZAW* 97 (1985): 23–35.

Collins, John J. *The Bible after Babel: Historical Criticism in a Postmodern Age*. Grand Rapids: Eerdmans, 2005.

Crawford, Sidnie White, Jan Joosten, and Eugene Charles Ulrich. "Sample Editions of the Oxford Hebrew Bible: Deuteronomy 32:1-9, 1 Kings 11:1-8, and Jeremiah 27:1-10 (34 G)." *VT* 58, no. 3 (2008): 352–66.

Cross, Frank Moore. *Canaanite Myth and Hebrew Epic: Essays in the History of the Religion of Israel*. Cambridge, MA: Harvard University Press, 1973.

Danelius, Eva. "Sins of Jeroboam Ben-Nabat, Part I." *JQR* 58 (1967): 95–114.

———. "Sins of Jeroboam Ben-Nabat, Part II." *JQR* 58 (1968): 204–23.

Davies, Philip R. "Josiah and the Law Book." In *Good Kings and Bad Kings: The Kingdom of Judah in the Seventh Century BCE*, edited by Lester L. Grabbe, 65–77. New York: T&T Clark, 2005.

De Wette, Wilhelm Martin Leberecht. *A Critical and Historical Introduction to the Canonical Scriptures of the Old Testament*. Translated by Theodore Parker. Vol. 2. Boston: Charles C. Little and James Brown, 1850.

———. *Dissertatio Critico-Exegetica qua Deuteronomium a Prioribus Pentateuchi Libris Diversum, Alius Cuiusdam Recentioris Auctioris Opus Esse Monstratur*. Jena, 1805.

Dietrich, Martin. "Martin Noth and the Future of the Deuteronomistic History." In *The History of Israel's Traditions: The Heritage of Martin Noth*, edited by Steven McKenzie and M. Patrick Graham, 153–75. Sheffield: Sheffield Academic, 1994.

Dietrich, Walter. *Prophetie Und Geschichte Eine Redaktionsgeschichtliche Untersuchung Zum Deuteronomistischen Geschichtswerk.* FRLANT 108. Göttingen: Vandenhoeck & Ruprecht, 1972.

Ben-Dov, Jonathan. "Some Precedents for the Religion of the Book: Josiah's Book and Ancient Revelatory Literature." In *Constructs of Prophecy in the Former and Latter Prophets and Other Texts,* edited by Lester L. Grabbe and Martti Nissinen, 43–64. Atlanta: Society of Biblical Literature, 2011.

Eagleton, Terry. *After Theory.* New York: Basic Books, 2003.

Edelman, Diana. "Solomon's Adversaries Hadad, Rezon and Jeroboam: A Trio of 'Bad Guy' Characters Illustrating the Theology of Immediate Retribution." In *The Pitcher Is Broken: Memorial Essays for Gösta W. Ahlström,* edited by Steven W. Holloway and Lowell K. Handy, 166–91. JSOTSup 190. Sheffield: Sheffield Academic, 1995.

Evans, Carl D. "Naram-Sin and Jeroboam: The Archetypal *Unheilsherrscher* in Mesopotamian and Biblical Historiography." In *Scripture in Context II: More Essays on the Comparative Method,* edited by William W. Hallo, James C. Moyer, and Leo G. Perdue, 97–125. Winona Lake, IN: Eisenbrauns, 1983.

Ewald, Heinrich. *Geschichte Des Volkes Israel.* 6 vols. Göttingen: Dieterichs Buchhandlung, 1843.

———. *The History of Israel.* Translated by R. Martineau. Vol. 1. London: Longmans, Green, 1869.

Eynikel, Erik. "The Portrait of Manasseh and the Deuteronomistic History." In *Deuteronomy and Deuteronomic Literature,* 233–61. Louvain: Peeters, 1997.

———. "Prophecy and Fulfillment in the Deuteronomistic History (1 Kgs 13; 2 Kgs 23, 16-18)." In *Pentateuchal and Deuteronomistic Studies: Papers Read at the XIIIth IOSOT Congress, Leuven 1989,* edited by C. Brekelmans and J. Lust, 227–37. Leuven: Leuven University Press, 1990.

———. *The Reform of King Josiah and the Composition of the Deuteronomistic History*. Leiden: Brill, 1995.

Fischer, David Hackett. *Paul Revere's Ride*. New York: Oxford University Press, 1994.

Fried, Lisbeth. "The High Places (Bāmôt) and the Reforms of Hezekiah and Josiah: An Archaeological Investigation." *JAOS* 122, no. 3 (2002): 437–65.

Friedman, Richard E. *The Bible with Sources Revealed: A New View into the Five Books of Moses*. San Francisco: HarperSanFrancisco, 2003.

———. "The Deuteronomistic School." In *Fortunate the Eyes That See: Essays in Honor of David Noel Freedman in Celebration of His Seventieth Birthday*, edited by Astrid B. Beck, Andrew H. Bartelt, Paul R. Raabe, and Chris Franke, 70–80. Grand Rapids: Eerdmans, 1995.

———. *The Exile and Biblical Narrative: The Formation of the Deuteronomistic and Priestly Works*. Chico, CA: Scholars Press, 1981.

Fritz, Volkmar. *1 and 2 Kings*. Translated by Anselm Hagedorn. Continental Commentaries. Minneapolis: Fortress Press, 2003.

Frost, Stanley Brice. "The Death of Josiah: A Conspiracy of Silence." *JBL* 87, no. 4 (1968): 369–82.

Gallagher, Catherine, and Stephen Greenblatt. *Practicing New Historicism*. Chicago: University of Chicago Press, 2000.

Garsiel, Moshe. "The Book of Samuel: Its Composition, Structure and Significance as a Historiographical Source." *JHS* 10 (2010): 2–42.

Gesenius, Wilhelm. *Gesenius' Hebrew Grammar*. Edited by Arthur Ernest Cowley and Emil Friedrich Kautzsch. 2nd English ed. Oxford: Clarendon, 1910.

Glatt, David A. *Chronological Displacement in Biblical and Related Literatures*. Atlanta: Scholars Press, 1993.

Gooding, David Willoughby. "Jeroboam's Rise to Power." *JBL* 91, no. 4 (1972): 529–33.

Gordon, Robert P. "Second Septuagint Account of Jeroboam: History or Midrash?" *VT* 25 (1975): 368–93.

Grabbe, Lester L., ed. *Good Kings and Bad Kings: The Kingdom of Judah in the Seventh Century BCE.* New York: T&T Clark, 2005.

Gray, John. *1 and 2 Kings: A Commentary.* 2nd ed. Old Testament Library. Philadelphia: Westminster, 1970.

Greenblatt, Stephen. *Learning to Curse: Essays in Early Modern Culture.* New York: Routledge, 1990.

Gressmann, Hugo. *Die Älteste Geschichtsschreibung Und Prophetie Israels.* Göttingen: Vandenhoeck & Ruprecht, 1910.

Hadley, Judith M. *The Cult of Asherah in Ancient Israel and Judah: Evidence for a Hebrew Goddess.* Cambridge: Cambridge University Press, 2000.

———. "Yahweh and 'His Asherah': Archaeological and Textual Evidence for the Cult of the Goddess." In *Ein Gott Allein? JHWH-Verehrung Und Biblischer Monotheismus Im Kontext Der Israelitischen Und Altorientalischen Religionsgeschichte,* edited by Walter Dietrich and Martin A. Klopfenstein, 235–68. OBO 139. Fribourg: Universitätsverlag, 1994.

Halpern, Baruch. "'Brisker Pipes Than Poetry': The Development of Israelite Monotheism." In *Judaic Perspectives on Ancient Israel,* edited by Jacob Neusner, Baruch A. Levine, and Ernest S. Frerichs, 77–115. Philadelphia: Fortress Press, 1987.

———. *David's Secret Demons: Messiah, Murderer, Traitor, King.* Grand Rapids: Eerdmans, 2001.

———. "Doctrine by Misadventure: Between the Israelite Source and the Biblical Historian." In *The Poet and the Historian: Essays in Literary and Historical Biblical Criticism,* edited by Richard E. Friedman, 41–73. Chico, CA: Scholars Press, 1983.

———. *The First Historians: The Hebrew Bible and History.* San Francisco: Harper & Row, 1988.

———. "Levitic Participation in the Reform Cult of Jeroboam I." *JBL* 95 (1976): 31–42.

———. "The Resourceful Israelite Historian: The Song of Deborah and Israelite Historiography." *HTR* 76, no. 4 (1983): 379–401.

Halpern, Baruch, and David S. Vanderhooft. "The Editions of Kings in the 7th–6th Centuries BCE." *HUCA* 62 (1991): 179–244.

Hardmeier, Christof. "King Josiah in the Climax of the Deuteronomic History (2 Kings 22-23) and the Pre-Deuteronomic Document of a Cult Reform at the Place of Residence (23.4-15*): Criticism of Sources, Reconstruction of Literary Pre-Stages and the Theology of History in 2 Kings 22–23*." In *Good Kings and Bad Kings: The Kingdom of Judah in the Seventh Century BCE*, edited by Lester L. Grabbe, 123–63. New York: T&T Clark, 2005.

Hays, J. Daniel. "Has the Narrator Come to Praise Solomon or to Bury Him? Narrative Subtlety in 1 Kings 1–11." *JSOT* 28, no. 2 (2003): 149–74.

Hendel, Ronald S. "Culture, Memory, and History: Reflections on Method in Biblical Studies." In *Historical Biblical Archaeology and the Future: The New Pragmatism*, edited by Thomas E. Levy, 250–61. London: Equinox, 2010.

Huizinga, Johan. "A Definition of the Concept of History." In *Philosophy and History: Essays Presented to Ernst Cassirer*, edited by Raymond Klibansky and Herbert James Paton, 1–10. New York: Harper & Row, 1963.

Joseph, Alison L. "The Portrait of the Kings and the Historiographical Poetics of the Deuteronomistic Historian." PhD dissertation, University of California, Berkeley. Ann Arbor: ProQuest/UMI, 2012. Publication no. AAT 3527138.

———. "Who Is Like David? Was David Like David?: Good Kings in the Book of Kings." *CBQ* 77 (2015): 20–41.

Kaufmann, Yehezkel. *The Book of Joshua*. Jerusalem: Ḳiryat-Sefer, 1959.

Keulen, P. S. F. van. *Manasseh through the Eyes of the Deuteronomists: The Manasseh Account (2 Kings 21:1-18) and the Final Chapters of the Deuteronomistic History*. Leiden: Brill, 1996.

———. *Two Versions of the Solomon Narrative: An Inquiry into the Relationship Between MT 1 Kgs. 2–11 and LXX 3 Reg. 2–11*. VTSup 104. Leiden: Brill, 2005.

Knauf, Ernst Axel. "Does 'Deuteronomistic Historiography' (DtrH) Exist?" In *Israel Constructs its History: Deuteronomistic Historiography in Recent Research*, edited by Albert de Pury, Jean-Daniel Macchi, and Thomas Römer, 388–97. Sheffield: Sheffield Academic, 2000.

Knoppers, Gary N. "Aaron's Calf and Jeroboam's Calves." In *Fortunate the Eyes That See: Essays in Honor of David Noel Freedman in Celebration of His Seventieth Birthday*, edited by Astrid B. Beck, John R Bartlett, Paul R. Raabe, and Chris Franke, 92–104. Grand Rapids: Eerdmans, 1995.

———. "The Deuteronomist and the Deuteronomic Law of the King: A Reexamination of a Relationship." *ZAW* 108, no. 3 (1996): 329–46.

———. "Dynastic Oracle and Secession in 1 Kings 11." *Proceedings, Eastern Great Lakes and Midwest Biblical Societies* 7 (1987): 159–72.

———. "Rethinking the Relationship between Deuteronomy and the Deuteronomistic History: The Case of Kings." *CBQ* 63, no. 3 (2001): 393–415.

———. "'There Was None like Him': Incomparability in the Books of Kings." *CBQ* 54, no. 3 (1992): 411–31.

———. *Two Nations under God: The Deuteronomistic History of Solomon and the Dual Monarchies*. Vol. 1, *The Reign of Solomon and the Rise of Jeroboam*. Harvard Semitic Monographs. Atlanta: Scholars Press, 1993.

———. *Two Nations under God: The Deuteronomistic History of Solomon and the Dual Monarchies*. Vol. 2, *The Reign of Jeroboam, the Fall of Israel, and the Reign of Josiah*. Harvard Semitic Monographs. Atlanta: Scholars Press, 1994.

Knoppers, Gary N., and J. Gordon McConville, eds. *Reconsidering Israel and Judah: Recent Studies on the Deuteronomistic History*. Winona Lake, IN: Eisenbrauns, 2000.

Kratz, Reinhard G. *Composition of the Narrative Books of the Old Testament*. Translated by John Bowden. London: T&T Clark, 2005.

———. *Die Komposition Der Erzählenden Bücher Des Alten Testaments: Grundwissen Der Bibelkritik*. Göttingen: Vandenhoeck & Ruprecht, 2000.

Kuenen, Abraham. *An Historico-Critical Inquiry into the Origin and Composition of the Hexateuch (Pentateuch and Book of Joshua)*. Translated by Philip H. Wicksteed. London: Macmillan, 1886.

———. *Historisch-Kritisch Onderzoek Naar Het Ontstaan En de Verzameling van de Boeken Des Ouden Verbonds*. 3 vols. Leiden: Engels, 1861.

Lakoff, George. *Women, Fire, and Dangerous Things: What Categories Reveal about the Mind*. Chicago: University of Chicago Press, 1987.

Lasine, Stuart. "Manasseh as Villain and Scapegoat." In *New Literary Criticism and the Hebrew Bible*, 163–83. Sheffield: JSOT Press, 1993.

———. "Reading Jeroboam's Intentions: Intertextuality, Rhetoric, and History in 1 Kings 12." In *Reading between Texts*, edited by Danna Nolan Fewell, 133–52. Louisville: Westminster John Knox, 1992.

Law, T. Michael. "How Not to Use 3 Reigns: A Plea to Scholars of the Books of Kings." *VT* 61, no. 2 (2011): 280–97.

Leuchter, Mark. "Between Politics and Mythology: Josiah's Assault on Bethel in 2 Kings 23:15-20." Paper presented at the 2013 Moskow Symposium, "Theorizing Ritual Violence in the Hebrew Bible," Brown University, May 5, 2013.

———. "Jeroboam the Ephratite." *JBL* 125, no. 1 (2006): 51–72.

Leuchter, Mark, and Klaus-Peter Adam, eds. *Soundings in Kings: Perspectives and Methods in Contemporary Scholarship*. Minneapolis: Fortress Press, 2010.

Levinson, Bernard M. "The Reconceptualization of Kingship in Deuteronomy and the Deuteronomistic History's Transformation of Torah." *VT* 51, no. 4 (2001): 511–34.

Lohfink, Norbert. "Was There a Deuteronomistic Movement?" In *Those Elusive Deuteronomists: The Phenomenon of Pan-Deuteronomism*, edited by Linda Schearing and Steven L. McKenzie, 36–66. JSOTSup 268. Sheffield: Sheffield Academic, 1999.

Longfellow, Henry Wadsworth. "Paul Revere's Ride." In *Selected Poems*, 148–52. Penguin Classics. New York: Penguin, 1988.

McCarter, P. Kyle. *2 Samuel*. AB 9. Garden City, NY: Doubleday, 1984.

———. "Introduction." In *1 Samuel: A New Translation with Introduction, Notes and Commentary*, 3–44. AB 8. Garden City, NY: Doubleday, 1984.

McKenzie, Steven L. *The Trouble with Kings: The Composition of the Book of Kings in the Deuteronomistic History*. VTSup 42. Leiden: Brill, 1991.

Monroe, Lauren A. S. *Josiah's Reform and the Dynamics of Defilement: Israelite Rites of Violence and the Making of a Biblical Text*. New York: Oxford University Press, 2011.

Montgomery, James A. *A Critical and Exegetical Commentary on the Books of Kings*. Edited by Henry Snyder Gehman. International Critical Commentary. New York: Scribner's, 1951.

Mullen, E. Theodore. "The Sins of Jeroboam: A Redactional Assessment." *CBQ* 49 (1987): 212–32.

Na'aman, Nadav. "Sources and Composition in the History of Solomon." In *The Age of Solomon: Scholarship at the Turn of the Millennium*, edited by Lowell K. Handy, 57–80. Leiden: Brill, 1997.

Nelson, Richard D. *The Double Redaction of the Deuteronomistic History*. Sheffield: JSOT Press, 1981.

———. "Josiah in the Book of Joshua." *JBL* 100, no. 4 (1981): 531–40.

Nicholson, Ernest W. *Deuteronomy and Tradition*. Oxford: Blackwell, 1967.

Noth, Martin. *The Deuteronomistic History*. Sheffield: JSOT Press, 1981.

———. *Könige.* Neukirchen-Vluyn: Neukirchener Verlag des Erziehungsvereins, 1968.

———. *Überlieferungsgeschichtliche Studien. Die Sammelnden Und Bearbeitenden Geschischtswerke Im Alten Testament.* Tübingen: Max Niemeyer, 1957.

O'Brien, Mark A. *The Deuteronomistic History Hypothesis: A Reassessment.* OBO 92. Fribourg: Vandenhoeck & Ruprecht, 1989.

Parker, Kim Ian. "Repetition as a Structuring Device in 1 Kings 1–11." *JSOT* 13, no. 42 (1988): 19–27.

Person, Raymond. *The Deuteronomic School: History, Social Setting, and Literature.* Leiden: Brill, 2002.

Pinsky, Robert. *The Life of David.* New York: Schocken, 2005.

Polzin, Robert. *Samuel and the Deuteronomist: 1 Samuel.* Bloomington: Indiana University Press, 1993.

Propp, William Henry. *Exodus 19–40.* AB. New York: Doubleday, 2006.

Provan, Iain. *Hezekiah and the Books of Kings: A Contribution to the Debate about the Composition of the Deuteronomistic History.* Berlin: de Gruyter, 1988.

———. "The Judgment Formulae of the Books of Kings." In *Hezekiah and the Books of Kings: A Contribution to the Debate about the Composition of the Deuteronomistic History,* 33–55. Berlin: de Gruyter, 1988.

Pury, Albert de, Jean-Daniel Macchi, and Thomas Römer, eds. *Israel Constructs Its History: Deuteronomistic Historiography in Recent Research.* Sheffield: Sheffield Academic, 2000.

Pury, Albert de, and Thomas Römer. "Deuteronomistic Historiography (DH): History of Research and Debated Issues." In *Israel Constructs its History: Deuteronomistic Historiography in Recent Research,* edited by Albert de Pury, Jean-Daniel Macchi, and Thomas Römer, 24–141 Sheffield: Sheffield Academic, 2000.

Rad, Gerhard von. "The Deuteronomistic Theology of History in the Books of Kings." In *Studies in Deuteronomy*, 74–91. Translated by David Stalker. London: SCM, 1953.

———. *Deuteronomium-Studien*. Göttingen: Vandenhoeck & Ruprecht, 1947.

———. *Old Testament Theology*. London: SCM, 1962.

———. *Theologie Des Alten Testaments*. Vol. 1. Munich, 1957.

Revere, Paul. "A Letter from Col. Paul Revere to the Corresponding Secretary [Jeremy Belknap]." 1798. Manuscript Collection, Massachusetts Historical Society. http://www.masshist.org/cabinet/april2002/reveretranscription.htm.

Rofé, Alexander. *The Prophetical Stories: The Narratives about the Prophets in the Hebrew Bible, Their Literary Types and History*. Jerusalem: Magnes , 1988.

Rogerson, John W. *W. M. L. de Wette, Founder of Modern Biblical Criticism: An Intellectual Biography*. JSOTSup 126. Sheffield: JSOT Press, 1992.

Römer, Thomas, ed. *The Future of the Deuteronomistic History*. Leuven: Leuven University Press, 2000.

———. *The So-Called Deuteronomistic History: A Sociological, Historical, and Literary Introduction*. New York: T&T Clark, 2007.

Rosenbaum, Jonathan. "Hezekiah's Reform and the Deuteronomistic Tradition." *HTR* 72 (1979): 23–43.

Rost, Leonhard. *The Succession to the Throne of David*. Translated by Michael D. Rutter and David M. Gunn. Sheffield: Almond, 1982.

———. *Die Überlieferung Von Der Thronnachfolge Davids*. Stuttgart: Kohlhammer, 1926.

Schearing, Linda, and Steven L. McKenzie, eds. *Those Elusive Deuteronomists: The Phenomenon of Pan-Deuteronomism*. JSOTSup 268. Sheffield: Sheffield Academic, 1999.

Schenker, Adrian. "Jeroboam and the Division of the Kingdom in the Ancient Septuagint: LXX 3 Kingdoms 12.24 a-z, MT 1 Kings 11-12; 14 and the Deuteronomistic History." In *Israel Constructs its History:*

Deuteronomistic Historiography in Recent Research, edited by Albert de Pury, Jean-Daniel Macchi, and Thomas Römer, 214–57. Sheffield: Sheffield Academic, 2000.

Schipper, Jeremy. "Hezekiah, Manasseh, and Dynastic or Transgenerational Punishment." In *Soundings in Kings: Perspectives and Methods in Contemporary Scholarship*, edited by Mark Leuchter and Klaus-Peter Adam, 81–105. Minneapolis: Fortress Press, 2010.

Schmid, Konrad. *The Old Testament: A Literary History*. Translated by Linda M. Maloney. Minneapolis: Fortress Press, 2012.

Schniedewind, William M. "History and Interpretation: The Religion of Ahab and Manasseh in the Book of Kings." *CBQ* 55, no. 4 (1993): 649–61.

Seeligmann, Isaac Leo. "Menschliches Heldentum Und Göttliche Hilfe: Die Doppelte Kausalität Im Alttestamentlichen Geschichtsdenken." *TZ* 19, no. 6 (1963): 385–411.

Van Seters, John. "The Court History and DtrH: Conflicting Perspectives on the House of David." In *Sogenannte Thronfolgegeschichte Davids: Neue Einsichten und Anfragen*, edited by Albert de Pury and Thomas Römer, 70–93. OBO 176. Fribourg: Universitätsverlag; Göttingen: Vandenhoeck & Ruprecht, 2000.

———. "The Deuteronomistic History: Can It Avoid Death by Redaction?" In *The Future of the Deuteronomistic History*, edited by Thomas Römer, 213–22. Leuven: Leuven University Press, 2000.

———. *The Edited Bible: The Curious History of the "Editor" in Biblical Criticism*. Winona Lake, IN: Eisenbrauns, 2006.

———. *In Search of History: Historiography in the Ancient World and the Origins of Biblical History*. Winona Lake, IN: Eisenbrauns, 1997.

———. "On Reading the Story of the Man of God from Judah in 1 Kings 13." In *The Labour of Reading: Desire, Alienation, and Biblical Interpretation*, edited by Fiona Black, Roland T. Boer, and Erin Runions, 225–34. Atlanta: Society of Biblical Literature, 1999.

Simon, Uriel. "I Kings 13: A Prophetic Sign—Denial and Persistence." *HUCA* 47 (1976): 81–117.

Smelik, Klaas A. D. "The Portrayal of King Manasseh: A Literary Analysis of II Kings XXI and II Chronicles XXIII." In *Converting the Past: Studies in Ancient Israelite and Moabite Historiography*, 129–89. Oudtestamentische studiën. Leiden: Brill, 1992.

Smend, Rudolf. "Das Gesetz Und Die Völker: Ein Beitrag Zur Deuteronomistischen Redaktionsgeschichte." In *Probleme Biblischer Theologie*, 494–509. Munich: Kaiser, 1971.

Smith, Mark. *The Early History of God: Yahweh and the Other Deities in Ancient Israel*. Grand Rapids: Eerdmans, 2002.

Spinoza, Benedict. *Tractatus Theologico-Politicus*. Amsterdam: Hamburgi, 1670.

Stavrakopoulou, Francesca. "The Blackballing of Manasseh." In *Good Kings and Bad Kings: The Kingdom of Judah in the Seventh Century BCE*, edited by Lester L. Grabbe, 248–63. London: T&T Clark, 2005.

———. *King Manasseh and Child Sacrifice: Biblical Distortions of Historical Realities*. Berlin: de Gruyter, 2004.

Sternberg, Meir. *The Poetics of Biblical Narrative*. Bloomington: Indiana University Press, 1985.

Sweeney, Marvin A. "A Reassessment of the Masoretic and Septuagint Versions of the Jeroboam Narratives in 1 Kings/3 Kingdoms 11–14." *Journal for the Study of Judaism in the Persian, Hellenistic and Roman Period* 38, no. 2 (2007): 165–95.

———. *First and Second Kings: A Commentary*. Old Testament Library. Louisville: Westminster John Knox, 2007.

———. *King Josiah of Judah: The Lost Messiah of Israel*. Oxford: Oxford University Press, 2001.

Talshir, Zipora. *The Alternative Story of the Division of the Kingdom: 3 Kingdoms 12:24a-z*. Jerusalem: Simor, 1993.

———. "Is the Alternate Tradition of the Division of the Kingdom (3 Kgdms 12:24a-z) Non-Deuteronomistic?" In *Septuagint, Scrolls and Cognate Writings*, edited by George J. Brooke and Barnabas Lindars, 599–621. Atlanta: Scholars Press, 1992.

———. "Literary Design—A Criterion for Originality? A Case Study: 3 Kgdms 12:24a-z; 1 K 11–14." In *Double Transmission Du Texte Biblique: Études D'histoire Du Texte Offertes En Hommage A Adrian Schenker*, edited by Adrian Schenker, Yohanan Goldman, and Christoph Uehlinger, 41–57. Göttingen: Vandenhoeck & Ruprecht, 2001.

Thomas, Benjamin D. *Hezekiah and the Compositional History of the Book of Kings*. Tübingen: Mohr Siebeck, 2014.

Tov, Emanuel. *The Text-Critical Use of the Septuagint in Biblical Research*. Jerusalem: Simor, 1981.

Trebolle, Julio C. "Kings (MT/LXX) and Chronicles: The Double and Triple Textual Traditions." In *Reflection and Refraction: Studies in Biblical Historiography in Honour of A. Graeme Auld*, edited by Robert Rezetko, Timothy H. Lim, and W. Brian Aucker, 483–501. Leiden: Brill, 2006.

———. "Redaction, Recension and Midrash in the Books of Kings." *Bulletin of the International Organization for Septuagint and Cognate Studies* 15 (1982): 12–35.

———. "Samuel/Kings and Chronicles: Book Divisions and Textual Composition." In *Studies in the Hebrew Bible, Qumran, and the Septuagint Presented to Eugene Ulrich*, edited by Eugene Charles Ulrich, Peter W. Flint, James C. VanderKam, and Emanuel Tov, 96–108. Leiden: Brill, 2006.

———. "The Text-Critical Use of the Septuagint in the Books of Kings." *Seventh Congress of the International Organization for Septuagint and Cognate Studies, Leuven 1989*, edited by Claude E. Cox, 285–99. Atlanta: Scholars Press, 1991.

Uehlinger, Christoph. "Was There a Cult Reform Under King Josiah? The Case for a Well-Grounded Minimum." In *Good Kings and Bad Kings: The Kingdom of Judah in the Seventh Century BCE*, edited by Lester L. Grabbe, 279–316. New York: T&T Clark, 2005.

Veijola, Timo. *Die Ewige Dynastie: David Und Die Entstehung Seiner Dynastie Nach Der Deuteronomistischen Darstellung*. Helsinki: Suomalainen Tiedeakatemia, 1975.

Waltke, Bruce K., and Michael Patrick O'Connor. *An Introduction to Biblical Hebrew Syntax*. Winona Lake, IN: Eisenbrauns, 1990.

Weinfeld, Moshe. *Deuteronomy and the Deuteronomic School*. Winona Lake, IN: Eisenbrauns, 1992.

———. "The Emergence of the Deuteronomic Movement: The Historical Antecedents." In *Das Deuteronomium: Enstehung, Gestalt, Und Botschaft*, edited by Norbert Lohfink, 76–98. Leuven: Leuven University Press, 1985.

Weippert, Helga. "Die Deuteronomistischen Beurteilungen Der Könige von Israel Und Juda Und Das Problem Der Redaktion Der Königsbücher." *Biblica* 53 (1972): 301–39.

Wellhausen, Julius. *Die Composition Des Hexateuchs Und Der Historischen Bücher Des Alten Testaments*. Berlin: Georg Reimer, 1889.

———. *Prolegomena to the History of Israel*. Edited by Douglas Knight. Atlanta: Scholars Press, 1994.

———. *Prolegomena zur Geschichte Israels*. Berlin: Reimer, 1883.

White, Hayden. *The Content of the Form: Narrative Discourse and Historical Representation*. Baltimore: Johns Hopkins University Press, 1990.

———. "Interpretation in History." *New Literary History* 4, no. 2 (1973): 281–314.

———. *Metahistory: The Historical Imagination in Nineteenth-Century Europe*. Baltimore: Johns Hopkins University Press, 1975.

Williamson, H. G. M. "Review of The Creation of History in Ancient Israel, by Marc Z. Brettler." *Journal of Jewish Studies* 47, no. 2 (1996): 352–55.

Wimsatt, William K., and Monroe C. Beardsley. "The Intentional Fallacy." In *The Verbal Icon: Studies in the Meaning of Poetry*, edited by William K. Wimsatt, 3–18. Lexington: University of Kentucky Press, 1954.

Wray Beal, Lissa M. "Jeroboam and the Prophets in 1 Kings 11-14: Prophetic Word for Two Kingdoms." In *Prophets, Prophecy, and Ancient Israelite Historiography*, edited by Mark J. Boda and Lissa M. Wray Beal, 105–24. Winona Lake, IN: Eisenbrauns, 2013.

Van Winkle, D. W. "1 Kings XII 25-XIII 34: Jeroboam's Cultic Innovations and the Man of God from Judah." *VT* 46 (1996): 101–14.

Zakovitch, Yair. "Juxtaposition in the Abraham Cycle." In *Pomegranates and Golden Bells: Studies in Biblical, Jewish, and Near Eastern Ritual, Law, and Literature in Honor of Jacob Milgrom*, edited by David P. Wright, David Noel Freedman, and Avi Hurvitz, 509–24. Winona Lake, IN: Eisenbrauns, 1995.

Zevit, Ziony. *The Religions of Ancient Israel: A Synthesis of Parallactic Approaches*. New York: Continuum, 2003.

Index of Authors and Subjects

Index of Scriptural References